Twentieth Century Architecture 5

Twentieth Century
Architecture 5

FESTIVAL OF BRITAIN

EDITED BY ELAIN HARWOOD AND ALAN POWERS

The Twentieth Century Society
2001

TWENTIETH CENTURY ARCHITECTURE
is published by the Twentieth Century Society
70 Cowcross Street, London EC1M 6EJ
© The authors 2001

NUMBER 5 · 2001 · ISBN 978-0-9529755-6-4 · ISSN 1353–1964

Twentieth Century Architecture Editorial Committee:
Elain Harwood, Alan Powers, Gavin Stamp
Guest editor: Simon Wartnaby.

Designed and typeset in Quadraat
and Festival Titling by Dalrymple.
Printed by BAS Printers Ltd.
Reprinted by Conti Tipocolor, 2011

This issue of Twentieth Century Architecture is made possible by
the generous financial support of: The Royal Commission for the
Exhibition of 1851, The Society of Architectural Historians of
Great Britain (a bursary from the Dorothy Stroud Bequest),
Architects Co-Partnership, The Fine Art Society PLC, Inch's
Books, Neville Conder, Trevor Dannatt, Paul Dixon, Helen Dorey,
Terry Farrell, Paul Finch, Jeremy Greenwood and Alan Swerdlow,
Elain Harwood, Michael Hopkins, Simon Jenkins, Patricia Long,
John McAslan, Fiona MacCarthy, Ian Mackenzie-Kerr, Bruce
MacTavish, Andrew Mackintosh Patrick, Sheila Manning,
and Marina Vaizey.

The Society gratefully acknowledges a grant from English
Heritage for part of the costs of its casework.

Contents

Foreword

ELAIN HARWOOD AND ALAN POWERS

The Festival of Britain is a large subject, on which only one major book has so far been published, *A Tonic to the Nation* (Thames and Hudson, 1976), edited by Bevis Hillier and Mary Banham, which accompanied a 25th anniversary exhibition at the V&A Museum. In commissioning articles for this 50th anniversary publication, it seemed sensible not to overlap with existing material, and to balance coherence with diversity. The articles therefore fall broadly into three categories, those which deal with antecedents, such as the history of the South Bank site before 1951 and the life story of Sir Gerald Barry, those concerned with the South Bank as the major artistic endeavour of the Festival, and those concerned with other manifestations of the Festival, more or less architectural in character.

Two or three major omissions will be spotted. There is almost no coverage of the Royal Festival Hall, chiefly because it has been so well described in a monograph by John McKean in the Phaidon 'Architecture in Detail' series, 1992. There is no article on Sir Hugh Casson, because his biography by José Manser, published by Viking in 2000, provides ample detail. There is no attempt to discuss the internal design of the pavilions and exhibitions on the South Bank. This subject has been omitted with regret owing to shortage of space, but researchers are commended to the archive of the Design Council at the University of Brighton (images of the Festival www.vads.ac.uk). There is no article on the landscape design of the South Bank, an important subject which we hope will be pursued by specialists in this field.

We are grateful to a number of people and institutions who have helped in the preparation of this journal, among them The National Sound Archive (Cathy Courtney and Melanie Unwin); Architectural Review photo library (Andrew Mead); the National Monuments Record; Christopher and Jackie Barry for loan of material from the Gerald Barry archive. Martin Packer has been generous in promoting our activities through its website devoted to the Festival, www.packer34.freeserve.co.uk. We are particularly grateful to those listed elsewhere who have made generous financial contributions which have enabled the Society to produce this journal in the fiftieth anniversary year of the Festival.

1 Le Corbusier Parle ... 1951

TRANSLATED BY EMMANUELLE MORGAN

Le Corbusier Parle ... 1951

TRANSLATED BY EMMANUELLE MORGAN

From a talk by Le Corbusier on a BBC Third Programme radio interview, recorded 10 July 1951 and broadcast 19 August 1951.

LE Corbusier was in England in the summer of 1951 to attend the CIAM conference at Hoddesdon. His radio talk, never previously published, was transmitted in French, and both a sound recording and a transcript survive in the BBC Archives. Two passages are marked as deletions on the transcript and have been omitted from this text, as have the two final pages, devoted to his painting. A large part of the talk is about the Festival exhibition 'Growth and Form' at the Institute of Contemporary Arts, devised by the painter Richard Hamilton and the biologist Lancelot Law Whyte, based on the classic investigation of design in nature, D'Arcy Wentworth Thompson's book, On Growth and Form, 1917.

The producer was Leonie Cohn, who specialised in architecture talks at the BBC for many years. She was attending the Hoddesdon conference and had the idea of getting Le Corbusier to record something. She recalls 'I dragged him into a taxi and brought him to the studio'. The transmission over a month later was introduced by John Summerson, a regular Third Programme broadcaster, who tried to explain why so much of the content of Le Corbusier's talk was not about architecture.

We are grateful to the Fondation Le Corbusier and the BBC Written Archives Centre at Caversham for permission to publish this text.

You would like me to talk about the English at the South Bank exhibition. It is with great pleasure that I do so. I talk to you as a man coming back from far away. My life, in particular in the last few years, has been spent looking at all sorts of countries, civilisations and customs, and I have constantly been asking myself many questions.

Air travel permits one to travel fast, to have direct sensations, and it has therefore allowed me to land in the heart of a very interesting country. I arrived last night and was thrown into the midst of the bustle of the South Bank, where I discovered a very amusing and very interesting exhibition. I have arrived straight out of an extremely intense CIAM congress held at Hoddesdon, which I have been attending for the past three or four days.

After experiencing the London suburbs, the buses and the tube, I finally reached the exhibition. Normally I hate exhibitions. Night came by and the miracle of electricity unravelled and I was very happy, I was astounded, delighted because I am an honest man and what struck me straightaway is the thing that exists very rarely in exhibitions: honesty.

This exhibition is honest, it is healthy, it is solid, it is full of vigour and verve, it is full of diversity, it is full of unity. It is not bad at all and one does not come across such an exhibition everyday, and I can assure you that I do not say that out of politeness. I was utterly delighted.

My delight increased for all sorts of reasons: maybe a little personal vanity. We went to visit the large auditorium which, whilst in the foyer, appeared to me familiar; however, its interior revealed an English creation that was extremely beautiful and that surprised me most. Well, it is wonderful! Truly, truly.

You seem, you English, not to find it very beautiful because young people created this admirable thing for you. They did it with knowledge, with respect of the world's physical laws – that is to say visibility, acoustics – and when one respects these laws, which architects have forgotten to do for at least a century, due to their academies and their schools with their *pompier* teachers ... . Well it is an extraordinary fortitude to find things which obey the rules and in this instance, the rules are mandatory: but imagination is also necessary.

We then went to a cocktail party to have a drink, where charming ladies from the County Council first explained to me what the County Council was. It would appear to be a very important body, as it is the London municipal advisory board and you know it is large. I would be very honoured to be part of the County Council but I can not accept because I am already crumbling under responsibilities. What is surprising is that the ladies next told me: 'well, it shows how well we had chosen!' I then replied: 'you have chosen admirably, it is admirable as, without a doubt, the whole world will admire your concert hall'. I tell you that in all honesty, as I was then introduced to the architects, who do not have white hair and who are not bald; it is astonishing as we normally wait for hair to fall before giving such commissions. However, I notice in this country today an extraordinary youthfulness, which I am familiar with, since I am on the best of terms with English architecture students, who for years have been calling me and inviting me, an invitation I have unfortunately not been able to take up. It is a very green youth, very clear, and extremely pretty to see.

One has believed a great deal that the modern was only to be found on the other side of the ocean, the opposite of Ango-Saxonism, but I do not agree. In America I battle with the superficial; when here, things are done seriously. Your entire country is indeed serious, with its admirable countryside and its trees, well planted, beautiful and well looked after. The roads are equally well maintained and built, and this is the spirit of your exhibition, with its well-crafted materials, precise technical drawings and imagination: it's ravishing.

It was raining last night by a stroke of luck, and under the rain I saw the Gardens of the Hesperides with their apple trees, the magical, red apples. I saw a blade which rises in the sky held by hardly nothing, defying all the laws of physics, and I saw a large building shaped like a crab-shell, light and held up by the

figure 1
Royal Festival Hall, 1951
(The Architectural Press)

lightest of cables, which despite my not having the time to visit it, waved at me in a friendly manner.

I was indeed very glad to nevertheless see it, and a while ago, just before this interview, I was made to wait inside the space where the 'Growth and Form' exhibition is, a room as small as your exhibition is large, and once again, I was delighted and enchanted. This exhibition is dedicated to life in all its forms, whether microbiological, micro-mineralogical, mathematical or even cosmic. The authors of this exhibition are sensitive and poetic as well as good observers, for they have recognised that nature is full of wonders which God has placed at our disposition. They have also made good use of the wonderful instruments of science, such as measuring, photography, cinema and lighting devices and, with these new mechanical and physical eyes and lenses, they have allowed us to see what our ancestors did not see. And they were astute enough to retain the poetry of the nourishment supplied by the universe and God for those who wish to open their eyes and ears, and look, see and understand.

This exhibition has touched me deep inside and it is very odd. I do not know if I am soon to become a British citizen: I do not think so, but I found in the 'Growth and Form' exhibition a purpose which has animated me for 30 years, because I can admit it now, I paint and sculpt. Let me tell you, if I do not bore you too much, and it leads me on to a big preoccupation of mine, which is the current atmosphere of the Arts and of the modern poetics. People, in the current upheaval, do not know what to talk about and who one should talk about, they do not know if there are Madonnas or muses, if there are Pharaohs or something else, or political battles or heroes, the tribunes, of the Waterloo Revolution. One deals with a subject and those who do not have a subject suddenly rush into the non-subject, this is to say abstraction, which they make a war horse, a victory. I shall not hide the fact that I was not very enthusiastic to leave our congress to come to the 'Growth and Form' exhibition, to see an exhibition of abstract arts, as they grandly call it, but I was delighted to find an exhibition which was of an art fantastically concrete.

Poetry is simply having very precise terms before our eyes, or at hand, and to place them in a sequence which shakes up, surprises and amazes. There is no need for rare words, rare situations, not at all, and the themes demonstrated in this exhibition are at the service of painting. Painting will be done. From my point of view, I was won over.

I am anti-school. I am going to confess to you that I left school at 13 because schools were very mean in the past, they were no fun. Nowadays they are charming, they are nice, schools welcome young people, unlike in the past, when schools were harsh. Schools have perpetuated authoritarian practices, the imposition of themes and beliefs which are debatable, this is what we call academicism and pompousness. Both strike throughout the world. It is banality that most men are eager to commercialise, to offer in the world, to sell and to buy, and these themes which I am telling you about allow us to get out of this deadlock, and allow unspoilt spirits to have all this scope ahead of them.

2 The South Bank site

GAVIN STAMP

The South Bank site

GAVIN STAMP

T HE Festival of Britain obliged London to look south across the Thames, if a little reluctantly.

The Surrey side, which was for so many years the object of all the architectural scorn of England, is now in process of redevelopment, the clamour of picks, power-drills and grabs filling the air. Plans for a massive embankment, public buildings, a great cultural centre, an exhibition site and gardens are going forward, and there is no doubt that a very fine result will be obtained. [1]

So wrote Sam Price Myers in his guide to *London South of the River* which appeared in 1949 (an enterprising title in the new 'Vision of England' series edited by Clough & Amabel Williams-Ellis and published by Paul Elek). By this time, London had at last woken up to the fact that the low-lying land contained by the great bend of the South Bank of the Thames was cartographically if not socially the centre of the capital. No wonder, therefore, that the principal site for what was officially described as a 'united act of national reassessment, and one corporate reaffirmation of faith in the nation's future'[2] to mark the centenary of the Great Exhibition should have been found in the heart of London on ground long neglected and on the bank of the Thames for so long ignored. Clough Williams-Ellis caught the mood of the day when he wrote

A full appreciation of the general transformation that has been wrought on the South Bank is impossible unless one can recall the dismal dilapidation to which London had for so long been indolently accustomed – at this of all places, its very centre. The 1951 Festival Exhibition served as an admirable new broom wherewith to sweep away the tangled squalor – a gay and inspiring broom, very welcome for itself as well as for effective spring-cleaning.[3]

The Crystal Palace had been first erected in Hyde Park; it would have been unthinkable in 1851 to clear a site for the Great Exhibition on land by the (stinking) Thames, however close to Westminster. The South Bank was then densely developed; part of it covered with warehouses and factories, the rest given over to unfashionable Georgian terraces whose occupants were engaged in activities which did not bear thinking about. A century later, however, things were very different: commercial pressures, population movement, slum-clearance and, above all, wartime bombing had converted the northern tip of Lambeth into a site ripe for coherent development.

The time seemed to have come, at long last, to integrate that sector of unknown territory defined by the quadrant curve of the river from Westminster to Blackfriars Bridge with the administrative and commercial capital on the opposite shore. A start had been made back in 1905 with the decision to build the County Hall, the headquarters of the London County Council, diagonally opposite Parliament on the South Bank. The Labour politician John Burns had seen this as an opportunity to 'lighten up a dull place, sweeten a sour spot, and for the first time bring the south of London into a dignified and beautiful frontage on the River Thames'.[4] Now the process of colonisation was continued by replacing wharves and jetties with a continuation of the river wall to mirror Bazalgette's Victoria Embankment. In the words of the guide to the Festival, 'This project ...

figure 1
The Thames Bank Site Model in the Festival of Britain Information Room, Savoy Court, in December 1948 (Gerald Barry archive)

1. Sam Price Myers, *London South of the River*, London, 1949, p.76.

2. Ian Cox, *The South Bank Exhibition. A Guide to the story it tells*, London, 1951, p.6.

3. In *Royal Festival Hall*, London, 1951, p.22.

4. Quote of 1905 in *Survey of London Monograph 17, County Hall*, London 1991, p.110.

5. Cox, op. cit., p.7.
6. John Pudney, *Music on the South Bank: An Appreciation of the Royal Festival Hall*, London, 1951, p.17.
7. Myers, op. cit., p.76.

has quite transformed the familiar patchwork of rubble and half-derelict buildings which had for so long monopolised the prospect from the North Bank'.[5]

The Festival of Britain, therefore, looked back across the Thames towards Westminster and Charing Cross as well as affording a fine prospect of the then unchallenged dome of St Paul's Cathedral to the east. No attempt was made to integrate the artfully irregular, picturesque plan of the South Bank Exhibition with Darkest Lambeth beyond. Along York Road a screen of tubular steel and canvas, designed by the Architects' Co-Partnership hid from the sight the shabby buildings alongside Waterloo Station, even though so many visitors entered through the adjacent Station Gate. Another light, decorative screen, designed by Edward Mills, ran along the York Road and Waterloo Road boundaries. Not to have turned the Exhibition's back towards the surrounding urban dereliction would have been inconceivable; the Festival was making a new start. It was to leave behind an important cultural monument – the Royal Festival Hall – as the focus of future redevelopment. Tribute may have been paid to the Crystal Palace with a miniature recreation of part of it (at the foot of the Shot Tower) but otherwise the Exhibition was intended to suggest modernity and so reflected the national rejection of the Victorian past and of what then seemed to be the sordid, compromised decades of the earlier 20th century.

Was the Festival site so derelict and worthless as architects, planners and politicians all assumed? Photographs and topographical drawings of the 1940s reveal that a number of Late Georgian terraced houses had managed to survive the Blitz while, a little further south, the lively street markets along the Cut and Lower Marsh indicated that local life continued undaunted. In his appreciation of the Festival Hall, John Pudney could insist that

Little has been lost intrinsically or architecturally by the clearance of the site. Throughout the first half of the twentieth century, the squalid survival of domestic architecture and the unkempt, disordered commercialism of this southern approach to the heart of London dismayed the eye and disturbed the public conscience.[6]

But the real character of this doomed area was suggested by Sam Price Myers:

Here, between Waterloo Bridge and Westminster Bridge, were some streets, much bombed, of late eighteenth and early nineteenth century houses. Seen on quiet Saturday afternoons or Sundays, when I usually visited them, they held both mystery and a stimulating beauty. Who lived in them? One saw little movement; doors were seldom opened and curtains, generally of yellowed lace and closely drawn, shut out the world. Some odd withdrawn life played itself out in these forgotten streets, and, with their end, goes a vision of graceful decay. I cannot remember ever having seen a child on their pavements or at their windows. There was something about Belvedere Road, Sutton Street, Chicheley Street and the rest that no stony embankment can replace; but we must hold to the eternal truth that, unless we turn our faces to the future, we are lost.[7]

I was born the year before the publication of Myers's book, so I do not remember the Festival of Britain but, as a child of the outer – Kent – suburbs, my early memories of the city's centre are of driving with my father through inner South London, whose incoherent dark shabbiness always had some atavistic appeal for me. I recall a large *graffito* on a wall by Vauxhall Bridge – 'Let Mosley Speak' – and, more happily, the giant red lion that then stood outside the Memorial Arch entrance to Waterloo Station. I associated the lion with the one holding a wheel in the British Railways coat of arms painted on the side of engine tenders; but I was wrong. A few years later in 1966 he was moved to the parapet of Westminster Bridge next to the County Hall where he was better placed, for he had long served as a sentinel overlooking the Thames.

The 'South Bank Lion' is the oldest surviving inhabitant of the Festival of Britain site. Indeed he was born there, in Coade's Artificial Stone Manufactory, in 1837 – at the very beginning of Victoria's reign but in the last year of life of the remarkable enterprise which stood on the future site of the Dome of Discovery. The lion was modelled by the sculptor W.F. Woodington and made of the won-

figure 2
Waterloo Bridge, the Shot Tower and the Lion Brewery seen from the Hungerford Bridge in December 1948 (Gerald Barry archive).

figure 3
Taking the Coade stone Lion from the parapet of the Lion Brewery, 2nd February 1949 (Gerald Barry archive).

derfully resilient artificial stone made to a secret formula established by Mrs Eleanor Coade. After the separate pieces of Coade stone had been cramped together, the Lion was painted red and hoisted up onto the parapet of the nearby new Lion Brewery. (A second, smaller lion was placed over the arched entrance in Belvedere Road and is now at the Rugby Union headquarters in Twickenham.)

Designed by Francis Edwards, who had once worked for Soane, this tall building – helpfully labelled 'BREWERY' in large letters below the lion – presented a giant Roman Doric order above an arcaded and rusticated basement fronting the Thames and was the most distinguished piece of architecture which stood on the Festival site. Damaged by fire in 1931 and hit in the war, it was demolished in 1948–49 to make way for the Royal Festival Hall. The lions, however, were saved by the London County Council after George VI expressed concern for them, and the bigger of the two (much more friendly creatures than the stiff, imperious lions that were the symbol for the Wembley exhibition in 1924) was repainted gloss red and placed on a modernistic plinth by a ticket office opposite the Waterloo Station Gate.

The Lion Brewery was illustrated and described in the 23rd volume of the *Survey of London* dealing with *South Bank & Vauxhall* or the northern part of the Parish of St Mary, Lambeth. It was published by the LCC in 1951 to coincide with the Festival, for the exhibition project had encouraged the Survey to look at a long-neglected area of inner London that was about to change dramatically. Covering ground stretching from Vauxhall to the modern site of the National Theatre, the volume deals with much more than the site immediately affected by the Festival; as the Preface explains, '[the book's] value as a record of the topography and buildings of North Lambeth will ... remain long after the South Bank Exhibition has become part of Lambeth history. At a cursory glance the area seems lacking in architectural and historical interest, but a detailed survey has proved richly rewarding'.[8]

The only really ancient monument still standing in the area was Lambeth Palace, but other long lost buildings – like Astley's Amphitheatre in Westminster Bridge Road – were remembered as were the various pleasure gardens which once operated near the Festival site before the brick terraces of houses were raised: Cupar's (or Cupid's) Gardens on the site of the Waterloo Bridge approach and, further south, Apollo's Garden, eventually closed by the magistrates. As with the preceding *Bankside* volume, published in 1950, and the contemporary volumes on the *Parish of St Pancras*, this study of the South Bank paid more

8. *Survey of London*, vol.23, *The Parish of St Mary Lambeth, Part 1, The South Bank & Vauxhall*, London, 1951, p.xxiii. Francis Sheppard records that Bankside was surveyed as it was felt that the Survey should look south of the Thames, and then the rest of Southwark was put on hold when the South Bank and Lambeth were surveyed because of the Festival.

attention to ordinary 19th-century buildings than the Survey of London would have done before the war. Late Georgian terraces that had survived in York Road and along the approach to Waterloo Bridge as well as Victorian churches such as St Andrew's, Coin Street, by S.S. Teulon were discussed and illustrated.

As regards the Exhibition site itself, however, the only other significant building mentioned, apart from some Regency houses in Belvedere Road, was the Shot Tower. Built in 1826 to the designs of D.R. Roper, it had remained in use for making lead shot right up until 1949. It might then have been demolished; instead, it was decided to retain all of it except the gallery chamber at the top. 'Many people, myself included,' recalled Gerald Barry,

figure 4
Tenison Street and Belvedere Road (foreground) seen from the Shot Tower in January 1949 (Gerald Barry archive)

at first thought that the Shot Tower should come down. It seemed to have little to say in terms of modern architecture and to be in danger of looking like an anachronism. I was quite wrong. I reckoned without the sentiment of the Londoner and without the tower's possibilities ... The Londoner loved it because it was familiar, and its familiarity was given a new, exciting appeal by reshaping its summit to accommodate a lighthouse and a radio telescope.[9]

Alas, this did not prevent its demolition a decade later to make way for the Queen Elizabeth Hall. Admittedly it had been intended to give the Shot Tower only a temporary lease of life but, as Clough Williams-Ellis put it, 'when the show is over, the felling of this old friend, so lately given due recognition and a new aesthetic purpose, would seem as cruel to some of us as would the removal of the Campanile from St. Marks'.[10]

The Survey of London volume indicates a growing interest in characteristic urban architecture already manifested by the publication of John Summerson's Georgian London in 1945. A wider interest in the history of the area – in its sociological and topographical complexity – was the inspiration for Forlorn Sunset, an historical novel by Michael Sadleir published in 1947 – the year of the conception of the Festival. A sequel to Fanny by Gaslight of 1940, Forlorn Sunset was, again, a work of a prurient investigation into the Victorian underworld illuminated by detailed urban history translated into fiction. Sadleir's novels are remarkable for their unpatronising evocation of Victorian life and for their historical and topographical accuracy. The South Bank area around Waterloo is only one of several locations for the action of the book, but the picture of it presented was the result of considerable research and was accompanied by a map of the area in about 1860.

9. Mary Banham & Bevis Hillier, A Tonic to the Nation. The Festival of Britain 1951, London, 1976, p.20.

10. Royal Festival Hall, London, 1951, p.22.

The focus of the narrative was Granby Street, the centre of an area of brothels between Lower Marsh and Waterloo Road whose 'career of brazen and crapulous infamy', Sadleir maintained, was 'without parallel in the history of nineteenth-century London'.[11] This was a phenomenon which seems to have escaped the attention of more recent social and urban historians, but if Granby Street is unknown today it is because both it and the surrounding streets were obliterated by the expansion of Waterloo Station after 1874. This particular pocket of vice lay to the south of the Festival site, but Sadleir also described the parochial responsibilities of the vicar of St John's, Waterloo Road, which included streets which would disappear under exhibition pavilions a century hence.

He had troubles in plenty of his own. Indeed, just because they were not, like Granby Street, utterly irreclaimable, the dark patches under his care were the more troublesome and heart-breaking. They were not the people themselves who drove him to despair. He might deplore their degradation, their turbulence and their squalor; he might observe with heavy heart, as he passed through Tenison Street or along his section of York Road, the perpetual in-and-out traffic, with drunken men in tow, of painted slatterns of all ages who kept an open door or hired six feet of flock on broken springs, somewhere upstairs behind the grimy frontages. But he did not condemn. What chance had these folk to be other than squalid and vicious?[12]

Sadleir's clergyman was fictional, but his church was real enough and it played a part in the Festival although it lay beyond the colourful screen walls enclosing the South Bank Exhibition. St John's, with its Greek Doric portico and prominent steeple next to Waterloo Station, is one of the so-called Waterloo Churches built in South London after the Napoleonic Wars. Designed by Francis Bedford, it was consecrated in 1824 and three years later James Elmes described it in *Metropolitan Improvements* as having 'some faults and many beauties ... this propriety of annexation and real beauty of proportion is absolutely destroyed by the atrocity of a steeple, the ugliest perhaps in London, which is straddled a cock-horse across the pediment'.[13] The interior was enhanced by Ninian Comper in 1924 but the interior was badly damaged in 1940. After a decade of standing open to the sky, it was restored by that dreary architect, Thomas H. Ford, as The Festival Church. 'Britain is a Christian community,' the official Festival literature could still confidently proclaim. 'The Christian faith is inseparably a part of our history. It has strengthened all those endeavours which this Festival has been built to display and the quality of our Faith will be exhibited not only in what is made for 1951, but in the manner of its making.'[14]

'The church of St John', Sadleir wrote, 'designed on classical lines by Bedford in 1824, was forceful and in an aggressive way a dignified building, but one little enough appreciated in the 'fifties and 'sixties, when parsonical gothic, however ill-assorted with its surroundings, was considered the only style worthy of the Establishment'.[15] Sadleir was perhaps revealing the tastes and prejudices of his own generation here, but he devoted a whole chapter to the history of the area. The South Bank was low-lying and marshy and so had long remained undeveloped. In the section of the Barkers' panorama of London taken from the roof of the Albion Mills by Blackfriars Bridge and looking south-west towards Westminster, it can be seen that, in 1792–93, most of 'Lambeth Marsh' within the bend of the river consisted of open ground on which trees were much more numerous than buildings. The possibility of residential development there emerged with the opening of Waterloo Bridge as a toll bridge in 1817. From this new river crossing, a long straight road was laid out to the Obelisk at St George's Circus, where it joined another radial road leading to the earlier handsome bridge at Blackfriars; houses soon followed, in new streets like Tenison Street whose names indicated that the ground landlord was the Archbishop of Canterbury.

The Waterloo Bridge Estate was one of several new developments in the area. It was built after 1824 by John Field to designs by the architect and antiquary, Lewis Nockalls Cottingham, who himself moved in 1828 into No.86 (originally

11. Michael Sadleir, *Forlorn Sunset*, London, 1947, p.26. Sadleir's picture of Granby Street was based on such books as *Ragged London in 1861* by John Hollingshead.

12. Sadleir, op. cit., p.54.

13. *Metropolitan Improvements*, 1827, quoted in *Survey of London*, vol.23, op. cit., p.32.

14. The Official Book of the Festival of Britain, London, 1951, p.20.

15. Sadleir, op. cit., p.52.

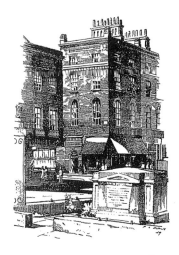

figure 5
Cottingham's Museum , 86 Waterloo
Road, seen from the churchyard of
St John's Church in 1949: drawing by
F.A. Evans in the *Survey of London*
volume.

No.43) Waterloo Road on the west side of the rising approach to the bridge. This end-of-terrace house was specially designed to contain his library and his huge and celebrated collection of architectural casts, models and objects. Cottingham's 'Museum of Mediaeval Art' was sold and dispersed in 1851, four years after its curator's death and exactly a century before the demolition of the terrace. In 1832, Cottingham had been able to claim that his collection had been viewed by 'several noblemen of acknowledged taste and many distinguished literary characters as well as by numerous professional friends'.[16] The Waterloo Road was certainly a partial success as a new transpontine suburb for a couple of decades, but the attempts to create respectable residential areas here was soon undermined by the advent of the railway.

The original terminus of the London & Southampton Railway was opened in 1838 out at Nine Elms, but in 1845 what became the London & South Western Railway planned an extension into central London and began buying up property for a temporary terminus by the Waterloo Bridge Road. The station opened in 1848 and the collapse of the railway building boom resulted in it becoming permanent.

The ruin of Waterloo Road as a street of residential decency was now complete. No nice family could have a home in the immediate neighbourhood of a big railway station. Think of the noise and crowds and smuts and general vexatiousness! But if the staid middle-class disliked a station at their doors, there were plenty of folk of other kinds who liked one very much , [17]

Sadleir's description of the area in the mid-19th century was the product of a highly developed historical imagination. Possibly he exaggerated the squalor – possibly not. The truth of his depiction is suggested by a few entries in the diaries of that high-principled and tortured investigator into low life, A.J. Munby. In March 1862 he crossed over Westminster Bridge, which was then being re-built, 'at the Surrey end of which I found a group of dustwomen, resting on their way home'. He arranged for one to be photographed at a nearby photographer's shop, and was then introduced to another girl – 'She's an envelope maker, Sir – there's lots of 'em hereabouts' – before being outraged by being offered much more than he wanted – 'was you in want of any ballet girls or poses plastiques? I can supply you Sir with girls ... '[18] On the other hand, three years earlier Munby had encountered a girl who had invested her earnings from prostitution in a coffee house on the South Bank. '"Quite true", she said simply. "I manage it all by myself, & can give you chops & tea – & anything you like: you must come and see me".' And so he did a few days later. 'Came back round by Waterloo Bridge, to seek for the Hampshire Coffee House. A small decent house just over the Bridge. I asked a policeman about it: Yes, it was quite respectable: never heard anything against it: didn't think bad women went there at all ... '[19]

We also have a first-hand account of the same area a few decades later in *Cock Sparrow*, the autobiography of that brilliant designer, Oliver P. Bernard (1881–1939), published in 1936. The first chapter is entitled 'Lambeth Days' and begins in 1887, Victoria's Golden Jubilee year, 'in Waterloo Road, in the borough of Lambeth, one day when for once that road was enlivened with bunting that limply festooned the shops, flour mills, shot towers and other premises forming the southern approach to a bridge named in commemoration of a military event.' This was because Bernard's first home was No.8 Waterloo Road, a little to the north of Cottingham's house in one of the terraces on the western side of the ascent to the bridge which were to be cleared for the Exhibition.

On this highway Bunny [i.e. Bernard] obtained his first view of humanity through various shop windows, behind some of which were Jewish tailors and tailoresses, squatting in open slavery ... The stench of other shops was not so interesting; that of a waxwork maker's and the stale odour of public houses were most repugnant. There was a wonderful fishmonger's, under the railway arch near York Road, over which trains thundered and whistles shrieked. Here everything smelled clean and cold; there were lovely blocks of ice and jolly

16. Janet Myles, L.N. *Cottingham 1787–1847. Architect of the Gothic Revival*, London, 1996, p.28. Cottingham's 1826 elevation for 80–86 Waterloo Bridge Road is illustrated on p.118 and in the Survey of London, vol.23.

17. Sadleir, op. cit., p.24.

18. Derek Hudson, *Munby: Man of Two Worlds. The Life and Diaries of Arthur J. Munby 1828–1910*, London, 1972, p.117.

19. Munby, op. cit., p.117.

salesmen who seemed to revel in this shop ... Nearby, at opposite corners of York Road, blue-chinned gentlemen in peculiar clothes, and fair-haired ladies, congregated as if waiting for something auspicious to happen; these street corners were an open market of human talent awaiting the pleasure of dictators who described themselves as dramatic and variety agents.[20]

Bernard's vivid recollections of the richness and variety of Cockney life in the streets to the north of Waterloo Station also included its seamier side, such as the life in the many public houses that lay on the many street corners. And then there was the nether region which lay physically below the bridge approach.

To the bottom of a flight of cavernous stone steps near Waterloo Bridge, one descended through a sickening presence of pink chlorate of lime, which free deposit was then a customary method of counteracting the consequences of inadequate public lavatories. By this descent one arrived in Belvedere Road, where there were other and smaller shops and hovels that smelt of dirt and decay, except one which overpowered all others with a concentrated reek of paraffin oil and pungent piccalilli. Left to his own innocent resources, Bunny sought the companionship of the horde of juveniles who belonged to this lower region, until one day his father traced him there and, after walking him home, thrashed him unmercifully without explaining the apparent social misconduct that merited such inexplicable punishment.[21]

By this time, the railway companies had done yet more damage to the area. Following a report by its secretary, Dr Samuel Smiles – better known as the author of *Self Help* and of biographies of the great engineers – the South Eastern Railway had ruthlessly driven an elevated railway line on arches from London Bridge over Waterloo Road (narrowly avoiding St John's Church) and York Road and so across the river to a new terminus on the site of the Hungerford Market at Charing Cross. This is the line that bisected the Festival site and its construction in 1862–64 ensured that the South Bank of the Thames remained industrial and shabby (although Charles Booth's *Descriptive Map of London Poverty* in 1889 indicates that the pockets of desperate poverty were further east and further south).[22]

The most regrettable aspect of this railway project was the removal of the first Hungerford Bridge, the suspension bridge designed by I.K. Brunel with architectural assistance on the towers from James Bunning. With a clear central span of 676 feet, it had opened on May 1st 1845 to provide a direct pedestrian route from the Hungerford Market and the Strand to Belvedere Road. On that opening day, 36,254 people passed over it, 20,000 in the first hour, and any unequal loading on the three spans was accommodated by rolling 'saddles' in the towers to which the chains were attached. These facts are worth repeating because of the contrast made with the farcical opening – and shutting – of the Millennium Bridge to Bankside a century and a half later. Henry Fox Talbot, the pioneer photographer, recorded the bridge when new and both the Shot Tower and the Lion Brewery are visible in the background of his early calotype.[23]

Unfortunately, during its short life, Brunel's beautiful bridge did not succeed either in improving the fortunes of the Hungerford Market or in reviving Belvedere Road as a residential area. The only boon of its replacement by the railway bridge was that the chains were taken to Bristol to complete Brunel's early and unfinished Clifton Suspension Bridge across the Avon. Otherwise, the arrival of the South Eastern Railway on the north bank of the Thames was disastrous in terms of civic amenity. Nobody has ever had a good word to say for the ugly lattice girder railway bridge – even if Claude Monet sometimes painted it in the London smog. Arthur Munby travelled on the new railway the day it opened, 11th January 1864, and was not impressed.

Our train went out of what lately was Hungerford market, over what was Hungerford Bridge: instead of the graceful curves of that, we now have a horizontal line of huge gratings, between the bars of which the folks on the footway stood to gaze at us. All the rest of the way, our Asmodeus machine looks over the roofs of poor men's houses which it has made horrible to live in, and passes across the sites of infinite dwellings destroyed ... Who

20. Oliver P. Bernard, *Cock Sparrow*, London, 1936, pp.1 & 13–14.

21. Bernard, op. cit., p.16.

22. On the map, the buildings lining Waterloo Road and York Road were coloured as 'Well-to-do. Middle Class' and the streets behind either 'Fairly comfortable. Good ordinary earnings' or 'Mixed. Some comfortable, others poor'. The streets marked blue or, worst of all, dark purple were around Coin Street to the east, and further south.

23. See Gavin Stamp, 'The Hungerford Market' in *AA Files* 11, Spring 1986, pp.58–70, and *The Changing Metropolis. Earliest Photographs of London 1839–1879*, London, 1984, p.156.

figure 6
The South Bank and Brunel's
Hungerford Bridge seen from the
Hungerford Market in c.1860 shortly
before the advent of the railway into
Charing Cross (Crown Copyright N M R)

are we that we should decimate the population and defile our children's minds with the sight of these monstrous and horrible forms, for the sake of gaining half an hour on the way to our work or our dinner?[24]

Schemes for the abolition of this railway bridge occupied the imaginations of architects and planners for over half a century, thereby diverting their attention to the possibilities for replanning the South Bank at the same time – displaying, of course, complete indifference to the buildings that stood there and the people that lived and worked in them.[25] The removal of the railway terminus at Charing Cross to Waterloo was first suggested by the new LCC as early as 1891. At the RIBA's international Town Planning Conference in 1910, a design by T.E. Colcutt was exhibited which envisaged the Charing Cross railway bridge replaced by a road bridge which was to be lined with two stories of shops leading to a South Bank laid out with boulevards and given an embankment (a continuation of the river wall being constructed in front of the new County Hall to the south).[26] The eastern focus of this axis was to be a grandly rebuilt Waterloo Station, with one side being the existing terminus of the London & South Western Railway and the other a new South Eastern & Chatham terminus for the railway cut back from Charing Cross. Indeed, it was in these Edwardian years that Waterloo Station was rebuilt with a new overall roof and external grand Classical facades – a slow process which culminated in the opening of the Memorial Arch in 1922. All this reflected the contemporary interest in the Grand Manner and in replanning cities on monumental and formal lines.

That the Charing Cross Bridge should be rebuilt as a road bridge was soon generally agreed and, after the First World War, the Dean of St Paul's suggested 'the blowing up' of the railway bridge 'as our National War Memorial'.[27] In 1916 a Bill for strengthening the existing railway bridge had been opposed by the recently founded London Society because 'it was obvious that, if this were done,

24. Munby, op. cit., pp.174–175; Asmodeus was the evil demon in the Apocryphal book of Tobit and appeared in Le Sage's *Devil on Two Sticks* hanging on the steeple of St Salvador's church and opening up the roofs of the houses below to expose the activities of their inhabitants.

25. Andrew Saint, 'A Pre-History of the South Bank', unpublished lecture, 1994.

26. *Royal Institute of British Architects, Town Planning Conference*, London, 10–15 October 1910, Transactions, London 1911, fig.9.

27. Sir Aston Webb, ed., *London of the Future*, by the London Society, London, 1921, p.21.

any proposal for removing the bridge would be rendered much more difficult'.[28] A new, war memorial bridge, aligned with the steeple of St Martin's-in-the-Fields and with triumphal arches at either end, was then proposed by Sir Reginald Blomfield and Sir Aston Webb together with the politician John Burns. In the introduction to a book on *London of the Future* published by the London Society in 1921, Aston Webb observed of the four iron railway bridges across the Thames that 'none are worthy to remain a moment longer than absolutely necessary, while Charing Cross Bridge is not worthy to remain at all' and noted 'the Government's support for the removal of the present station to the southern side, the construction of a fine road bridge in place of the existing unsightly railway bridge, and the erection of a national memorial on the site of the present station'.[29]

In his contribution, on the subject of 'The Surrey Side', Paul Waterhouse proposed a wide new avenue running from the new bridge to St George's in the Borough and a new railway station east of Blackfriars Road. A large square would occupy the present site of the Festival Hall. He was certain that 'The centre of gravity of London is going to shift southward. I do not suggest that the heart of London will cross the water, but I do suggest and prophesy that the occupation of Surrey land by official, Imperial, national and influential tenants is sure to come and to come quickly'.[30] In the same book, Sir Arthur Fell, MP, wondered

Is there any ordinary Londoner who could name any buildings or monuments south of the Thames beyond St Thomas's Hospital and Waterloo Station? ... The London County Council Town Hall, when finished, will be a beginning, and when the new bridge and great station are added, the very heart of this neglected London will be opened up and other improvements will follow, and the south of the river will be raised from the deadly torpor which has overshadowed it for the past forty years. It was quite different fifty years ago. At that time Astley's Theatre was fashionable and all London flocked to see Miss Ada Menken as 'Mazeppa' on her barebacked steed. The 'Old Vic', as it was called, drew all London for its pantomimes and its transpontine blood-curdling drama.[31]

By 1932, Harold P. Clunn in *The Face of London* could claim that, 'By universal consent Charing Cross Bridge is now doomed and, whatever the present difficulties, its destruction will play a most important part in the reconstruction of London'.[32] The situation was, however, by now complicated by the debate about whether to restore or replace John Rennie's magnificent Waterloo Bridge, which had begun to show symptoms of serious settlement in 1923–24 and was anyway too narrow to accommodate the rails for the trams the LCC wanted to take across the Thames

28. *London of the Future*, p.19. The London Society had been founded in 1912.

29. ibid., pp.25 & 20.

30. ibid., p.135.

31. ibid., p.123.

32. Harold P. Clunn, *The Face of London*, London, 1932, p.116.

figure 7
Waterloo Bridge and the Shot Tower in c.1880 seen from the North Bank (Crown Copyright NMR)

33. Robert Byron, *How We Celebrate the Coronation*, London, 1937, p.13; Edward Walford, ed., *Old and New London*, London, n.d., vol.3, p.292.

34. A perspective by William Walcot of his 1926 design for a double-decker road and rail bridge was in the possession of the late Roderick Gradidge.

35. Arthur Keen, *Charing Cross Bridge*, London, 1930, p.vi.

36. *The Architects' Journal*, 11th December 1929, pp.902–903.

37. Byron, op. cit., pp.14–15.

at this point. The consequence was a battle between those who wished to rebuild Waterloo Bridge and the advocates of saving what Robert Byron rightly described as 'the best bridge London ever had' (and Canova had considered 'the noblest bridge in the world ... alone worth coming from Rome to see') by having a new Charing Cross Bridge for road traffic instead.[33]

The many different schemes for a road bridge were discussed and illustrated in the book by Arthur Keen published in 1930. Although a double-decker Charing Cross Bridge for both road and rail traffic was also proposed in the 1920s, most suggestions involved removing the railway and covering the South Bank with wide new streets and squares between vast new stations.[34] In the preface to Keen's book, the Earl of Crawford and Balcarres, chairman of the new Royal Fine Art Commission, wrote that 'much against my will he convinces me that the picturesque must give way to sterner things, and that the attractive wharfs and warehouses of old Lambeth must vanish, to be replaced by something more useful, and let us hope effective and in its own way impressive'.[35] In 1928 the Royal Commission on Cross-River Traffic produced a scheme for a new Charing Cross Bridge which was heavily criticised for crudely accommodating road traffic at the expense of wider architectural and town planning considerations.

Tempers become even more frayed the following year when a new scheme by the LCC with the Southern Railway for rebuilding the Charing Cross Bridge and for a new station at Waterloo was opposed by the RIBA and others, despite having Sir Edwin Lutyens, 'Architect Laureate', as consultant to give it respectability. The criticism was just: Lutyens's job had been to apply elevations to the massive commercial blocks which were to face the river either side of a grand square, but most objectionable was the fact that the whole area between the new axial avenue and Waterloo Road was to be occupied by a new railway terminus to serve Kent while a new avenue from the bridge would suddenly bend to arrive at a giant roundabout on the site of the Old Vic. As the *Architects' Journal* commented in 1929: 'The layout of the roads on the Surrey side, judged from the aesthetic point of view, can only be described as hideous, and must be the work of men untrained in that particular type of intellectual activity which is required for the achievement of civic design'.[36]

The Bill for the new bridge was defeated in Parliament, and the Charing Cross Bridge project came to epitomise what was wrong with London, with the Ministry of Transport, the London County Council, the Borough of Lambeth, the RIBA, the Southern Railway and the other interested organisations and individuals all having different and often conflicting ideas about the best solution to a universally recognised problem. It was in this context that Gerald Barry published a National Plan in 1931 with his own proposals for roads and railways on the South Bank [for which see the essay by Suzanne Waters in this journal].

Lutyens resigned from the RIBA when he was criticised during this controversy, but, in the event, the Southern Railway could not afford to abolish Charing Cross Station and its attendant and universally execrated bridge and so it was Waterloo Bridge that went, despite its supreme merit as a work of art. This foul deed was done by Herbert Morrison, as Leader of the Labour-controlled LCC, in 1934 in defiance of the expressed wish of Parliament to preserve Rennie's bridge. Political expediency and utilitarian thinking triumphed over wider considerations and the best long-term solution. As Byron observed in his 1937 conservation polemic, *How We Celebrate the Coronation*, 'If this is public welfare, I prefer Colonel Blimp. He is wolf all over. The party of planners and beautifiers dresses itself up like sheep'.[37]

Considering this civic debacle, the only consolation is that the old Waterloo Bridge was replaced by a fine new structure by Rendel, Palmer & Tritton, with Sir Giles Scott acting as consultant. Apart from this gratuitous rebuilding, however, nothing came of all the grand plans so that, for the South Bank, the most exciting artistic moment before the Festival was possibly when Comper reviewed the entire crews of two battleships at the Union Jack Club in the Waterloo Road with a view to finding an ideal model for a proposed naked male figure of Victory on his Welsh National War Memorial in Cathays Park in Cardiff. He found what he was looking for in the manly shape of Able Seaman Fred Barker.[38]

After 1940, when the Luftwaffe began to make its own contribution to the replanning of London, further grand designs emerged. In 1942 a committee of Royal Academicians under the chairmanship of Lutyens published *London Replanned*, a depressing vision of axial vistas and roundabouts. South London was to be completely transformed: a giant circular park was proposed at St George's Circus, the Charing Cross Bridge was to be rebuilt (of course) and 'the Surrey bank of the River ... developed with Embankment gardens and office buildings' while the clock was to be turned back a century by taking the Waterloo terminus back to Nine Elms. Naturally, 'It is anticipated that the older portions of the district will be entirely rebuilt'.[39] The second report of the R.A. Planning Committee, published in 1944 as *Road, Rail and River in London*, was little better, envisaging embankment gardens and commercial buildings lining the Thames.

The County of London Plan prepared for the LCC by J.H. Forshaw and Patrick Abercrombie and published in 1943 was less formal in conception. In this, detailed proposals were published for the South Bank, which in the long term – following the removal of riverside industrial activity – was to have two theatres to the north of a new road running across the future Festival site and a swimming pool and a youth centre to the south, all on a more informal layout (by Arthur Ling) reflecting the influence of Continental modernism. Here was the genesis of the idea of a cultural centre on the South Bank, but its inspiration came from the Shakespeare Memorial National Theatre Committee which had approached the LCC for a new site instead of South Kensington and were offered one between the Waterloo and Hungerford Bridges in 1942 – for which the now elderly and ailing Lutyens produced a sketch design.[40]

'It is one of the great anomalies of the capital,' wrote Forshaw and Abercrombie,

that while the river, from Westminster eastwards, is lined on the north side with magnificent buildings and possesses a spacious and attractive embankment road, the corresponding south bank, excepting St. Thomas's Hospital and the County Hall, should present a depressing, semi-derelict appearance, lacking any sense of that dignity and order appropriate to its location at the centre of London and fronting onto the great waterway. This gloomy aspect is intensified to-day by war damage ... Cleared of its encumbrances, equipped with a continuous strip of grass and a wide esplanade ... this area, extending on the front as far as London Bridge and inland to York Road, Stamford Street and Southwark Street, might well include a great cultural centre, embracing, amongst other features, a modern theatre, a large concert hall and the headquarters of various organisations.

This scheme, of course, 'would involve the removal of the present railway bridge at Charing Cross'.[41]

According to yet another plan for rebuilding the South Bank, made by Charles Holden after the war for both the LCC and the Ministry of Works, the Charing Cross Bridge would be rebuilt in 1971–74. By that date the river would be lined with government offices (like a succession of Senate Houses) together with an hotel and the projected National Theatre and concert hall. This uninspiring vision, following on from Abercrombie, was accepted in 1948 but was immediately superseded by the proposal for the Festival Hall and the South Bank Exhibition. Meanwhile, despite the best laid plans of knighted architects and of politicians, and in defiance of damage caused by a flying bomb in 1944, the wretched railway bridge obstinately continued to allow green electric trains to rattle into Charing Cross Station.

Such is town planning in London, a city in which – on the whole, perhaps, fortunately – the enduring reality of bricks and mortar tends to defy the grand vision and the desire to make all things new. Indeed, the survival of the

figure 8
Tenison Street and the Shot Tower in 1940, pencil drawing by Ailwyn Best. (Andrew Sanders)

38. Anthony Symondson, *The Life and Work of Sir Ninian Comper 1864–1960*, London, 1988, p.22.

39. *London Replanned, The Royal Academy Planning Committee's Interim Report*, London, 1942, p.25.

40. Illustrated in A.S.G. Butler, *The Architecture of Sir Edwin Lutyens*, vol.3, London 1950, pl.63. The LCC had successfully promoted a Bill to acquire Thames-side land to control development in 1934 and more land was acquired by compulsory purchase in 1938 to permit the building of an embankment wall.

41. J.H. Forshaw & Patrick Abercrombie, *The County of London Plan proposed for the London County Council*, London, 1943, pp.130–131.

intractable railway viaduct across the cleared site designated for the Festival became a principal generative factor in the evolution of the 'egg in the box' solution for soundproofing the Royal Festival Hall, even though the site and levels of the new concert hall were fixed in the belief that it would eventually be replaced by a road bridge. Fifty years on again, the Hungerford Railway Bridge is still with us, ugly as ever, along with that single survivor from the South Bank Exhibition, the Royal Festival Hall, while the Shot Tower and the Dome of Discovery have needlessly disappeared. It is a story as sad as it is farcical.

To get a sense of what the old, shabby, Late Georgian Waterloo that was sacrificed for the Festival looked like, to imagine the South Bank of Michael Sadleir, Sam Price Myers and Oliver Bernard, it is now necessary to go east of Waterloo Road and its dreadful, destructive roundabout to explore the streets and terraces around Roupell Street (saved from comprehensive redevelopment a decade later by local opposition). I wish I had seen the Festival of Britain but, even more, I would like to be able to remember the South Bank before the Exhibition arrived. 'One of the principal aims of the Festival is to bring to the British way of life some enrichment that will endure for long after the Festival year is over,' explained the official Guide. 'It is fitting, therefore, that the main national Exhibition should be the first occupant of a site which has been so long abandoned by human enterprise and so newly won from the river'.[42] But that last statement was a lie.

Owing, in part, to the malevolence towards the exhibition structures displayed by the new Conservative government elected in 1951 and the cynical indifference of the Minister of Works, David 'Smarty Boots' Eccles, the legacy of the Festival on the South Bank was unresolved planning and incoherent, windswept spaces; a no man's land in which a handful of aspiring cultural buildings are compromised by unresolved walkways and unpleasant underpasses and all overshadowed by the mediocrity of the Shell Tower and the criminal inhumanity of the Waterloo roundabout. This incomplete vision, this distorted memory of what once was, and could have been – still cut in half by that railway viaduct – has yet to be resolved. It would take much more than the Festival of Britain to overcome London's traditional snobbish prejudice against the Surrey side of the Thames (although the wonderful 'London Eye' wheel together with Tate Modern in Bankside Power Station may now have succeeded in doing this). Much as I admire the Festival Hall (and the Hayward Gallery), I would rather see the Shot Tower and Cottingham's terraces still standing today as well, while I deeply lament the passing of old Waterloo Bridge and the Lion Brewery. But at least the dear old South Bank Lion is still with us, even if stripped of his red livery.

ACKNOWLEDGEMENTS

I am most grateful to Andrew Saint for his advice and help on the various abortive schemes to rebuild the Charing Cross Bridge and replan the South Bank; to Rosemary Hill for her advice and for reminding me that L.N. Cottingham once lived in the Waterloo Road; to Alan Powers for reminding me that Oliver Bernard did so too; and to Andrew Sanders for more local information. As I once regularly walked over the Hungerford Bridge when I lived nearby in Pocock Street, I still feel wistful and proprietorial about the poor old South Bank: hence this essay.

42. Cox, op. cit., p.7.

3 Colour Plates

Below · The Festival site seen from across the Thames by Westminster Pier.
(Michael Cooke-Yarborough / C20 Society)

Opposite · Tetrahedral screen to York Road. Architects' Co-Partnership.
(Michael Cooke-Yarborough / C20 Society)

Dome of Discovery, with Transport and Royal Festival Hall and Shot Tower.
(Michael Cooke-Yarborough / c20 Society)

Concourse, with entrances to The Land and People of Britain. H.T. Cadbury-Brown.
(H.T. Cadbury-Brown)

Left to right: 1851 Centenary Pavilion, Harbour Bar, Edward Mills's screen; Homes and Garden Pavilion to the rear with John Piper mural and Yacht Basin in foreground. (Michael Cooke-Yarborough / c20 Society)

Chicheley Street entrance, with York Road screen, Administration Block to left, unfinished. (Michael Cooke-Yarborough / c20 Society)

Top · The '51 Bar by Leonard Manasseh, with Daphne Hardy's concrete sculpture underneath, and County Hall behind. The white structure to the left was the water tank.
Below · The '51 Bar by night. (Michael Cooke-Yarborough / C20 Society)

Right · Skylon and the Concourse by night. The lights were set in jars into the concourse.
(Michael Cooke-Yarborough / C20 Society)

The Concourse by night, seen from the Regatta Restaurant, showing the Transport Pavilion on the left, with locomotive in front (Arcon), the entrance from Waterloo Station lit up (Gordon Tait), and the York Road screen and Dome of Discovery to the right. (H.T. Cadbury-Brown)

The Architects' Co-Partnership's screen to York Road by night.
(Michael Cooke-Yarborough / C20 Society)

The Boat Dock by night, with the entrance to the Shot Tower alongside and Gordon and Ursula Bowyer's 'Sport' behind.
(Michael Cooke-Yarborough / C20 Society)

The Lion and Unicorn Pavilion and Unicorn Café by night, with Hungerford Bridge, the York Road entrance and Upstream section behind.
(Michael Cooke-Yarborough / C20 Society)

Previous Page • View of the South Bank site from across the river by night; the Royal Festival Hall with its original façade is in the centre, with the Shot Tower to the left and Skylon to the right. (Popperfoto)

Above • Inside the Lion and Unicorn Pavilion. Dick Russell and Robert Goodden. (Michael Cooke-Yarborough/C20 Society)

Sir Hugh Casson, 'Dome of Discovery under construction' (courtesy of Alan Irvine and Sir Hugh Casson Ltd.)

In Search of Sir Gerald Barry, the man
behind the Festival of Britain

SUZANNE WATERS

In Search of Sir Gerald Barry, the man behind the Festival of Britain

SUZANNE WATERS

H ATEFUL *schooldays at Marlborough and the war itself turned me into a rebel all right. My generation (what was left of it) were Angry Young Men. But we also believed in Utopia.*[1]

This quote from an unfinished draft of Sir Gerald Barry's autobiography sums up the essence of the man who became the Director General of the Festival of Britain.

When we look back at the Festival and the personalities involved, much of the writing has focused on the figures of Herbert Morrison and Hugh Casson, but owing to the lack of writing and research into his life, little is known about the Director General, Gerald Reid Barry (1898–1968). A recent interview with Max Nicholson, his friend and sparring partner for over twenty years, has revealed much more about this highly imaginative, witty, warm, humane man. As the former editor of the *Week-end Review* and the *News Chronicle*, he was well suited to his role as Director. He himself declared, and Max Nicholson confirmed, that the roots of the Festival lay in the ideas about politics, architecture and life expressed by Barry and his contemporaries during the interwar period.

Barry was born in Surbiton, the son of a clergyman who moved soon after to Norfolk. He later recalled his childhood being extremely sheltered. This sheltered rural idyll was brought to an abrupt end when Gerald was sent to Marlborough College, which he loathed. Yet he was influenced by two masters. One was his history tutor John O'Hagan, whose tutorials taught Barry 'to read to think, and the magic of standing on one's head and seeing the world upside down.'[2] He was to need such skills for the Festival. The other influence, far less benign but just as deep, was a bullying master called Sandford, whom Barry likened to a monkey, 'I cannot think of him to this day half a century later, without my anger and detestation rising.'[3] It was this master's particularly brutal bullying of a pupil that made Barry into a rebel. That was the lasting legacy of Marlborough. At 18, he joined the Royal Flying Corps and it was the senseless slaughter he witnessed in the War that reaffirmed his desire to fight for a better world.

In 1924 at the age of 26, Barry became editor of the *Saturday Review*, which opened many literary and political doors. He found his milieu in the 'unexpected company' of Margot Asquith, Hilaire Belloc, J.M. Barrie, G.K. Chesterton and J.B. Priestley amongst others.[4] He also sought to make the periodical 'an organ of the most persuasive kind of Conservatism', relating to principle rather than Party.[5] But a clash with the new owner over Lord Beaverbrook's United Empire Party, which advocated a free trade policy within the Empire but excluded Europe (a foreshadowing of Beaverbrook's isolationist views) led to his resignation in January 1930, taking most of his staff with him. Barry disliked the idea of the *Saturday Review* being used as a vehicle for Beaverbrook's propaganda for the Party. It was this stance for editorial independence that remained at the root of Beaverbrook's later hostility to the Festival of Britain.

Two weeks later on the 14 February, the *Week-end Review*, appeared with Barry as editor.[6] Financed by Samuel Courtauld, it was intended to be to be a review of 'politics, books, the theatre, art and music'. The Paper got off to a resounding

1. Folder no.57, draft autobiography, Sir Gerald Barry papers, British Library of Political and Economic Science (BLPES).
2. ibid.
3. ibid.
4. ibid.
5. Sir William Haley 'Gerald Barry', in E.T. Williams & C.S. Nicholls, eds. *Dictionary Of National Biography* (1961–1970), Oxford University Press, 1981, p.76.
6. *Week-end Review*, 14 March 1930.

figure 1
The Queen, Ralph Tubbs and Gerald Barry looking at the Dome of Discovery. 2 May 1950 (Gerald Barry archive)

7. ibid.
8. ibid.
9. *Week-end Review*, 14 February 1931, supplement in BLPES folder no.46.
10. ibid.
11. ibid.

start, with many messages of support including one from the Prime Minister, Ramsay Macdonald, who said 'it was essential that there should be an independent and intelligent journalism in this country'.[7] Other well wishers included Herbert (later Viscount) Samuel, Stanley Baldwin, John Galsworthy and Sir Edwin Lutyens. Its emphasis was on airing of current political issues and encouraging the arts, continuing the format of intellectualism and politics developed in the *Saturday Review*. Regular poetry competitions were held, book reviews and essays on architecture. One long standing contributor was Barry's friend the architect Clough Williams-Ellis, who wrote a series of articles on ten British cities entitled 'What is Wrong with England'? These were written at the height of Williams-Ellis's involvement in campaigning for the environment.

The articles reflected Barry's concern over environmental issues such as ribbon development, bypass bungalow architecture and filling stations, then spreading throughout the country. In his introduction to the series, Barry laments the lack of effective planning legislation in this area and describes Clough as looking at these cities in terms of their amenities and architectural standards.[8] One of the features of the magazine was the column 'This England' compiled from strange newspaper stories submitted by readers and selected by Barry as expressive of the English character. This feature was maintained when the *Week-end Review* merged with the *New Statesman and Nation* in 1934 and has remained a weekly item in the *New Statesman* ever since.

Amidst the crisis of 1931, when Ramsay Macdonald's government was facing severe economic depression and high unemployment, Barry launched one of his most ambitious projects. On February 14 the *Week-end Review* issued as a supplement a document called the National Plan, compiled by the young Max Nicholson (born 1904). Described as 'a manifesto for a radical change in how to govern a nation,' it proposed a series of state controlled organisations and a reorganisation of the state by function and was extremely wide ranging. Analogies can be drawn with the Soviet Five Year Plans, and it is significant that 'plan' remained a key word for the period, amongst all the political parties. The basic objective of the National Plan was to replace 'the present chaotic economic and social order with a national planned economy, capable of working with other planned economies both within the Empire and abroad.'[9] An important aim was the establishment of a standards and design institute to revitalise industry. It also included a drastic reorganisation of the civil service and other bureaucratic bodies.

The National Plan was sent out to a number of prominent people, politicians, including Sir Oswald Mosley, (whom Barry knew and had interviewed) economists civil servants and scientists. Sir Robert Donald, a member of the Royal Commission on Local Government, thought it a 'stupendous conception'.[10] Others such as J.T. Longstaff then President of the Royal Geographical Society, interpreted it as 'fascist'. Though Barry's response to this was to point out that whereas, 'fascist' indicated a militarist solution, his plan was a civilian one. Oswald Mosley also supported it but preferred greater state control. Barry argued for a well planned economy with a mixture of state control and responsible self government.[11] He also favoured a general streamlining of bureaucracy, an approach he strove to implement in his role as Director General of the Festival.

Amongst the many proposals in the National Plan was a London Planning Commission to sort out the 'wasted south bank between the Thames, Vauxhall, the Oval, Elephant and London Bridge.' The programme for this commission anticipated one of the main purposes of the Festival in proposing that;
'*the whole jungle might be cleared away with provision for gathering all the railway lines, electrified and running below the surface into a single spacious Terminus, the rest of the site being given over to public and business buildings, standing at ample distances apart, instead of lining cramped, mean corridor streets ... and the streets of this quarter would bear no relation to the existing tangle, but would provide new broad straight avenues ... a rectangular grid replacing inherited banks and curves.*'[12]

In 1931, Barry was elected to the Political Economic and Planning group (PEP), in charge of press and publicity. Formed as a direct result of the *Week-end Review's* National Plan, it was a think-tank, including Max Nicholson, Julian Huxley and Sir Basil Blackett, a director of the Bank of England as chair, with the architectural patron Jack Pritchard as author of an alternative national plan.[13]

A weekend was spent at Dartington generating ideas, with the owner, Leonard Elmhirst who contributed £1,000 to funds. The group's central aim was to co-ordinate any problems involved in the production of the National Plan ready for its implementation by 1934.[14]

The *Week-end Review* was a critical success, but not a financial one. In 1934, it became part of Kingsley Martin's *New Statesman*. Barry then joined the *News Chronicle* as features editor, becoming editor in 1936. A liberal left leaning paper, it was known for its championing of the 'underdog' and espousal of just causes.

In his draft autobiography Barry refers to this as a period of continuous campaigning, on the political, and artistic fronts. The link between these was exemplified by the *News Chronicle* schools competition in November 1936. The brief was to design a mixed senior elementary school for 480 children in an urban area and for a mixed school for 160 children in a rural area. The *Architects' Journal* reported on Fleet Street's bewilderment at having a national newspaper run an architectural competition, with prizes totalling £1,200, a vast sum for the period.[15]

Architectural Design, though, praised the *News Chronicle* for its approach and hoped that the competition would 'banish the dirty brown (paint) from our elementary schools'.[16]

Henry Durell, Colin Penn and Felix Walter won the first category. The second category was won by Denis Clarke Hall, and a version was built at Richmond, Yorkshire, whose design pointed to the post-war revolution in school design. It was this campaign that led to Barry being elected as an Associate of the RIBA in 1940, an achievement of which he remained 'phenomenally proud'.[17]

Barry's passion for architecture was continued in his commissioning of Paul Reilly, then his features editor at the *News Chronicle*, to travel around the country photographing buildings and writing about them as a regular feature. Another of his fellow journalists was Philip Furneaux Jordan (brother of the architect and AA teacher Robert) who was also features editor and foreign correspondent.

As Bevis Hillier describes in his introduction to the book, *A Tonic to the Nation*, 1976, Hugh Casson was already well known to Gerald Barry before the Festival as a contributor to the *News Chronicle*, writing articles like 'What to do with the cupboard under the stairs' and the future of architecture. Ralph Tubbs was also an adviser to the *News Chronicle* as well as being the author of two popular Penguin books on architecture, *Living in Cities*, 1942, and *The Englishman Builds*, 1945.

In 1939 Barry commissioned the architect F.R.S. Yorke to modernise two cottages, a blacksmith's shop and forge that he had bought in Sutton, on the Sussex Downs. Yorke opened up the interiors, added a double height music room at one end of the two buildings and provided a sun roof and terrace to the rear, while maintaining the eighteenth century street facade. Inside were polished wood floors and tubular steel furniture, alongside the occasional heirloom. This juxtaposition of old and new was emblematic of Barry's progressive approach.

Barry did not stop campaigning on the political front. In 1934, he contributed to a collection of essays entitled *Challenge to Death*, along with a number of writers, and artists, including Rebecca West, Vera Brittain, H.G. Wells, Winifred Holtby, Edmund Blunden and an introduction by Viscount Cecil. Though written from a broadly left wing perspective, the majority of the ideas expressed a pacifist viewpoint, reflecting the general concern that Europe was heading for another war. Barry's contribution argued that the isolationist policy of Beaverbrook would not prevent war. During the summer of 1938, at the height of appeasement leading up to the Munich conference in September, Barry was in secret talks with an eminent German economist, opposed to the Hitler regime,

12. ibid. (see also Gavin Stamp's article in this journal)

13. Jack Pritchard, *View from a Long Chair*, Routledge, 1984, pp.64–5. See also John Pinder, ed., *Fifty Years of Political and Economic Planning*, Heinemann, 1981.

14. op. cit. BLPES folder no.1, diary.

15. *Architects' Journal*, 5 November 1936, pp.624–6.

16. *Architectural Design and Construction*, November 1936 p.3.

17. op. cit. BLPES folder no.47.

who was trying to prevent the war, which he perceived as inevitable. Although unable to publish these talks, Barry believed that if the 'press of the democratic countries remained silent then they are breaking their own moral and spiritual code.'[18]

In 1947 Barry resigned from the *News Chronicle*, over issues of editorial independence. As he says in his draft autobiography 'I was never much of a diplomat, especially on international affairs.' But it was also prompted by his belief in an intelligent, independent and populist newspaper, and these values were at the heart of his aims for the Festival of Britain.

THE FESTIVAL OF BRITAIN

In 1945 John Gloag, a well-known authority on contemporary design, wrote to *The Times* about having a festival to celebrate the centenary of the 1851 exhibition. This was quickly followed up by Barry, who wrote an open letter in the *News Chronicle* on the 14 September addressed to Sir Stafford Cripps, President of the Board of Trade, advocating a great trade and cultural exhibition to coincide with the centenary of the Great Exhibition. The proposed event was intended as a means of stimulating good design, advertising British products and attracting foreign orders and tourists.[19] The idea was not new, for as early as 1943, the Royal Society of Arts had issued a proposal along similar lines, but it was Barry who brought these ideas to fulfilment.[20] Cripps replied in his own handwriting in red ink that he thought 'perhaps it might be a good idea.'[21]

At the same time the government set up a departmental committee under Lord Ramsden to look into the possibility of holding such an exhibition in 1951. In 1946, the Ramsden Committee concluded that a large scale international exhibition was beyond Britain's means, and considered various alternatives including a British Industries Fair, with a separate exhibition of industrial design. In April 1947, the Arts Council recommended that a cultural exhibition be held in London and other centres around the country. Once the international exhibition was dropped, it was suggested that there be a Festival of the Arts, a film festival, an exhibition of industrial design and a scientific exhibition. Cripps, as President of the Board of Trade considered a cultural festival of this nature outside his remit, but recommended Herbert Morrison, who was then without departmental responsibilities, be put in charge. Herbert Morrison and Clement Atlee chose the name 'Festival of Britain' in January 1948.[22]

The Festival Council was set up in 1948, with General Lord 'Pug' Ismay, formerly Churchill's Chief of Staff, as Chairman. His appointment defused some of the hostility of the right wing press, but Barry had to endure the sniping of Beaverbrook press (chiefly by the *Daily Express*) throughout the three years of run-up to the Festival. But as one of Barry's friends observed, 'will you tell the Chairman sometime that it isn't comparable with the war when we had the drawback of having the Beaver on our side, whereas now we have the advantage of having him against us.'[23]

Among the other council members were the M P and journalist A.P. Herbert, who was a regular contributor to both the *Week-end Review* and the *News Chronicle*, along with Leonard Elmhirst, T.S. Eliot and Kenneth Clark.

For Barry, the Festival was a 'natural culmination of the battles of the previous twenty years', and 'the hopes in three dimensional projection of a brighter and better future.'[24] His championing of the arts was different from that of the Arts Council, which was perceived as being concerned only with high culture.[25] Rather, through the *Week-end Review* and the *News Chronicle*, Barry promoted a much broader and populist approach to the arts, including architecture, which he wanted to be seen as having a social dimension, as reflected in the schools competition.

The appointment of a celebrated editor of a left leaning newspaper was inspired. For the designer James Gardner it was 'a stroke of luck for us designers

18. BLPES folder no.5.
19. Unpublished text Elain Harwood on Post War English Architecture.
20. A1/B1/PRO/WORK 25/7.
21. BLPES folder no.34.
22. Elain Harwood op. cit.
23. BLPES folder 66.
24. BLPES folder 57, draft autobiography.
25. Margaret Garlake, *New Art, New World British Art in Postwar Society*, Yale University Press, 1999, p.19.

... panting in the wings and hoping.'[26] Barry had a good media profile, he had been broadcasting since 1929, and had contributed articles to the *Radio Times* and *The Listener*. Barry saw the Festival as an expression of the British way of life, its achievements, past and present, 'the people's show' and a continuation of the notion of Englishness expressed in the *Weekend-Review*.[27] He also got on well with Pug Ismay and managed Morrison, about whom Barry said that the best thing he (Morrison) did was to let them get on with it.[28]

On 1 April 1948, Barry took up his appointment with Leonard Crainford as his secretary, 'in three austerely equipped rooms in the Royal Society of Arts offices and a somewhat sketchy telephone service'.[29] In the following eight weeks, Barry and his colleagues thrashed out the main themes of the Festival. This was to be an integrated or combined exhibition for the sciences and arts, with a separate science exhibition and architecture exhibition and most important to Barry a series of nationwide events. There was also to be a mobile travelling exhibition.[30]

Significantly, Barry proposed a streamlining of the organisation of the Festival, firstly by placing all its six constituent bodies (quangos as they would be called today) under one roof and secondly, by putting the physical organisation and finance of the exhibition under the Central Office of Information (one of the constituent bodies). This was intended to offset some of the Council of Industrial Design's (COID) responsibility in these areas. Barry preferred the Council's role should be to endorse design standards for the exhibition of industry, worthy of the Festival. Barry was also largely responsible for the content of the Festival. He set up a small creative panel of designers (the Presentation Panel) which he chaired, whose task was to translate the Festival theme into concrete exhibition terms.[31] After a number of meetings, Barry quickly realised that he needed designers who could visualise in three dimensions what the public wanted, and appointed a team including Misha Black,[32] James Holland, Ralph Tubbs and Hugh Casson as Director of Architecture, later joined by James Gardner, to do just that. Gardner was appointed as one of the Festival designers on Gordon Russell's recommendation, and because of his work as Chief Designer for the *Britain Can Make It* exhibition, in 1946. This exhibition had been part of the COID's post-war campaign for good mass market design, as a means of stimulating the economy, encouraging unity and breaking down class barriers. All were to be members of the Presentation Panel.

Such personalities were critical to the success of the Festival, as Barry was keen to have good people who would work well together. Hugh Casson, as Director of Architecture, had worked for him at the *News Chronicle*, and Gordon Russell (Director of the COID) who represented the Council on the Executive Committee, was also a personal friend. Good organisation was key and covered all aspects from accommodation, food, catering, paint supplies, even ensuring an adequate supply of whisky in 1951.[33] Ismay compared it to Operation Overlord in 1942.[34] It allowed Barry, though, to concentrate on the ideas and values of the Festival.

In 1949 the Festival Office was set up in 2 Savoy Court, where most of the constituent bodies except the Arts Council were housed, which made day-to-day running much easier. Although in overall control, it has been difficult to pinpoint specific projects that Barry was involved in. He was certainly instrumental in some of the most important areas, such as the development of the Festival Gardens in Battersea Park.[35] James Gardner, Chief Designer of Battersea, recalled that Barry initially found the Festival 'too clinical for his tastes.'[36] In July 1948, Barry had a private meeting with the stage designer, Oliver Messel, who suggested a Tivoli style gardens be put on as part of the Festival celebrations.'[37] The idea had already been mooted during a discussion of the Executive Committee in June 1948 of holding a fun fair at the South Bank site, when Dudley Ryder from the COID said that 'it should not be the usual English type, but something along the lines of Tivoli'.[38]

26. James Gardner, *The Artful Designer*, Centurion Press, London, 1993, p.167.

27. PRO/WORK 25/21.

28. BLPES folder 47.

29. May 1948 (PRO/WORK 25/46).

30. ibid.

31. ibid.

32. Misha Black also worked on *Britain Can Make It*.

33. PRO/WORK 25/46.

34. AI/B6/PRO/WORK 25/7.

35. See Becky Conekin's article in this Journal.

36. James Gardner, in Mary Banham and Bevis Hillier, eds, *A Tonic to the Nation*, London Thames and Hudson, 1976, p.118.

37. PRO/WORK 25/21, Barry to Ismay, 13 August 1948.

Behind the scenes at Battersea, Barry, Casson and Gardner were working to-gether. Gardner recalls Barry showing him and Casson an old mezzotint of Vaux-hall Gardens saying that, 'we will design an elegant pleasure garden, and it will be upstream well away from the South Bank, and we keep its treatment strictly to ourselves ... no committees'.[39] Though Barry could not escape committees, he whittled down the organisation of Battersea to four people but had to accept the creation of the Festival Gardens Company Ltd, to finance the project, with George Campbell from the Treasury holding the purse strings and Sir Henry French as managing director.[40] Barry's advice remained that he wanted the gar-dens to be elegant and fun, in sharp contrast to the modernity of the South Bank, so when Gardner wanted to have a spiral stair leading to a tree walk, Barry agreed to it.

Barry visited Rome in May 1950 to look at the use of floodlighting on historic buildings, fountains and the dramatic effect of gas flares, subsequently used at Battersea and the South Bank. Taken round the Piazza Campidoglio at midnight by the Chief City Engineer he found the effects 'most breathless and moving.'[41]

Throughout the three years, Barry kept up the momentum, not only amongst the committees, but also with the media. The Presentation Panel and Executive Committee met on a weekly basis and there were regular weekend conferences at his house. He lived and breathed the Festival. Barry, Morrison and Ismay en-

figure 2
F.R.S. Yorke, Extension to The Forge, Sutton, W. Sussex, 1939, for Gerald Barry (Gerald Barry Archive)

38. A5/B1/PRO/WORK 25/46.
39. Gardner, op. cit., p.172.
40. A2/A6/PRO/WORK 25/21.
41. BLPES folder 34.

sured the participation of the Royal Family; Princess Elizabeth was already President of the Royal Society of Arts, and it was not difficult to persuade the King and Queen to be patrons of the Festival. Likewise, he maintained public interest with his regular radio broadcasts and the competition for the naming of the Skylon. As a newspaperman, he recognised the importance of deadlines and the role of the press in such a major event. He never let go of the positive, upbeat image of the Festival, despite reservations expressed by some members of the Festival Council, after the budget was cut by £1.5 million in 1949, to £11,300,000.[42] The outbreak of war in Korea in June 1950 gave further reason for press sniping.

In his series of radio broadcasts, Barry stated that the Festival's purpose was 'intensified, rather than diminished by the world situation, and 'that she [Britain] should demonstrate her strength and resilience.' He believed that an element of light heartedness was necessary and it 'will do our austerity-ridden people no harm to have an opportunity of letting off a little steam.' [43] Keen to attract overseas visitors, in July 1950 he sent four red London buses on a European tour to publicise the Festival. Comparing them to E.M. Forster's 'Celestial Omnibus' that broke the rules: 'The four buses instead of running along the streets of London were about to tour the roads of Europe.' [44] They were to visit Sweden, Denmark, Holland, Belgium and Luxembourg and the city of Hamburg. This was all part of the gaiety and colour that Barry intended; nor was the Festival confined to London but it was to be nationwide and with a 'chain of significant events in towns and villages.'[45] Apart from the official exhibitions at Edinburgh, Glasgow and Belfast, these ranged from tree planting, sporting displays, and placing seats on the village green to local arts exhibitions and concerts and the painting of public buildings.

Over the Festival period from May to September, the nationwide events were well attended, the South Bank received 8.5 million visitors, and overall figures reached 18.5 million. Throughout, Barry was determined to maintain high standards of industrial design, hence the COID's involvement in the Festival. He wanted them to have full responsibility for the choice of every single manufactured exhibit in the official Festival exhibition, resulting in the 1951 Stock List. The aim was that such goods should be available to buy, unlike the *Britain Can Make It* exhibition which was dubbed, the 'Britain Can't Have It Exhibition' by some critics. During and after the Festival, Barry with his friend Gordon Russell, had sought to establish a permanent exhibition centre. But it was Barry, who had the political influence, through writing and arranging meetings with David

figure 3
Herbert Morrison and Hugh Casson at a private preview of the preliminary designs for the South Bank 27 May 1949 (Gerald Barry archive)

figure 4
The King, Gerald Barry and Hugh Casson. 2 May 1950 (Gerald Barry archive)

42. op. cit. A5/A2/PRO/25/44, Festival Council meeting 11 October 1949.
43. BLPES folder 46, draft of radio broadcast.
44. *A Tonic to the Nation*, p.16.
45. BLPES folder 34.

figure 5
Visit of Members of the Council &
Executive of the Festival of Britain to the
South Bank. 4 May 1950. From left:
Ralph Freeman, Misha Black, Hugh
Casson, Sir Wynn Wheldon, Sir Harry
Lindsey, Sir Alan Herbert, Jean Mann,
Sir Frederick Bain, Lady Megan Lloyd
George, Sir Henry French, John Ratcliff,
Sir Alan Barlow, Cecil Cooke, Gerald
Barry, Leonard Crainford, Ralph Tubbs,
Brig. Greenfield, Col. Neil. (Gerald
Barry archive)

46. ibid.
47. Personal diary entry, 8 March 1951, lent by
Jackie Barry.
48. BLPES folder 59.
49. *A Tonic to the Nation*, p.38.
50. Garlake, op. cit., p.223.
51. Personal conversation with Max
Nicholson 31 March 2001.

Eccles (Cripps's successor) who brought about the creation of the Design Centre in 1956.[46]

Throughout the Festival Barry remained 'hands on', despite his considerable powers of delegation, but maintaining such high standards exerted its toll. The early months of 1951 were spent travelling around the country, attending meetings and lamenting the awful weather. A typical day included a meeting to discuss the proofs of the official guides, viewing Mitzi Solomon Cunliffe's statue, 'Root Bodied Forth', at the sculptor's workshop, considered by some to be 'indecent'. In March, exhausted by his travels, he spent a day in bed catching up only to be visited by the 'full horrors of Battersea', with 'Morrison thirsting for French's blood' recalling 'that all our troubles stemmed from Stafford Cripps's misbegotten child Festival Gardens Co' which was making a huge loss.[47]

Inevitably, the end of the Festival was something of an anti climax;
Tonight, the managers of the Festival Gardens are going to set the Thames on fire, the show goes on. Before attending this symbolic spectacle, the Controller and I will dine quietly together at my club and tell sad stories of the death of kings.[48]
Afterwards Barry hoped that the Festival or some of its structures would remain for another year and Morrison had assured him of a similar post that would challenge his abilities. But with the fall of the Labour government that autumn this was not to be. The new Minister of Works, David Eccles set about demolishing the South Bank exhibition buildings, saying that he did not wish to become the 'caretaker of empty and deteriorating structures'.[49] Perhaps his agreement to allow the Design Centre to go ahead was either a fit of conscience or a tribute to Barry's powers of persuasion. Of the buildings on the South Bank, Jane Drew's Thameside Restaurant survived ten years and, of the art works, the sculptures fared best. Many of the commissioned pieces ended up in museums and schools or public spaces around the country. Very few reliefs and murals escaped, although John Piper's external mural from the Homes and Gardens Pavilion is still in storage.[50]

For Barry, the Festival had brought him great acclaim and recognition in the form of a knighthood in 1951. Afterwards, he found himself something of a 'stranded leviathan' as he sought to find something worthy of his talent. In 1952, he became adviser on public policy to the National Farmers' Union, a position far removed from his Festival role, but evidence of his wide ranging curiosity. Architecture and design, though, remained at the top of his list of interests. Alongside his project for the Design Centre, he became a consultant to the London County Council for the development of the Crystal Palace site and later he chaired the Barbican Committee. In 1958, he joined Granada Television, where he was able to convey his personal enthusiasm for good architecture and design through his educational programmes.

His taste and judgement was much admired and his company was in great demand at informal get-togethers as well as more serious occasions, but his great genius was getting people to talk to him and being able to encourage others. He also had a knack of seeing the bigger picture, to the extent that he would glide away in his own magic world, be impossible to contact for several days and return rightly confident that he would be instantly forgiven for any resulting crisis.[51] Like Don Quixote, in some ways he never grew up, but if he had, then we would not have experienced his vision behind the Festival of Britain, unlike the earnestness which beset the Millennium Dome.

5 The Expression of Levity

ALAN POWERS

The Expression of Levity

ALAN POWERS

THE English enjoy themselves sadly ('Les anglais s'amusent tristement') was one of Gerald Barry's favourite quotations, taken from the Duc de Sully. The Festival of Britain, in his mind, at least, was to be a lesson in enjoyment for people who had lost the knack of it, for his experience had shown him how pleasure was the basis of civilisation. To make this a political platform, as Barry did in his career as an editor, is more difficult than to take an opposite course by exhorting people to suffer. In Hugh Casson, Barry found the ideal collaborator for the exploration of lightness, and the cohesion of the buildings on the South Bank demonstrated a unanimity of feeling among architects and designers about the means by which pleasure and enjoyment could be achieved as an architectural goal. Philip James, the secretary of the Arts Council, stated in the introduction to their 1951 exhibition of festivities of the past, 'Splendid Occasions', 'the art of public rejoicing is in danger of becoming one of the lost arts'. Lost but rediscovered in 1951, now apparently lost again. The experience of recent years suggests that there is nothing the nation likes more than a good funeral.

Posterity's verdict on the South Bank of 1951 has been surprisingly negative, as if its physical destruction at the end of the season required verbal salt to be ploughed into the ground too.[1] Some iron entered the soul of architecture after the Festival (and England was far from unique in this respect). The underlying dynamics of Festival design on the South Bank are worth trying to capture in the light of such commitedly adverse interpretation.

TOWARDS AN ARCHITECTURE OF LEVITY

'No, Sir, the skylon has no purpose. It is not functional in any way. It does not light the Festival; it burns with its own inner light. It's not even a phallic symbol or a totem pole. It has no social significance; it doesn't stand for Democracy, Freedom, Progress, or the Future Happiness of Man. It doesn't stand at all; it could stand on the ground, but it doesn't.'[2] This opening passage from an anonymous commentary on the Festival from the *New Statesman* picks out the most overt demonstration of a literal levity in the visual expression of weightlessness. Interestingly, it suggests the move away from a literal or coded symbolism, as found in nineteenth century eclecticism or even in a number of modern movement buildings, towards an integration of symbolism in the irreducible form of a building, despite the denial implicit in the text just quoted. Upward movement and the expression of weightlessness were typical of many of the South Bank buildings. This symbolism did not have to be read, merely experienced.

Investigation of structures, like the Skylon, based on minimal members in compression and tension, was undertaken by Buckminster Fuller during the 1940s at a time of intense creativity. The discovery, by one of Fuller's students, Kenneth Snelson, of the first 'tensegrity structure' took place in Chicago in 1948. Fuller's name is not normally invoked in discussion of the Skylon, but it compares to the central spine of the 1932 Dymaxion House, and some of the earlier rejected design ideas described by Sir Philip Powell are similar to the helium balloons illustrated in Fuller's magazine, *Shelter*. The reliance on tension for

figure 1
Gordon Cullen and D. Dewar Mills, cover for *Architectural Review*, South Bank Exhibition Special number, August 1951. The original caption for the cover read 'The South Bank exhibition may be regarded as the first modern townscape, not only by virtue of the fact that its buildings and furnishings are designed in the contemporary idiom throughout, but equally because its layout represents that realisation in urban terms of the Picturesque, in which the future of town planning as a visual art assuredly lies. One of the most successful features of the exhibition seen from this point of view is the way in which existing buildings lying outside the boundaries of the site have been brought into the picture; practical recognition is thus given to a truth which town planning theory is apt to overlook – that in the modern world the town planner's job is as much a re-creation of the old (through the establishment of new relationships between it and the spectator) as the creation of what is physically new. The cover, with a diorama showing the houses of Parliament, Whitehall Court and St. Paul's superimposed on a plan of the exhibition, emphasises this significant aspect of the South Bank achievement.'

1. See Reyner Banham's essay 'The Style: 'Flimsy ... Effeminate?' in Bevis Hillier and Mary Banham, eds. *A Tonic to the Nation*, Thames and Hudson, London, 1976 and Barry Curtis, 'One Continuous Interwoven Story (The Festival of Britain)', 1985, reprinted in *The Block Reader in Visual Culture*, Routledge, London, 1996, pp.209–20. For my own earlier attempt to characterise the antecedents of the Festival style, see ''The Reconditioned Eye' – architects and artists in English Modernsim' *AA Files* 25, Summer 1993, pp.54–62.
2. 'Festival Diary' by 'Critic', *New Statesman and Nation*, 5 May, 1951, p.497.

49

3. Joachim Krause and Claude Lichtenstein, eds, *Your Private Sky, R. Buckminster Fuller, the art of design science*, Baden, Switzerland, Lars Muller, 1999, p.392.

4. The roof structure is illustrated and described in *Architectural Design*, July 1951, p.213.

5. The structure was illustrated as the frontispiece to Neville Conder, *Modern Architecture, Art and Technics*, London, 1950.

6. Bryan Appleyard, *The Pleasures of Peace*, Faber and Faber, London, p.30–1.

7. *The Sphere*, 2 June 1951, p.359.

strength, seen in the bicycle wheel, was the basis for a reversal of classical structure. As Joachim Krause and Claude Lichtenstein write, for Fuller, 'tensegrity is also a philosophical model of coherence. By what is it held together then, if not the compact mass? By increasingly thin tensile members that border on the spiritual.'[3]

Not many buildings had the Skylon's liberty to be purely themselves, but the idea of not touching the ground was one of the more obvious Festival devices. Some exhibits, like tractors, were hung on wires. The Dome of Discovery was held on slender raking struts. Many designers used the device of the 'flashgap', a recessed horizontal line, usually black, where a column meets the floor or the ceiling, or where a building meets the ground. This negative inversion of the classical moulding was introduced into the buildings of Berthold Lubetkin and Tecton in the mid 1930s, notably the Finsbury Health Centre, and is one of the sources of visual unity in the Royal Festival Hall. Where classicism expresses the solidity of coursed masonry, occasionally relieved by beautifully framed openings, its modern antonym, unable to defeat gravity, attempted a conjuring trick which, although it became a cliche after a while, was perhaps consonant with the upward thrust of the Festival.

Not all suspension produces an effect of upward movement. Among the engineering achievements of the South Bank was the roof of the Fairway Café, designed by Michael Grice of Architects Co-Partnership, which was required to be fitted beneath the Chicheley Street screen with its triangular canvas pennants. The roof was a prestressed concrete diagrid, only 15 inches in depth, making a 50 foot square roof without columns, achieved with unseen tension cables running though it, engineered by Ove Arup and Partners.[4]

Suspension is a practical device for temporary architecture, applied to the big top or as used by Le Corbusier in his Pavilion du Temps Moderne at the Paris exhibition of 1937. The Porte d'Honneur at the same exhibition by Jacques Debat-Ponsan, a mast with guy ropes descending onto a single point on the plinth, was perhaps another Skylon precursor, although easily outdone by Powell and Moya.[5] Sketches of masted structures by Howard Cleminson, an AA student who committed suicide in 1939, published in *Focus* 4, were recognised by his contemporaries as precursors of the Festival, and Gerald Barry's first idea for the Festival was to use a series of tent structures, whose association with festivity is axiomatic. Reyner Banham pointed out the inspiration provided by a suspended canopy by Renzo Zavanella at the Milan Fair in 1948, fringed with bunting, but whether or not the English designers remembered where they had first seen such ideas, they were generic to the period.

ILLUMINATION

Light is the opposite of dark, as well as of heavy. The South Bank frequently elided its two meanings, not only literally in its use of electric light by night and large windows by day, but in its use of decorative colour as a means of stimulating the perception of light. Illumination is also an inner quality of the mind, capable of being stimulated by external conditions. The Festival consciously attempted to make these connections, and as Bryan Appleyard writes, 'What was being celebrated at the Festival was not Imperial pomp but British ingenuity and humanity, the wonders of science and the sheer lightness of the world to come. It was an attempt to will into existence a prevailing myth, Humanist and reasonable, which would sweep away the darknesses of the past and replace them with towns as picturesque as the countryside.'[6] Not only was the South Bank given 'the most spectacular illuminations London has ever known', specially striking after years of blackout, but older buildings throughout the country were floodlit for the first time.[7]

Light was one of the themes linking science and art in the Festival. Radar, which, through British ingenuity, had helped to win the war, was a recurrent motif in Humphrey Jennings's film, *Family Portrait*, made for showing in the Telekinema. The 'Magic Mirror' which Sir Francis Drake's Spanish adversaries believed him to possess in order to see beyond human vision became a metaphor not only for radar, but also for qualities of creative intuition in all fields. The Shot Tower on the South Bank was fitted with a radar scanner to emphasise this.

KINETICS

David danced before Saul to lift him from depression. The expression of movement is fundamental to the Festival's aesthetic of pleasure, and its most evident point of contact with the mainstream of modernism. It is not hard to see movement expressed in the plan of the South Bank, with printed arrows on the plans and the testimony of photography and film to show how the winding, climbing, turning circulation pattern brought visitors close to the experience of dance, even if they did not stay in the evening to take a partner and circle around the open-air dance floor, as many did. Turning wheels in the sky provided a pattern for movement on the ground. Perhaps the presiding geniuses of the Festival were two artists whose work was not present there. The first would be the American sculptor Alexander Calder who was often in England in the later 1930s, demonstrating his toy-like circus to private parties in Ben Nicholson's studio, or at John Piper's farmhouse. Calder's discovery of the mobile as a modern art form brought modernism and childhood wonder back together. The second genius would be Lázsló Moholy-Nagy, resident in Golders Green from 1935 to 1937, and one of the designers, before his departure for the USA, of the MARS Group exhibition of 1938. The other chief designer of MARS in 1938 was Misha Black, who was in charge of the upstream half of the South Bank, and whose role, relative to Hugh Casson's overall brief, has tended to be overlooked. It is hard to make exact connections with Moholy, apart from the impression he left in England that modern design was about to penetrate the greatest mysteries with the simplest intuitive means. In an article in *Industrial Arts* in 1936, Moholy dreamed of 'Light in Communal Festivals' where coming generations 'from airplanes and airships … will be able to to enjoy the spectacle of gigantic expanses of illumination, movement and transformation of lighted areas, which will provide new experiences and open up new joy in life.'[8] He also suggested projecting advertisements onto the clouds at night. The South Bank did not exactly provide these experiences, but in his last book, *Vision in Motion*, 1947, published the year after his death, Moholy made a plea for the underlying political importance of understanding the world as a set of relationships in space and time, which he described as '*the* key to our age', whose understanding 'will help in grasping future problems and vistas, enabling us to see everything in relationship'; and furnishing us 'with the right concept of cooperation and defence against aggression, where again time and space are inextricably intertwined.'[9]

In his book *Exhibition Design*, 1950 (Architectural Press), Misha Black indicated through illustrations how suspension and illusory weightlessness were part of an international exhibition style long before 1951, claiming that the 1938 MARS show 'heralded a new approach to contemporary exhibition design'. As a designer experienced in many wartime exhibitions, Black also stressed the importance of freedom of movement within a display area and the need to choreograph the visitor's experience, writing that 'the visitor should feel free to flit from exhibit to exhibit as his fancy moves him.'[10]

LANDSCAPE AND PICTURESQUE

Movement was perhaps the key aspect of the Picturesque movement of the late eighteenth century which was applied by the designers of the South Bank, under the inspiration of the *Architectural Review*. The Picturesque, both as originally

8. L. Moholy-Nagy, 'Light architecture', *Industrial Arts*, 1/1, London, Spring 1936, reprinted in R. Kostelanetz, ed., *Moholy-Nagy, an anthology*, Da Capo Press, New York, 1970, p.159.

9. L. Moholy-Nagy, *Vision in Motion*, Paul Theobald, Chicago, 1947, p.266.

10. Misha Black, ed., *Exhibition Design*, Architectural Press, London, 1950, p.32.

11. Clough Williams-Ellis in *Royal Festival Hall*, Max Parrish, London, 1951, p.60.

stated by Sir Richard Payne Knight and Uvedale Price in the 1790s, and as reinterpreted in the 1940s, is a many-sided sensibility, manifesting all the opposites of categorisation and Cartesian thought. Its pragmatism and opportunism were recognisably English, and this understanding informed the acceptance of the irregularities of the South Bank site, where variations in level were deliberately preserved. The *Architectural Review*'s coinage of the term 'townscape' was part of a didactic attempt to transfer landscape design principles of kinetic space relationships to all situations, making a division between two opposed types of modern architecture, those which retained some of the formal plan symmetries of classicism, seen by an ideal eye, and those which accepted the shifting viewpoint of experience.

One of the important early statements of the townscape principle in the *Architectural Review* was 'Exterior Furnishing', January 1944, written, as was the main text of the canonic 'Townscape' article of December 1949, by the proprietor of the magazine, H. de Cronin Hastings, but unsigned. In this article, Hastings drew analogies between the jumbled, personalised aesthetic of private spaces, mingling old and new objects with varieties of texture and pattern, and the reality of the external environment, where instead of the tidying up which both modernists and classicists seemed to demand, a principle of 'live and let live' would produce visual stimulus and encourage a more tolerant attitude. Hastings proclaimed the political content of the picturesque, as a movement for freedom and social justice, in a manner which his critics have chosen to ignore, preferring to see in the *Review*'s endeavour only nostalgia and weak pragmatism. Hastings defended the taste of the common man on the basis of a personal philosophy that found the marvellous in the everyday, and wished to inspire creators to do the same.

Landscape was not only a design feature but in many ways the dominant metaphor of the South Bank. Apart from its literal representation in plant material and gardening, the idea of naturalness was allied to the idea of growth, and the conditions required for it: sunlight, air and water. The wych elm, the sole tree existing on the site, was treasured and accorded a position of honour at the entrance to the Festival Hall. Other mature trees were brought in to keep it company, in an inversion of the situation of the Crystal Palace where the building design was adapted in order to accommodate existing trees in the transept. The theory and practice of landscape design had been in the process of development in parallel to architecture in the course of the 1930s and 40s, with visionary moments in which landscape was presented as something beyond style and beyond nationality, although also something where the English could pride themselves on a national tradition. Reyner Banham's 1976 article (see footnote 1) resolves its petulance with the South Bank by admitting the success of the landscape.

Movement was emphasised by the novel attention given to outdoor floorscape as a way of relieving monotony underfoot. Landscape was used for theatrical effect, as Clough Williams-Ellis wrote in the souvenir volume on the Royal Festival Hall, describing aspects of the building now very largely lost, 'the division between indoors and out and the transition from one to the other has been softened and made less abrupt and arbitrary by ingeniously dodging trees and flower-beds about, apparently at haphazard' creating 'a cunningly woven web of eye-traps, of false perspectives, of flower groups half hidden and half revealed in succeeding planes' which required active participation from the spectator, 'some effort to see what is not there, but what has been subtly implied.'[11]

The Upstream half of the exhibition dealing with 'The Land' reinforced the hermeneutic property of landscape. This counterbalanced weightlessness with features which have tended to be forgotten, like the 'Minerals of the Island' pavilion by Michael Grice of Architects' Co-Partnership which took the form of a three-sided windowless black cone, from which smoke issued at the top, and included a simulation of a coal mine.

Most international exhibitions represented the home, through model houses, reconstructions of the past or imported exotics. The South Bank gave special emphasis to the representation of the home, chiefly in the Homes and Gardens pavilion, and in other respects to the wider idea of a homeland. The avoidance of imperial themes, in contrast to the Wembley exhibition of 1924 and Glasgow 1938, deliberately pushed attention back to the physical and social character of Britain which Gerald Barry and his associates believed had been neglected for too long. The outdoor spaces of the South Bank were presented in the form of outdoor rooms, with varied transitions between them. The sanctification of the home was an aspect of the Arts and Crafts movement transmitted to Modernism and examination of the irreducible essentials of the home had occupied English architects in the later 1930s, who began to see modern architecture in close relationship to vernacular as an expression of domesticity in its patterning of indoor and outdoor space, and even in the more literal signifiers of house, such as the pitched roofs, garden gates and chimney stacks seen in the Norfolk council houses of Tayler and Green that were given Festival of Britain Architectural Awards. These challenged the modern movement to accept them on a level of pure functionalism, as well as on grounds of local distinctiveness and familiarity.

In some ways the most radical aspect of the South Bank (and more obviously the case with Battersea) was to risk two modes which architecture had mostly made other to itself: the expression of femininity and childhood, both closely linked to the home, but equally reasons why domesticity has so often been marginalised. Lewis Mumford, writing for an English readership in 1943, saw the war as proof of the failure of 'our too masculine, too life-denying society'. Perhaps, he wrote, 'the best slogan for the coming age is that for the life boats: women and children first.'[12] The Welfare State gave the best available conditions for promoting such needs on a practical level, and many architects in local authorities designing schools and housing were working to find appropriate formal expression for these values.

Exposing the denial of the feminine has become a theme in recent critical writing on architecture. At the South Bank, only a few actual women designers were employed, but the adoption by male designers of colour and ornament seems to underlay a deeper disquiet among adversaries of the Festival. Reyner Banham's essay in *Tonic to the Nation* took the phrase 'Flimsy and Effeminate' from Lionel Brett for his discussion of the South Bank, putting it as a question. There is certainly a gender issue involved, and the unspoken fear may not be one of women as such, but of homosexuality, in a culture that was, for a liberal élite, surprisingly intolerant of any minority sexual orientations, and particularly panicked by their public manifestation. The defection of Burgess and McLean to the USSR in March 1951 seemed to prove the point. The legacy of that time has been that gay modernist architects, such as Herbert Tayler and David Green, felt compelled to remain silent about this important aspect of their creativity and social mission, as did Henry Morris, the patron of the Cambridge Village Colleges which in many ways were precursors of the Festival spirit, and Lord Forrester, the patron of the Brynmawr Rubber Factory.[13] Architecture is still edgy about such matters, and even in more liberal times, a similar anxiety attended the appearance of postmodernism in the 1970s and 80s. Thus the pendulum has tended always to be pushed back towards the straight-faced rigidity which modernism habitually adopts. Levity becomes suspect.

LUDIC LEVITY

In 1943 in New York, the historian Siegfried Giedion, the painter Fernand Leger and the architect J.L. Sert composed a manifesto, 'Nine Points on Monumentality', an odd title which chiefly makes sense when it is considered, in the words

12. Lewis Mumford, *The Social Foundations of Post-War Building*. Rebuilding Britain Series, No.9, London, Faber & Faber Ltd. 1943, p.40.

13. See Chris Waters, 'Disorders of the Mind, Disorders of the Body Social: Peter Wildeblood and the Making of the Modern Homosexual' in Becky Conekin, Frank Mort and Chris Waters, eds., *Monuments of Modernity, Reconstructing Britain 1945–1964*, Rivers Oram Press, London and New York, 1999.

14. Joan Ockman, *Architectural Culture 1943–1968, A Documentary Anthology*, Rizzoli, New York, 1993, p.27. The manifesto text is reprinted ibid., pp.29–30.

15. Introduction to Kenneth Clark, 'Ornament in Modern Architecture', *Architectural Review*, December 1943, p.147.

16. Clark, ibid., p.150.

17. Lionel Brett, 'The South Bank Style', *Observer*, 6 May 1951.

18. Osbert Lancaster, 'The Death of Modern Architecture', Broadcast 7 October 1951, text in *Architects' Journal*, 18 October, 1951, pp.465–8.

of Joan Ockman, as a call for 'collective or symbolic content.'[14] As Reyner Banham pointed out in 1976, their manifesto seems almost to describe the South Bank, although it was not published until 1956. One aspect of this revision and, in some respects reversal, of the pure modernism of the 1930s was the question of ornament. Although the Festival is often associated with an ornamental revival, the actual buildings of the South Bank displayed little beyond some flat geometric patterning. This could claim sources in British vernacular, many of them explored in articles in the *Architectural Review*, and corresponded to practice in Sweden and other countries respected for their modern architecture. In 1943, the Review published an article by Kenneth Clark on 'Ornament in Modern Architecture'. The unsigned introductory words ask: 'If for good reasons [decoration] cannot exist, is not the architecture of the twentieth century doomed to remain sterile, because devoid of play and joy?'[15] Clark attributed the death of ornament in the nineteenth century to 'the measuring mind' and the division of labour. 'We shall have no ceremony in life, and no ornament in architecture, until some new and promising faith reintegrates our lives.'[16] Perhaps the South Bank went some way to achieving this reintegration, since, as Lionel Brett wrote in the *Observer* in 1951, the visual language of the mid century which it represented was based, not on ornament in any recognisable sense, but on 'engineering touched with magic, or in other words the marriage of science and art.'[17]

There was still the sense of a missing link, whether between artistic professionals and their public or between present and past. Ornament loomed in the gap, and was normally refused by architects who had been trained to use it, but felt it could carry no meaning. Osbert Lancaster, cartoonist, member of the editorial board of the *Architectural Review* and designer of parts of the Festival Gardens, asked in a radio broadcast in October 1951 whether the modern movement, understood as functionalism, was not in fact over when the South Bank had so convincingly demonstrated an architecture of pleasure. 'If a really live and profitable movement is to develop from this beginning,' Lancaster said, 'then many of the most cherished illusions of Modern Movement will have to go overboard.'[18] He went on to describe the situation in terms of language, regretting that the rhetorical repertory of modernism was inadequate to enthuse an uneducated public, however valuable it may have been as a training course. The demonstration at the South Bank of techniques of architectural language and rhetoric is fundamental to its interpetation, since the expression of levity was achieved in so many ways.

Themes of social cohesion through the largely non-verbal rhetoric of play were explored in Johan Huizinga's book *Homo Ludens, A Study of the Play Element in Culture*, published in English in 1949. The author had lectured on this subject in London after 1933, and before the first Dutch edition of 1938. There is no direct evidence of Huizinga's influence on the Festival of Britain, but his book comes closest of any text of the period in explaining why Gerald Barry might have thought enjoyment needed to be the main message of the Festival. The book is a plea for the seriousness of play, its integral role in the arts, and the dangers of neglecting it. Huizinga ranges over play in many cultures and spheres, He proposes that play is therapeutic for society as much as for individuals. The nineteenth century lost the play instinct. In the twentieth, sport tries to fill the role of play, but owing to its commercialisation, does not substitute for the sacred festivals of archaic cultures, which brought health and happiness to society. 'This ritual tie has now been completely severed', Huizinga wrote, 'sport has become profane, "unholy" in every way and has no organic connection whatever with the structure of society.' Art had become equally divorced from its original links with public and social activity, influenced by connoisseurship and the market, even if its specialisation was a form of game, and science has suffered similarly from the loss of its ludic element.

Huizinga also sees the distortion of play as one of the symptoms and devices of totalitarian regimes, indulging in 'puerilism of the lowest order: yells or other signs of greeting, the wearing of badges and sundry items of political haberdashery, walking in marching order or at a special pace, and the whole rigmarole of collective voodoo and mumbo-jumbo.'[19] Therefore, Huizinga sadly concluded in 1938, play proper has been in decline since the eighteenth century, displaced by corrupted substitutes. A democracy desperately needs its play.

England gains a special mention for having held on to important aspects of play in its parliamentary democracy, as well as having the word 'fun' in its language, which he claims, in long passages of philology, has no exact equivalent in any other. Huizinga's text offers a version of a widely-held belief that the special virtues of English culture lay in the ability to hold contradictory views in balance. Gerald Barry's 'This England' column in the *Week-end Review*, cut like a documentary film from news clippings, might serve as an example of the contradiction of mocking while celebrating. The Festival of Britain had a large task of trying to recreate a language of communal celebration, of a kind emphasised by Huizinga as an important aspect of archaic societies now lost. Sacred play, he explained, takes place in a temporary world within the world, marked off for the purpose, as was the South Bank site, with its conscientious efforts to block out the surrounding buildings. It takes place according to a cycle of time, as the Festival did in its recalling of 1851, and it works as a form of magic, 'actualising by representation'. The South Bank paradoxically reinvented the city in the image of the home, two categories which long-standing convention had made strangers to each other, yet for any theorist who believed in the fundamental correspondence between home, city and sacred space, there was no paradox, each level merely unfolding into the next. Play is therefore one way of describing the priestly function of the artist.

Why did the South Bank move some of its visitors to tears? The categories explored in this article are all emotive in different respects. Their combination and synthesis in a physical and optical experience in 1951 could be overwhelming, while also being essentially familiar. The effect was similar to what is supposed to take place in church and the South Bank played on the very areas that Protestantism (and, by extension, the mainstream of modern architecture) mistrusts: colour, femininity, lightness, extravagance, secularism and communal participation, while luring its target home audience with a mirror portrait of their better selves. It seems to have filled some gap left by the absence of religion, a gap neither specific to a protestant condition nor to an English one, but rather a general one of the modern world, of the kind identified by Freud in *Civilisation and its Discontents* (first published in English in 1930) and Jung in *Modern Man in Search of a Soul* (1933). These texts, like Clark's strictures on 'the measuring mind', identified the source of the problem in distant times, and called for a radical reorientation, to be achieved partly by overcoming the guilt about pleasure imposed by the church. Levity does not operate in isolation, but is part of a systemic loop, in which its opposites are also contained, as Clough Williams-Ellis emphasised when quoting fom the American author Don Marquis, to make a point about the essence of the South Bank: 'Levity is the result of spiritual and aesthetic poise. A person who is groping and struggling for such poise is worried and grave. All progress is towards levity through gravity. Weight then wings! But it is the wings which are the goal, not the weight. Not wings to fly solemnly with; wings to frivol with. You cannot worry them into existence. You may get them by acting as if you already have them and thinking you have them.'[20]

If a stylistic analogy to the South Bank as a design phenomenon should be sought, it is surely with the baroque, a period and an associated mood which swings in and out of favour through the history of English architecture, depending much on the temper of feeling towards mainland Europe.[21] In its aims and achievements, the South Bank epitomised the ludic aspect of modern

19. J. Huizinga, *Homo Ludens*, Paladin, London, 1970 p.232.

20. Don Marquis, extract from *The Almost Perfect State*, quoted by Clough Williams-Ellis in letter to the *New Statesman*, 12 May, 1951, p.534.

21. It is interesting, although perhaps of minor significance, that Sir Leslie Martin's doctoral thesis (a rare endeavour for an architect of his generation) was on the Spanish Baroque architect Churriguera.

architecture, so at odds with much that is normally understood as proper to it. Writing in 1976, Banham suggested that the influence of the Festival on the next generation of English architects was entirely negative, naming James Stirling in this respect. At that date, such a view seemed correct, but Stirling's later development, in the use of coloured surfaces, historical references, elaborate architectural landscapes and promenades and jokes, caused John Summerson to title an article about his Staatsgalerie design, 'Vitruvius Ludens'.[22] Here, perhaps, the Festival influence can be recognised and reassociated with the curiously unexplored question of play and its wider significance.

22. John Summerson 'Vitruvius Ludens', *Architectural Review*, March 1983, pp.19–21.

6 'A Good Time-and-a-half was had by All'

H.T. CADBURY-BROWN

figure 1
Entrance to The Land of Britain by H.T.
Cadbury-Brown. (Cadbury-Brown)

'A Good Time-and-a-half was had by All'

H.T. CADBURY-BROWN

H.T. (Jim) Cadbury-Brown had won a competition in 1937 for a series of ticket agencies and parcels offices for the Big Four private railway companies (a first, pre-nationalisation example of them collaborating together as British Railways), and had gone on to design stands for Chance Glass, Turners Asbestos Cement, and the Federation of British Industries. He had met Hugh Casson when a student, and they had collaborated on the MARS *exhibition in 1938. The other commissioned architects had similarly important experience of exhibition design. The Festival was the first time that Betty, an American architect who came over to work for Ernö Goldfinger, worked with her future husband.*[1]

1. In conversation with Elain Harwood and with comments from Betty Cadbury-Brown, August 2000.

I WAS invited to work on the South Bank by Hugh Casson. One of Hugh's great strengths was that he knew so many people in the art world, everybody trusted him and he never let them down. He had also worked as Astragal in the *Architects' Journal*, which introduced him to many more people. His assistant was John Ratcliff, a nice man, who co-ordinated the architects in a service way and represented them at meetings. Later Howard Lobb, already Chairman of the advisory Architectural Council, was brought in to ensure that the work was completed to time, and succeeded only in infuriating the architects and designers who were happily working together.

Everybody knew each other. After Cambridge Hugh Casson had come to study at the Bartlett School of Architecture, but shared the social life down the road at the Architectural Association, where I was studying. Later we and others, including Frederick Gibberd and Ernö Goldfinger, collaborated on the MARS Group Exhibition held at the Burlington Galleries in January 1938. Ralph Tubbs and I had been at the Architectural Association together and had subsequently shared a flat in Clarges Street. Because of his gammy knee, Tubbs was unfit for war service and had served as a firewatcher at St Paul's Cathedral; in London in the war he had met Henry Moore, Graham Sutherland and knew many artists. He had also been secretary of the MARS Group. Casson wanted people who would 'pull together', as they had on the MARS show, because everything had to be done very quickly, without fighting each other. Many of the group had worked together in architectural offices, for example Bronek Katz, Reginald Vaughan and Ralph Tubbs had all worked for Max Fry before the war – and with so few offices designing modern buildings then everybody did know each other.

Just about the only architect to qualify after the war, and the youngest of the group, was Leonard Manasseh, who won a competition for a high-class restaurant and bar, a reduced version of which was built as the '51 Bar.

Control of the exhibition was in the hands of an inner group, led by Casson with Misha Black and Ralph Tubbs as architects, and James Holland and James Gardner as designers. Black had been the design co-ordinater for the MARS Group show, and Ralph Tubbs had worked for exhibitions for CEMA (Council for the Encouragement of Music and the Arts), and his two books for Allen Lane, *Living in Cities* (1942) and *The Englishman Builds* (1945) had also prompted exhibitions. Allen Lane of Penguin Books was an important figure in creating the culture of the times, selling well-written and well-presented books on a range of intellectual subjects at just 6d each. Their broad appeal showed that it was possible to get complicated ideas across to a largely under-educated population. Gerald Barry was to my mind the whole begetter of the Festival of Britain project, and he belonged to the same Liberal Left that marked British consciousness at the time.

Exhibitions really began with the Great Exhibition in 1851. It was the granddaddy of them all.[2] You can see how horrible much of the design was in 1851, how much better it had become by 1862, and how much better still it was at the Festival.

There was a terrific feeling of optimism. It was joyous to work on, the first big anything, after years of small exhibitions, alterations, and a little housing work. There were people who objected to the Festival as an unnecessary expense, but far greater was the sheer sense of pleasure after ten years without building. There was a real sense in which the Festival marked an upturn in people's lives. The timing was just right – if it had been done a few years earlier there would have been less money, fewer materials. It was an event for a new dawn, for enjoying life on modern terms, with modern technology. That was the real reason for the exhibition, and it marked a brighter socialism. There was a real sense of celebration, that anything was possible, and that British technology was good – as shown by inventions such as radar, television and the jet engine. There were commercial elements in the displays, but they were carefully integrated within the broad umbrella of the overall design. And I think everybody liked it. It was the first time that Britain had had open-air cafés and restaurants – and our weather's not that bad. Though we didn't expect that people would dance in the open air every night.

Misha Black organised the 'Upstream' section and Casson the 'Downstream' section. The 'Upstream' section, devoted to 'The Land of Britain', was more important than the 'Downstream' section devoted to human achievement or 'The People of Britain', because it was so much larger and more coherent. 'Downstream' was dominated by the Royal Festival Hall, which was a separate commis-

2. Cadbury-Brown slowly began to collect prints of the Great Exhibition, some of which still grace his walls, and he showed me catalogues of both the 1851 and 1862 exhibitions. The close relationship between modern architecture in England and history seems first evident in 1951.

figure 2
Dome of Discovery with the rock garden and entrance to the Land of Britain Pavilion by H.T. Cadbury-Brown. (The Architectural Press)

sion. Casson and Black made the major appointments, although the architects, as co-ordinators for each of the 22 or more sections, could either chose works of art from a common pool bought or commissioned by the Arts Council, or invite some individual designers and artists to fulfil specific needs. There were common standards, such as the width of stairs and gangways, so that issues of public safety were resolved by this framework. Other common elements saved time, money and arguments – notably a standard range of 'Festival' paint colours, so that if you specified 'blue', for example, you knew what you were getting and there could be no disputes.

The architects would propose an idea for the pavilions, which went to 'the panel' – the Council of Architecture. Then, once this basic design was approved,

each pavilion was allotted a designer, whom you had to work with. I was allotted James Gardner and Victor Rotter, who had done some very good work for the Coal Board at Olympia fairs. In the pavilions the script people were important. The engineers were Freeman, Fox and Partners, who as successors to the firm Fox and Henderson had a direct link back to the Great Exhibition, and the contractors were Costains, who built the whole of 'Upstream'. The close collaboration with the Freemans, father and son, and with the contractors was one of the pleasures of the Festival, in contrast to the feeling of distance or of working with a committee that you find on larger jobs. When I explained my idea for the central support of the cones, Sir Ralph Freeman's only comment was 'And I expect you want it to stand on a glass ball?' At the end of the process the costs were reconciled by a quantity surveyor. It was a good way to work. But I was determined to be my own landscape architect, having developed a feel for landscape when studying under Geoffrey Jellicoe at the Architectural Association.

My section (SB 12) was a complex brief, that knitted together the 'Upstream' and 'Downstream' sections and many of the individual pavilions. The main entrance to the Festival from Waterloo Station was through an arched entrance by Gordon Tait of Sir John Burnet, Tait and Partners. You were then faced with a choice of routes. On either side I did two semi-circular entrances or 'cones', one red, one blue, which served as porticoes leading you either through the pavilions of the 'Land' side or – via a complex route under the arches of Hungerford Bridge – of the 'People' side. The organisation of specific routes through the exhibits was one of the great advantages the Festival had over the Millennium Dome, with its introverted pods of displays or 'zones'. At the Festival everything was very tight; you could comprehend it in a single visit. The alternative to the two routes was the 'Concourse' ahead of Tait's entrance, the broadest open space in the Festival – leading to the river and culminating in a fountain display overlooking

figure 3
The Fountains at the end of the Concourse, overlooking Whitehall Court by H.T. Cadbury-Brown. (London Metropolitan Archives)

figure 4
Fountains. (The Architectural Press)

Whitehall Court, which formed the focal terminal of this axis. In fact it was part of a bigger idea that the 'inner group' had of taking the axis right up Northumberland Avenue to Trafalgar Square, but this had to be abandoned for lack of money. Nevertheless the fountains on the South Bank had 2½ times more water than those in Trafalgar Square.[3]

The South Bank fountains were particularly fun to design. I went to Versailles, and was shown the Chateau d' Eau by the engineer there: a building which looks just like any other part of the vast chateau complex, but which contains enormous storage tanks of water. The terraces of fountains were then fed in sequence by gravity. I was particularly interested in the fountain jets, the brass nozzles like the

3. The Trafalgar Square fountains were unveiled in 1947.

figure 5
Entrance to The People of Britain Pavilion by H.T. Cadbury-Brown. (Cadbury-Brown)

mouthpieces on a trumpet whose shapes dictated the form of the fountain. Those at Versailles were the originals. But I didn't just want fountains, I wanted gas jets underneath the water to burn above (like Christmas pudding!). This was deemed too dangerous by the authorities. So instead there were gas torchères set between the fountains, behind a little handrail and lip where the public could run their hands in the water and smaller jets creating a 'mist'. The fairway itself was set with electric lights in the pavement – cats eyes for roads were only just beginning to make an appearance, and for the short duration of the exhibition it was deemed sufficient to set bulbs under covers like jam-jars within the paving – the result was no more explosive than were the gas jets. There is little difference in designing something that will last for a few months or up to two years. There is a big difference between this and designing something that would be more permanent. As the buildings were temporary, we could be experimental, but then – as there were so few products in production – we had to be. This was the era before even curtain walling had reached Britain, and there were few lightweight materials suitable for exhibition work.

On the downstream 'People' side, I did a two-storey steel-framed pavilion reminiscent of the recent work by Mies van der Rohe. There was a water feature, with a small bridge and containing a seated figure by Heinz Henghes; and the Turntable Café. The designers realised that the pavilion was a strongly architectural statement and allowed it to read for itself, putting most of the display work into the arches of Hungerford Bridge. The turntable was an extension to the railway line to Charing Cross Station for turning engines around. Artists with whose work I was involved included Henry Moore, Barbara Hepworth, and David McFall. Julian Trevelyan did a mural in the Turntable Café, where there was also a stone carving by Anna Mahler and Felix Topolski painted a very large mural under the railway arch by Belvedere Road.

figure 6
Entrance to The People of Britain Pavilion by H.T. Cadbury Brown. (Cadbury-Brown)

On the 'Land' side I gave the designers a freer hand. My original drawings for the entrance envisaged a great shaggy outcrop of fissured rock, designed to make as great a contrast as possible with the sophistication of 'People' opposite – it was perhaps not as fissured as I would have liked. Graham Sutherland painted a large mural in the Land of Britain, and surprised everyone by using pastel yellows and lilacs.

My site with its two entrances was a critical one because it contained much of the underlying structure of the exhibition. In particular it had to link up all the other buildings in the Upstream site: it had Brian O'Rorke's 'Country Pavilion' next to the Land entrance, while the Concourse connected the Dome of Discovery, Skylon, and Sea and Ships Pavilion on one side, and Arcon's Transport building on the other. Little extra jobs included designing plinths for many of the sculptures, such as Barbara Hepworth's *Contrapuntal Forms*, originally sited next to the Dome and now in Harlow. The Dome of Discovery was a very good building. The concept was one of the first to be developed in 1948, and it had to be 365 feet across, just as the Millennium Dome *had* to be 365 metres. The concept may have been led by the snappy name. It was a real dome (not a tent like the modern

Dome), but ribbed in great circles in three dimensions, and thus entirely triangulated. These legs were hinged, so that the structure could expand and contract yet be braced against the wind from any direction. There was a bid to keep the Dome and Skylon (which was lovely),[4] but instead there was wanton destruction on a political level. The Tories hated the Festival, because it was successful and largely left-wing. The excuse given was the high value of the site. Yet in 2000 it is still empty.

The best thing about the Festival was seeing one's own buildings. But also the totality of the thing – it was full of joy, with concourses full of people. The preparation in so short a time was frantic – remember the stomach ulcers? I don't remember any strikes or labour problems. That said, everybody worked long hours, and overtime payments grew as the exhibition neared. That's why Casson said, 'And a good time-and-a-half was had by all'.

4. There was a detailed proposal by the LCC to move the two to Crystal Palace Park, which they had recently acquired.

7   Festival of Britain South Bank Tour

ELAIN HARWOOD, ANNIE HOLLOBONE
AND ALAN POWERS

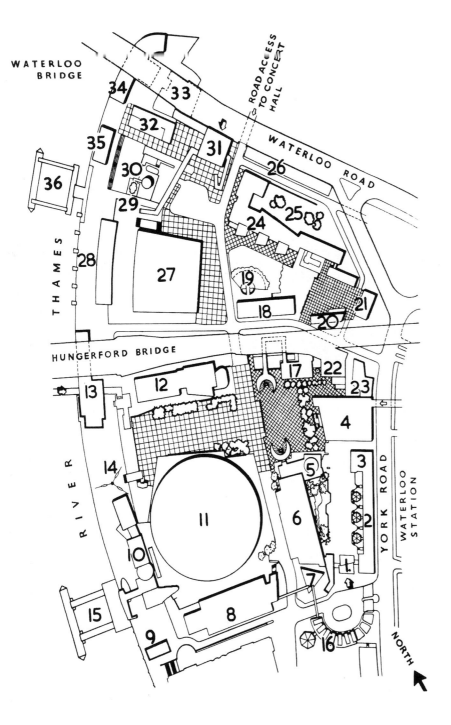

WATERLOO
BRIDGE

34 33

ROAD ACCESS TO CONCERT HALL

35 32 31
36 30 29
28 27
THAMES

HUNGERFORD BRIDGE

13 12 14

RIVER

11 10 15 9 8

WATERLOO ROAD

26 25 24 19 18 21 20

17 22 23
4
3 5 2
6 7
16

YORK ROAD

WATERLOO STATION

NORTH

Festival of Britain South Bank Tour

ELAIN HARWOOD, ANNIE HOLLOBONE
AND ALAN POWERS

'AS soon we pushed through the turnstiles and past the impatient attendants, there was a surprise, a sudden sense of space and leisured gaiety.' (Patrick O'Donovan and Hugh Casson, commentary to *Brief City*, 1952).

'We wanted to get our effects inside the exhibition, so that as soon as people went through the gates they were in an extraordinary, huge, exciting toyshop right in the middle of London, with different views coming to them and at them all the time.' (Hugh Casson).[1]

York Road entrance: Gordon Tait of Burnet Tait and Lorne. The high entrance over a footbridge from Waterloo Station is distinctive for its tall laminated trusses made of timber given by British Columbia and designed by the Timber Development Association. The interior of the Rocket cafeteria underneath was by Kenneth Cheesman, where the trusses formed giant braces,

figure 1 The view from the York Road entrance (The Architectural Press)

figure 2 Inside The Rocket, mural by Betty Swanwick (Crown copyright N M R)

and there was sculpture by Mitzi Cunliffe and Peter Peri.

Chicheley Street entrance and offices, plus Fairway Café and Minerals Pavilion: Michael Grice of the Architects' Co-Partnership, with Ove Arup and Partners. This included offices for Festival management staff, a V I P lounge with its own garden, the entrance from Chicheley Street and screen to road. The offices were housed in eight individual 'boxes' (also known as 'carry cots' and designed by A C P partner Kenneth Capon) suspended over a solid ground floor and overlooking a courtyard garden, and following the curve of the road behind. They were screened from York Road by a high steel scaffold set with canvas tetrahedral 'flags'.

' ... a tetrahedron without the bottom, in canvas, screens, and I thought, 'Well, that's easy to make.'

figure 3 Mitzi Cunliffe, *Root Bodied Forth*, looking towards the Land of Britain and Dome of Discovery (The Architectural Press)

figure 4 The Fairway (The Architectural Press)

1. Hugh Casson, 'Putting on a Show', R I B A Christmas Holiday Lectures, 1951–2; 2 January 1952, p.64; R I B A Manuscript Collection.

figure 5 Payboxes at Chicheley Street entrance (The Architectural Press)

figure 6 York Road screen and kiosk (The Architectural Press)

figure 7 The 'Carry Cot' offices by Chicheley Street (The Architectural Press)

2. Michael Grice: National Sound Archive. National Life Story Collection: Architects' Lives, interview by Alan Powers, March 2000.

3. The Times, Festival of Britain Supplement, n.d. c.8 May 1951, p.6.

4. Hugh Casson: National Sound Archive. National Life Story Collection: Architects' Lives, interview by Cathy Courtney, February 1990. F1089–90. We are grateful to the Casson family for permission to quote from this interview.

One doesn't realise. So anyway, they're to be in canvas, these diamonds, and it was pointed out to me that canvas stretches, so much percent in the warp, and so much percent in the weft. So, you know, it seemed to me interesting but somewhat theoretical. But in fact, all the canvas was in diamonds, of which there were thousands, and were attached by springs which were made and designed by Terrys, of the angle poise. That lot had a slightly different tension to this lot, and the actual canvas things themselves not just a simple piece, you don't cut a diamond of canvas. No. No. We had to get them made by some sailmakers called Rase and Lapforth (Michael Grice)[2]

Alongside, the Minerals Pavilion was conceived as a truncated tetrahedron clad with concrete coal-faced blocks and mounted on a podium covered with grass which concealed the main exhibition space – 'a coal mine turned inside out', as The Times put it.[3] A high-level walkway linked the building to the Power and Production Pavilion (see below).

Entrances to The Land of Britain and The People of Britain sections, with Turntable Café: H.T. Cadbury-Brown. Assistants: on the Land side, R.W. Finch, on the People side Elizabeth Dale and Peter Softley, who also helped with the general layout of the Concourse. Assistant for Turntable Café, R.W. Finch. Interiors by V. Rotter, James Gardner and (for the café) Bliss and Subiotto. Landscaping for 'Land' by Peter Youngman, with water garden by J. Kasamoto, for the rest Frank Clark and Maria Sheppard with Cadbury-Brown. Sculpture, *Woman with Pitcher*, in Turntable Café by Anna Mahler. Seated figure in pool by Heinz Henghes. Sculptures on Concourse by Henry Moore, Barbara Hepworth (*Contrapuntal Forms*), and David MacFall. Julian Trevelyan mural in the Turntable Café. 'Felix Topolski did a huge history of the British Empire, [*Cavalcade of Commonwealth*] under the arches. It was absolutely enormous, about 30 feet high, by about 60 feet long.' (Hugh Casson).[4]

figure 8 The Concourse, looking towards the People of Britain and Transport (The Architectural Press)

figure 9 Entrance to the Land of Britain (The Architectural Press)

The concourse truly came into its own at night, when it became the centre for impromptu dancing. The axis was determined by the position of the entrances from Waterloo and from the Bailey Bridge. 'Here we made use of a trick. We decided to try to make people think, when they came to the main piazza, that the buildings that in fact were on the other side of the Thames were at the far end of the piazza. That meant that we had to pretend that the river was not there. We lowered the level of the main assembly place or piazza by two feet, and at the end we put fountains ... You see a terrific view, but you cannot walk to it because the river is in between, and so you get the best of both worlds.' Whitehall Court was decorated with lights, so that at night it became 'a sort of fairy castle suspended in the air.' (Hugh Casson).[5] It is indicative of the Festival's sense of history that Cadbury-Brown went to Versailles to research the development of fountain jets. But he also wanted gas jets underneath to create flames. This was deemed too dangerous by the authorities, so instead there were gas torchères, and smaller jets creating a 'mist'.

The alternative to perambulating the concourse was to follow one of the two prescribed routes through the exhibition, and Cadbury-Brown designed two aluminium cones as porticoes to these routes, one red, one blue. For the 'Origins of the People' he designed a glazed Miesian building that formed a dignified and uncluttered entrance. A tortuous route then threaded between the arches of Hungerford Bridge, while to the side he designed a little café with a Japanese garden. On the other side, the 'Origins of the Land' was by contrast rough and totally enclosed, designed to express a geological rockfall in reinforced concrete.[6] Cadbury-Brown wrote that 'the most up to date idea which I have been nursing was some reinforced brickwork spanning a 12' opening (just for the heck of it) and

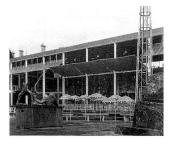

today the contractors talked me into having a hidden steel beam behind.' (H.T. Cadbury-Brown)[7]

The Country pavilion: Brian O'Rorke, assisted by Gordon Lie and Colin Laird. Display design by F.H.K. Henrion. 'An outsize Dutch barn' (Brian O'Rorke).[8] R.T. James and Partners, structural engineers, Peter Youngman landscape. This simple building was in two sections: one dedicated to 'The Natural Scene' had as its centrepiece a great plaster tree; the other, 'Countryside', had to cope with large numbers of animals

figure 10   The Turntable Café, with portable signpost by Robin Day and Milner Gray (The Architectural Press)

figure 11   The Natural Scene and The Country pavilion from the Fairway, with the Dairy Bar, and Henry Moore's *Genesis* (The Architectural Press)

5.   Hugh Casson, 'Putting on a Show', RIBA Christmas Holiday Lectures, 1951–2; 2 January 1952, p.66; RIBA Manuscript Collection.

6.   Notes supplied by section architect for Casson's lecture at the RIBA, 24 March 1950. PRO WORK 25/43, A3/6. Conversation with Jim and Betty Cadbury-Brown, August 2000.

7.   ibid.

8.   Brian O'Rorke, from notes prepared by the architects for a lecture given by Casson at the RIBA on 24 March 1950. They are in A3/6, PRO WORK 25/43 A3/6.

figure 12   Looking across the Concourse from the People of Britain, Heinz Henghes's sculpture in the pool below. (The Architectural Press)

figure 13   Tractor Display inside The Country pavilion (The Architectural Press)

figure 14 Minerals of the Island (Mining) and Royal Pavilion (The Architectural Press)

figure 15 Minerals of the Island (Mining) (The Architectural Press)

figure 16 Power and Production, featuring the 'biggest glass window in the world', with County Hall behind (The Architectural Press)

kept on site, from prize cows to hives of bees. 'The agricultural pressure group said they couldn't have the same horses all through the exhibition, had to change the breed every week. So Henrion had to put in his budget, this sort of thing ... Then he had to find somebody to make a huge bee, about 14 foot long, which was quite difficult. What sort of fee do you pay them? How long is it going to take? And what are they going to make of it? You see these were all totally new problems.' (Hugh Casson)[9] 'The service requirement seemed particularly complex: the valuable horses which arrived without horseshoes and for which daily transport had to be provided to take them to Hyde Park for exercise; the daily delivery of plankton from the Lake District as a diet essential to all the live fish exhibits; or the breeding of 5,000 butterflies, a year in advance, so that a new batch could be supplied once a week for the "Live Butterfly" window: this in turn made it necessary to organise Boy Scouts all over

the country to dig up the appropriate wild flowers which alone would feed the particular butterfly species, delivered in that week ... Over five months, five thousand prize animals – bulls, cows, horses, sheep, goats, chickens and ducks – had to be exhibited as they were so valuable that none of them could be shown for longer than a few weeks.' (F.H.K. Henrion).[10] On the ground floor was a Dairy Bar selling milk.

'In front of the building is a sunken stream, meandering naturalistically among reeds and boulders; beyond it the visitor can see into the open side of the building.' (The Times)[11]

'The 'Country' Pavilion has a faintly Japanese air, perhaps only because the whole thing is based on long, narrow shapes, bound into firm rectangles – a most accomplished design, this.' (John Summerson)[12]

Power and Production Pavilion: H.J. Reifenberg and G. Grenfell Baines of BDP, engineer F.J. Samuely. Sculpture on the wall of the western hall representing electricity, heavy and light industry by Karel Vogel. The building was entered from the Raw Materials Pavilion to the east, at first floor gallery level. It was thus possible to look down on the large industrial exhibits and out over the river through a completely glazed west end, claimed by the manufacturers Pilkington's to be the largest sheet of glass in the world. The external bas-relief was by Karel Vogel and the Camberwell School of Arts and Crafts. On the first floor was a self-service cafeteria, The Whistle.

figure 17 The entrance to Power and Production (The Architectural Press)

The '51 bar and Roof terrace: Leonard Manasseh, assistants Ian Baker and Lois Hutchings, Felix Samuely engineer. This scheme began as a competition for a restaurant, won by Manasseh in November 1949 out of 67 entries and with Patrick Gwynne as a close runner up. It was curtailed when the budget for the South Bank was cut in 1950, and Manasseh was left to design just the bar. 'The brief was to make a coherent and unified whole out of the following miscellaneous requirements – a luxury bar and roof terrace, a substation, a block of public lavatories ... their planning had to prevent any unorthodox entry from Chicheley Street.' (Leonard Manasseh).[13] Manasseh did his own landscaping. The attenuated female figure, sculpted in concrete by Daphne Hardy Henrion and as skeletal as the building, is now in Manasseh's own garden at Highgate. 'Recalling the curious lanky grace of the Dinkas in the Sudan' (*Illustrated London News*)[14]

The Bailey Bridge and Regatta Restaurant. Misha Black and Alexander Gibson of the Design Research Unit. A temporary footbridge was erected by the Royal Engineers from the bottom of Northumberland Avenue leading directly to the site, and was one of the busiest entrances. 'As the South Bank is part of London that people ordinarily do not go to very much we must try somehow to link the South Bank with the North Bank and make it easy to go from one to the other.' (Hugh Casson).[15] At its southern end it was supported on the steel frame of the restaurant, a precast, pre-stressed structure with an aluminium roof. There were platforms on two levels, the upper one a semi-open bar and promenade deck overlooking the river, with a restaurant (again with an open-air section) below, and a garden behind it, complete with a transplanted 40' tree and a pool. 'The Zecora acununata on the Regatta Restaurant came into leaf in late May, dropped its leaves in Autumnal display in early July and broke into spring foliage in August', (Frank Clark, landscape designer.)[16] The kitchens were underneath. Copper abstract piece by Lynn Chadwick. Mural on terrace by Laurence Scarfe, and on restaurant wall (in ceramic) by Victor Pasmore. This was the centrepiece for Mark Hartland Thomas and Helen Magaw's scheme of furnishings and tableware using patterns inspired by X-ray crystallography.

'The slick decorative Regatta Restaurant makes great play with its flights of steps and reminds me to say that stairs, steps, ramps and overhead ways are brilliantly handled throughout the exhibition.' (John Summerson) [17]

figure 18 Installing the Zecora acununata outside the Regatta Restaurant (Gerald Barry archive)

9. Hugh Casson, National Sound Archive F1089–90.

10. F.H.K. Henrion, 'The Agricultural and Country Pavilion', in Banham and Hillier, *A Tonic to the Nation*, London, Thames and Hudson, 1976, pp.106–7.

11. *The Times*, Festival of Britain Supplement, n.d. c.8 May 1951, p.6

12. John Summerson, *New Statesman and Nation*, 12 May 1951, p.529.

13. Leonard Manasseh, notes prepared by the architects for a lecture given by Casson at the RIBA on 24 March 1950. They are in A3/6, PRO WORK 25/43 A3/6.

14. *Illustrated London News*, May 26, 1951, p.856.

15. Hugh Casson 'Putting on a Show', Christmas Holiday Lecture, RIBA, 2 January 1952, RIBA Archives, p.57.

16. Frank Clark, in Festival of Britain, Final Report no.3; A1/A3/8, PRO WORK 25/53.

17. John Summerson, *New Statesman and Nation*, 12 May 1951, p.529.

figure 19 The landward flank of the Regatta Restaurant, looking towards Sea and Ships and Nelson Pier (The Architectural Press)

figure 20 Julian Trevelyan mural in The '51 bar (Crown copyright NMR)

figure 20 The Dome of Discovery, with Sea and Ships beyond (The Architectural Press)

figure 21
Sea and Ships (The Architectural Press)

18. *Architectural Review*, vol.110, no.656, August 1951, p.89.

19. Explanation accompanying the competition entry by Powell and Moya, assisted by Martin Hurley and James Gowan, A4/C7, PRO WORK 25/43.

20. Hugh Casson, 'Putting on a Show', RIBA Christmas Holiday Lectures, 1951–2; 4 January 1952, p.93; RIBA Manuscript Collection.

21. 'Critic' in *New Statesman*, 5 May 1951, p.497.

22. John Summerson, *New Statesman and Nation*, 12 May 1951, p.529.

Sea and Ships Pavilion: Basil Spence. Interior designers James Holland and Basil Spence. This was constructed as a largely open structure, of 40–45 ft high latticed frames at 20 ft centres. Murals, flags, sculptures, and model ships were suspended from the main structure. The upper levels had concrete floors surfaced with ships decking, cork or rubber. The story of shipping was dealt with in six sections: the history of sailing ships, the marine engine and its development, the principles of mechanical propulsion, shipbuilding, special ships and fisheries. One of the main features was a 40' square relief sculpture of *The Islanders* by Siegfried Charoux. Other art included murals by John Hutton, Tristram Hillier, James Boswell (Fisheries), G. Skolly (Shipbuilding); *Neptune* sculpture by Keith Godwin, a mobile fountain, *Windjammers*, by Richard Huws, and a fountain by Maurice Lambert. The ship models were by Bassett Lowke Ltd.

'Sums in miniature the multi-level-internal-external type of planning in which the exhibition specialises.' (*Architectural Review*)[18]

Alongside, the Nelson Pier built by the LCC included a self-service cafeteria, The Skylark, also designed by Spence.

figure 22 John Hutton's mural at the Sea and Ships Pavilion (Crown copyright NMR)

figure 23 The Dome of Discovery, with Power and Production in the foreground, Sea and Ships to the left (London Metropolitan Archive)

Vertical Feature – Skylon, by Powell and Moya, engineer Felix Samuely. 'To act as a pointer or beacon and to be the main vertical element in the exhibition. To be clearly visible by day and by night.' (Powell and Moya)[19] It was nearly 300ft high, and its width was 70ft at the pylon.

'Skylon was put up in a scaffold 30ft high, then hauled up on to an immense ice cream cone, and then built up on top with little panels, each panel about the size of a door.' (Hugh Casson)[20]

'The Skylon is a cone of light in a dark world.' (*New Statesman*)[21]

'a silly toy, a pretty toy and a dangerous one, whose merciless descending point is luckily just out of reach', (John Summerson, *New Statesman*)[22]

'Its precision and elegance make it a fitting symbol for an exhibition at which the world of modern science is lavishly on display.' (*The Times*)

'And the Skylon? Well, that was a simple formula in three dimensions, a clear statement in steel and aluminium and wire. Every part of it did precisely the job it was designed to do. And what was that? Why, simply to hang upright in the air and astonish.' (Patrick O'Donovan and Hugh Casson, commentary to *Brief City*, 1952)

Transport: Arcon (Rodney Thomas). The form was determined by the requirement to display 'full-sized examples of locomotives, cars, aeroplanes and portions of ships ... the endeavour has been to express the character of each form of transport differently, but at the same time design the building as a whole.' (Rodney Thomas)[23] There were five sections in two main buildings, one large, one small, hugging the Hungerford Bridge as the most appropriate place to exhibit transport.

The Dome of Discovery: Ralph Tubbs. Assistants Michael Pattrick, Frank Tischler and Keith Bennett. 'The basic concept of this dome, the largest in the world, is to contrast the visual solidarity of a series of sweeping horizontal galleries of reinforced concrete with the extraordinarily lightness of the vast aluminium saucer dome which spans out and beyond all the galleries and which is supported on very light tubular steel struts.'[24] It was also the largest aluminium structure erected by that date. The dome was built up of ribs, in three directions and thus triangulating the structure while allowing it some flexibility to move. Geometry, particularly circles and cones, played an important part in the design, for the concrete exhibition galleries formed a series of concentric circles underneath the circles of the aluminium ribs. Much of the exhibition material was crammed into the Dome, as it was the only truly dark space on the site.

John Ratcliff claimed that it grew out of the concept of a giant 'Big Top'.[25] For Casson it was 'a great brain, that is why we kept it rather dark inside. The idea was that we know very little even now about what is going on in the world, and so the inside of the dome is dark, like ignorance, with occasional patches of light where there are sparks of knowledge, where people have found out things.'[26] It was rather more than twice the size of the Perisphere at the New York World's Fair of 1939–40, or, as Tubbs claimed later 'it was twice the length of the axis of the Albert Hall'.[27] 'If one is to have a dome in

an exhibition it has to be the largest dome in the world. We wondered how large to make ours, and someone said that 365 was an easy number to remember, and so we said we would make it 365 feet.' (Hugh Casson)[28]

'It was the largest dome that had ever been built. It was rather like a ship. It was a live thing, it moved and strained with the changes of weather and temperature. Its roof was both carried and tethered by these slender spars that were hinged and could move and give a little when the wind caught the side of the building. The side walls supported nothing. They were no more than curtains against the light and weather and they were not the

figure 24 Inside the Dome of Discovery (The Architectural Press)

figure 25 Looking across to Transport, with the entrance to the Downstream section to right under Hungerford Bridge (The Architectural Press)

23. Rodney Thomas, from notes prepared by the architects for a lecture given by Casson at the RIBA on 24 March 1950. A3/6, PRO WORK 25/43 A3/6.

24. Ralph Tubbs, in PRO WORK 25/43.

25. John Ratcliff, 'Architects and the Festival of Britain', in A Tonic to the Nation, p.110.

26. Hugh Casson, 'Putting on a Show', RIBA Christmas Holiday Lectures, 1951–2; 31 December 1951, p.21; RIBA Manuscript Collection.

27. Ralph Tubbs, in Fay Sweet, 'Oh brave new world that had such buildings in it', The Independent, 8 May 1991, p.19.

28. Hugh Casson, 'Putting on a Show', RIBA Christmas Holiday Lectures, 1951–2; 2 January 1952, p.59; RIBA Manuscript Collection.

29. G.W. Stonier, New Statesman and Nation, 28 April 1951, p.473.

30. John Summerson, New Statesman and Nation, 12 May 1951, p.529.

31. Hugh Casson, National Sound Archive F1089–90.

32. Conversation with Sir Peter Shepheard, 6 October 2000.

same distance from the edge all the way round. You could walk round this thing and at every pace the proportions, the shape and the view changed. It was not simply a gigantic mushroom. It was a considered work of art as well as an achievement in engineering.' (Patrick O'Donovan and Hugh Casson, commentary to Brief City, 1952)

'A curved silver lid against the blue, and of course the biggest dome in the world, or what would it be doing here?' (New Statesman)[29]

'A saucer dome nearly four times as big as that of Santa Sophia is not necessarily four times as impressive and, in fact, as you enter, might just as well be a flat girder roof.' (John Summerson)[30]

Outside, 'there was a sort of Arctic Theatre, and [some husky dogs] gave a performance every hour. They sort of came in artificial snow, and barked, and were fed, and had to be exercised every day.' (Hugh Casson)[31]

Lion and Unicorn Pavilion: R.D. Russell and Robert Goodden.
Assistants John Morton, K.G. Browne, T.M. Lupton. Russell and Goodden also did the interiors. Engineers R.T. James and Partners. Consultant for Lamella roof, E.

Lewis. The Lion and Unicorn Pavilion was unusual in that Robert Goodden and Dick Russell designed both the building and the display, with texts by Laurie Lee to a brief by Hubert Philips. It truly caught the English spirit in all its ambiguity and whimsy. Peter Shepheard recalls seeing drawings by Casson for the pavilion much as built, and has suggested that he had a firm hand in its evolution; certainly the name was his.[32] The structure was a steel frame carrying a Lamella timber truss roof of English oak, which overswept the side walls in an upwards curve that served to

figure 28 Fred Mizen, Corn figures of the Lion and Unicorn (The Architectural Press)

figure 26 The Lion and Unicorn Pavilion (The Architectural Press)

figure 27 Inside the Lion and Unicorn Pavilion (The Architectural Press)

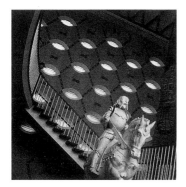

figure 29 The White Knight
(The Architectural Press)

figure 30 The Unicorn Café
(The Architectural Press)

33. Margaret Casson, National Sound Archive F1234–5.

34. R.D. Russell and Robert Goodden, in *A Tonic to the Nation*, p.97.

35. Robert Lutyens, *Country Life*, 27 April 1951, p.1273.

36. Wells Coates, in PRO WORK 25/43.

37. John Summerson, *New Statesman and Nation*, 12 May 1951, p.530.

brace it. The open, barn like quality enabled the entrance frontage to be entirely glazed, and for the side-walls to have only eye-shaped portholes, which formed a tear-like pattern down the long elevation and limited views of Hungerford Bridge. The long mural inside was by Kenneth Rowntree, and showed scenes from British history.

'It was just about us, the people. There were three huge features down the centre of the hall. They were huge sort of vertical things. The judge, for instance, was a wonderful great vertical form with a red robe falling right down and his wig on top. It's all in the detail which really counted. The church had a huge stone cross. They all had to be designed to go in various bases down at the bottom and have a lot of wording and so on.

'There was a flight of birds going right the way through this huge hall, which was symbolising liberty. They were made by some-body in a mould and they hung from the ceiling in a great flight, flock, going as if out of the window at the end, and a few outside. They were lovely.' (Margaret Casson)[33] Even the name was symbolic, the Lion standing for 'the more de-pendable traits of the national character, the Unicorn for the more volatile' (Russell and Goodden).[34] The exhibit ended with landscapes by Gainsborough, Constable, Turner and Paul Nash, and a bell specially cast by the Whitechapel

foundry, rung by remote control daily and which is now the tenor bell of Kelvedon Church, Essex.

'There is glass on one side, and a Victorian wallpaper on the other, punctuated by glass eyes. The ceiling supports, among innumera-ble other objects, a flight of doves issuing from a wicker cage. Strung along the gallery in Baroque frames are blackboard texts from Shake-speare and the Bible. The visitor says: 'Dear me! How very amusing!' Then one remembers the theme to which the Pavilion is dedicated and one is frankly a little appalled.' (Robert Lutyens).[35]

The pavilion also included a tented cafeteria, The Unicorn, slung from two 70' high masts, and landscaped with a moated forecourt by Peter Shepheard.

Television: Wells Coates. Assistant Peter Bender, who did an external mural. Interior by Denys Hinton, landscaping by Peter Shepheard. Coates conceived this tour through the story of television as a 'mystery *cave*: an aquarium with multiple effects, designed for the dithyram-bic spectator' behind an abstract representation of a cathode ray tube, in the form of a mural by Mary Fedden. The structure itself was 'simple' and partially open on the ground floor, the main display being above. (Wells Coates).[36]

Telecinema: Wells Coates. Assistant Peter Bender. Mural by John Armstrong. Interior by Denys

figure 31 Mary Fedden and Barbara Jones painting the mural for the Television Pavilion (Fox Photos Ltd.)

figure 32 Looking from under Television, with mural by Peter Bender, through the courtyard to Homes and Gardens, and with Edward Mills's Administration Building behind (The Architectural Press)

figure 33 Entrance to Homes and Gardens (The Architectural Press)

figure 34 John Piper, *The Englishman's Home*, in Homes and Gardens (Crown copyright NMR)

Hinton, landscaping by Peter Shepheard. Features included stereoscopic films using a modified Dudley system of polarisation, requiring glasses, and a new form of borderless screen developed by Coates (and later used by Ernö Goldfinger for his Odeon, Elephant and Castle). The availability of non-flammable film by the end of 1950 enabled the projection box to be incorporated within the body of the auditorium, which was rectangular for acoustic reasons, and clad in a 'quilted' finish under a framework roof described by Coates as a 'lobster claw'.

'Wells Coates's 'Television' and his 'Telecinema' are both excellent, probably, indeed, the most mature and finished architecture on the site and the only architecture that surrenders nothing to decorative facility. These form two elements in a wonderfully pretty group, planned like an old village, with a green along which are ranged the dainty porticoes and courts of Homes and Gardens.' (John Summerson)[37]

Homes and Gardens: Denis Clarke Hall/Bronek Katz and Reginald Vaughan. Assistant Ursula Meyer. Katz and Vaughan conceived their pavilion as a Dutch barn, with subsidiary structures of tubular scaffolding clad in asbestos and brick. They designed the interiors themselves. Sculpture by John Matthews, mural, *The Englishman's*

Home, by John Piper. Landscaping by Peter Shepheard, incorporating gilded bronze sculpture by Jacob Epstein in the pond outside the tea garden – the Garden Café. The entrance range was designed by Denis Clarke Hall in canvas.

figure 35 Looking to the Shot Tower, with Homes and Gardens on the right and the rear of the Royal Festival Hall (detailed by Trevor Dannatt) to the left (The Architectural Press)

'You are confronted, in despite of the invitation extended by the bold inscription, not with a doorway but with a blank wall, given some degree of formality by a piece of sculpture centred on it. As you move forward there is a sense of gathering confinement, which is suddenly dispelled a few paces further on by an unexpected view to the left, across a lawn, a sunken pool, a sculptured figure and the distant shot-tower – a playback, as it were, of the view you have lately left.' (*Architectural Review*)[38]

Downstream Landscaping: Peter Shepheard. Winkfield Manor Nurseries, Ascot. 'The landscape work consists of the design of all the space between the buildings, walks, terraces, paving, steps, and of the gardens in this space, flowerbeds and boxes.' Shepheard's best-known work here was the moat garden outside the Unicorn tea-room, the moat protecting the plants and ensuring nobody could

figure 36 The Exhibition entrance from Waterloo Bridge (The Architectural Press)

leave without paying for their tea. 'I looked around for some big, beautiful boulders, and found some in a Yorkshire quarry which I placed along the concrete edges of the pool. I strewed the edges of the water with the boulders. When the Festival closed the boulders were rescued, and found their way to schools and housing schemes – I kept meeting them for years afterwards.'[39] He also landscaped the former dock area by the Shot tower, with a sculpture by Karin Jonzen.

Thameside Restaurant, Harbour Bar, Health, The New Schools, Nursery vaults exhibition and walkway to Royal Festival Hall: Jane Drew of Fry and Drew.

'At first the only decision that was made was that most of the restaurants should be on the riverbank. As no riverbank had been built at that time, it meant that we need not fret about that for a few months.' (Hugh Casson).[40]

Maxwell Fry didn't want to get involved in the Festival as he didn't think architecture should be 'a temporary affair'. But Drew considered that it was 'a great opportunity to try out things.'[41] The site included the vaults under Waterloo Bridge. Assistants J.C. Todd, Z. Borowiecki, C.S. Knight, M. Pain, S. Gardiner, with interiors by Ward and Austen (restaurants), Peter Ray (health hall), Neville Conder (schools and vaults). Engineers, Ove Arup and Partners. The restaurant was well supplied with art – a mural screen by Ben Nicholson, *Turning Forms* by Barbara Hepworth, *Birdcage* by Reg Butler, and a fountain by Eduardo Paolozzi – the first time that Paolozzi had ever exhibited anything.

'I had an idea that instead of having a flat mural it would be nicer for Ben's mural to curve. Ben thought this would be a marvellous idea. [He] said to me would I please see that all the workmen who were putting up his mural wore white gloves. So I went off to Selfridges and got I think five dozen pairs of white gloves. Ben said to me that I hadn't put a curved glass in front of his curved thing, but of course I hadn't any money. But I said I could put a ha ha, with pebbles. And I saw him off on a train to St Ives quite happy, but he got out half way home and phoned me. He said I only put those pebbles there to give the public some ammunition to throw

38. *Architectural Review*, vol.110, no.656, August 1951, p.96.

39. Conversation with Sir Peter Shepheard, 6 October 2000.

40. Hugh Casson, 'Putting on a Show', RIBA Christmas Holiday Lectures, 1951–2; 2 January 1952, p.59; RIBA Manuscript Collection.

41. Jane Drew, National Sound Archive. F8637–8. Lecture at Courtauld Institute, London, 10 November 1995.

figure 37 Thameside Restaurant (The Architectural Press)

figure 38 The Broadwalk, Thameside Restaurant (The Architectural Press)

figure 39 Walkway to the Royal Festival Hall for those not visiting the Festival (The Architectural Press)

42. Jane Drew, National Sound Archive.

43. Jane Drew, National Sound Archive.

44. Lynn Chadwick, National Sound Archive. National Life Story Collection, Artists' lives, interviewed by Cathy Courtney, April-May 1995. C466/28.

45. Jane Drew, National Sound Archive.

figure 40 Sport (The Architectural Press)

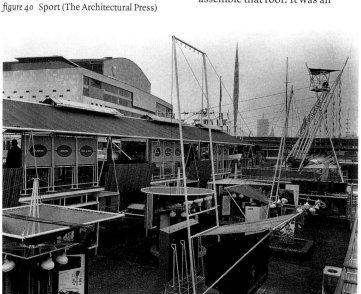

at him! I pointed out they were all cemented down.' (Jane Drew)[42]

This section incorporated the entrance from Waterloo Bridge, under a feature tower. 'I did what was then completely new, I had an all glass lift. In order that people could go up and see. A viewing tower in which people could see everything and be seen.' (Jane Drew)[43] The lift had a hanging mobile at its summit by Lynn Chadwick. 'This was a building in the form of just a framework. I put in these canvas triangles, like a ship's sails you know, like the little sails you have in a yacht, in the front ... But the mobile, that's where I found that it is impossible to have a mobile in the top of this tower, you see, and the wind was blowing through, and although the bits were very heavy, it still wasn't very satisfactory.'[44]

The Thameside Restaurant, raised over the river wall, enjoyed spectacular views, and was retained as a café for the riverside walk until the self-service facility was built in the lower floor of the Royal Festival Hall in 1962–4. The Thameside Restaurant was entirely prefabricated, for speed. 'We got the girls who made the aeroplane wings to come up and they took less than a week to assemble that roof. It was an aluminium surface, just like an aeroplane wing. It came up on lorries from Bristol.' (Jane Drew)[45]

Sculpture, *London Pride*, by Frank Dobson, near main entrance to the Royal Festival Hall.

Sport: Gordon and Ursula Bowyer.
Assistants Ward Koss and John Reid with Kenneth Grange as graphic and display designer; engineer Lawrence Kinchington. Gordon and Ursula Bowyer (née Meyer) had earlier helped on Homes and Gardens, and were initially invited only to design the interiors for Sport. This was the last section to be begun, because it was dependent on the completion of the river wall. Drew's assistants were too stretched to produce a detailed design for this section, so the newly married Bowyers took on the whole section. 'If the Design Panel were all under 45, our team were all under 30. Anything was possible in those days ... Our brief was to tell the story of Sport in Britain and to include every conceivable one but naturally giving more prominence to soccer, cricket, tennis and golf than fencing, beagling and falconry. Some historical material was included, especially about the ones that started in Britain – a surprising number. This meant trips to Lords, Wimbledon, etc to borrow exhibits; to visit a real tennis court and see what it looked like and to select the latest well-designed sports equipment – the COI made sure of that! We decided to form a series of double height space frames viewable from ground and first floor levels which would accommodate a high proportion of the exhibits. These were glazed where necessary and protected from above by canvas awnings. There were also a number of free-standing independent displays between the main structure and the river. Stairways were planned at each end of the building and a viewing platform projected over the river. Some sports of course, have very little equipment and here we had to use various

display techniques to overcome this, produced by two very talented artists and designers, Henry and Joyce Collins. Their boxing figure in stitched leather, slightly over life-size, was superb. I'm not sure that I ever quite forgave Sir Hugh Casson for acquiring this at the end of the Festival!' (Gordon Bowyer)[46]

Shot Tower, The Centenary Pavilion and transformer room: Hugh Casson and Leslie Gooday. The only building for which Casson accepted full responsibility was for the remodelling of the 1826 Shot Tower already on the site as a lighthouse and pigeon loft, with a steel platform on top used for demonstrating radar. 'Inside, … we thought about having a fountain, or waterfall, but couldn't get the pressure. In the end we had a lot of dangling balls.' (Hugh Casson).[47] An army anti-aircraft gun carriage was mounted on top that allowed the radar dish to circulate through 360 degrees and to rise from horizontal to vertical. An old brick

building alongside was retained as a control room. A centenary display commemorating the 1851 Great Exhibition was held in a small structure reminiscent of the Crystal Palace, placed high to demonstrate 'its elegance and frailty'.

Boat building display and garden: Hugh Casson and Leslie Gooday. Peter Shepheard landscape, R.T. James and Partners engineers. A covered display of boat building, developed only in 1950, using a surviving dock retained on the site. The circulation was planned so that visitors approaching the boat building shed should see

figure 41 The 1851 Centenary Pavilion
(The Architectural Press)

figure 42 The Riverwalk, Seaside. Painted bollard by James Fitton
(The Architectural Press)

figure 43 The Boat Pool, with Shot Tower to left and Waterloo Bridge beyond
(The Architectural Press)

46. Gordon Bowyer, September 1998.
47. Hugh Casson, 'Putting on a Show', RIBA Christmas Holiday Lectures, 1951–2; 4 January 1952, p.84; RIBA Manuscript Collection.

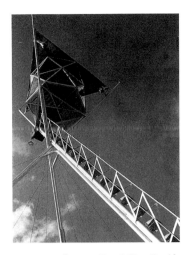

figure 44 Crow's Nest, Seaside
(The Architectural Press)

48. A3/6. Notes supplied by section architect for Casson's lecture. PRO WORK 25/43. Anthony D. Hippisley Coxe, 'I enjoyed it more than anything in my life', in A Tonic to the Nation, op.cit., p.88.

49. Edward Mills, notes supplied for Casson's lecture, 24 March 1950, in A3/6, PRO WORK 25/43.

50. Ruari McLean, quoted in A Tonic to the Nation, p.17.

figure 45 Administration Building and Waterloo Road Screen
(The Architectural Press)

through it to the garden beyond, but actually watch the displays well clear of the circulation route.

Seaside: Eric Brown and Peter Chamberlin. 'Six tapered tubular steel masts, braced and guyed by cables. Booms stick out to support inverted pyramids of canvas, which create a velarium canopy, and have to be supported by very heavy concrete foundations. In addition there is a small bar, restaurant and viewing point over the landing stage, supported by two continuous lattice girders designed to resemble the structure of a seaside pier' (Peter Chamberlin). Festival rock ('How do those letters get inside the sticks of rock? What was it that the Butler saw?'), donkey rides and Donald McGill postcards represented the 'essentially English' seaside.[48] Part of the structure was retained as a walkway and viewing platform until the Royal Festival Hall was extended in 1962. Brown and Chamberlin also designed the buildings on the Rodney Pier alongside.

'The British Seaside was celebrated in a crowded corner by the river, a mixture of rock shops, of roundabouts, of donkeys, of pointless models that merely pleased, of bright temporary awnings and bits

of rope and netting. Altogether it somehow captured that inexplicable lift of the heart, that hurrying into sandals and sports shirts, that placid sitting on the sands, that brief forgetting of the office and factory which happens when the British go down to the seaside for their holidays.' (Patrick O'Donovan and Hugh Casson, Brief City, 1952)

figure 46 The River Wall, Seaside
(The Architectural Press)

Administration and Staff Canteen: Edward Mills. A long, horizontal building below Waterloo Bridge, incorporating a screen that shielded the exhibition site. Mills conceived the building as 'a backcloth, light and colourful in appearance but not distracting from the varied shapes of the purely exhibition designs.'[49] It comprised a steel frame set over the brick basements of shops formerly on the site. It contained the first-aid point, maintenance workshops, electric substations, staff rooms and a canteen.

Building for the BBC and GPO: Drake and Lasdun. A small structure for outside broadcasts and technical facilities, set under the terrace to the Royal Festival Hall. Engineer Walter Goodesmith.

'Personally, on that first morning when first saw the Festival looking across the river from Charing Cross Station, it was so utterly beautiful and exciting that I wept.' (Ruari McLean)[50]

'‘No visible means of support’:
Skylon and the South Bank

SIR PHILIP POWELL

'No visible means of support':
Skylon and the South Bank

SIR PHILIP POWELL

O NLY two structures at the South Bank were the result of competitions, held in November 1949. One for a restaurant and bar attracted 68 entries and was won by Leonard Manasseh. The competition for 'a vertical feature' was more enthusiastically supported, with 157 submissions. The brief suggested that it could be 'completely abstract in conception or related to the theme of the exhibition', and had in itself to be 'a demonstration of the originality and inventiveness of British designers.' It could be three-dimensional, or be made of such transitory elements as water, gas, balloons or coloured lights. 'Mechanical, electrical and hydraulic effects' were encouraged. The only other condition was that it had to relate to the Dome alongside, whose design had already been fully determined.[1]

Many entries were from regional practices or groups of students. There was also a striking number of submissions by non-architects, including Duncan Grant and Quentin Bell. The clear winner was 'Skylon', a tensile structure designed by Philip Powell and Hidalgo ('Jacko') Moya with the engineer Felix Samuely. A young James Gowan assisted with the drawings for the scheme. The twelve-sided body of Skylon was 250' high in itself and nearly 300' when suspended, but only 13'6" wide at its maximum point. It was made of 12' braced steel panels which were bolted on site and covered with stain-finished aluminium louvres which diffused light by day and were lit up at night with tungsten lamps mounted up the inside of the frame. This 28 ton body was supported at its bottom point by a system of three twin cables forming a cradle, which passed over the tops of three pylons and down to foundation anchorages spaced 70' apart. Three guying cables from the same anchorages supported the upper part of the body at its widest point, which received extra stiffening.[2] In their submission Powell and Moya called it 'a pointer or beacon', explaining that its design was created to take up as little ground space as possible.[3] While historians can compare the relationship between the tall, slender Skylon and the rotund Dome of Discovery to that between the Trylon and the Perisphere at the 1939–40 New York World's Fair, this was not obvious to the architects at the time.[4]

Nearly all the so-called modern architects had been plucked by Casson, at least all those of his generation, so most of the entries were from very young

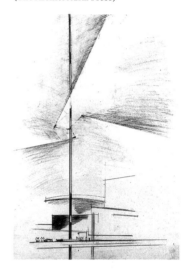

figure 1
Vertical feature Competition.
Winning design by Powell and Moya,
an impression by night.
(The Architectural Press)

figure 2
Vertical feature Competition. The Third
Prize winning design by P.A.R.
Dickinson. 2 January 1950. (The
Architectural Press)

figure 3
Lord Ismay & Gerald Barry with Michael & Philip
Powell and Hidalgo Moya, and their model of their
model of the winning design for Skylon. After the
presentation of prizes at County Hall. 16 January 1950.
(Gerald Barry archive)

1. Assessors' report, 1949, in A1/J2 – A1/J8,
PRO WORK 25/20.
2. Building, vol.26, no.6, June 1951, p.214.
3. Powell and Moya, assisted by Martin
Hurley and James Gowan, A4/C7, PRO WORK
25/43.
4. From a conversation between Sir Philip
Powell and Elain Harwood on 9 October 2000.

architects, including many students, or unknown regional firms. Dick Levine came second; he knew Misha Black and the Design Research Unit although he was not strictly a member of the practice – otherwise he wouldn't have been able to enter. Third was Peter Dickinson, a fine architect who, sadly, died very young.

Jacko and I did separate entries. I did a pyramid, a slightly tapering thing, with a zig-zag bracing and a coloured pattern, but Jacko's first sketch felt so right that there was no point going further and we collaborated after that. But it was Moya who evolved the design. One earlier idea we had was for a helium gas balloon, a bit like a barrage balloon on end, but there wasn't enough helium in the world to fill it, and it would have cost £10 million if there had been. Jacko drew up the final twelve-sided scheme, with Felix Samuely as engineer. Samuely used fewer supports and neater guys than was believed possible. This is because the cables were prestressed, they could act in compression as well as tension. Samuely had taught us at the AA, and advised us at Churchill Gardens, though the City of Westminster preferred to employ the more experienced Scott and Wilson as engineers because we were pretty unrespectable and very young.

The structure was erected in sections, and then the aluminium louvres were fixed. The wind moving through them caused a whistling sound, so that Skylon seemed to hum. The louvres were highly silvered, so that they reflected by day. At night they really glowed when the lights inside were lit up. The lights strung inside were one of the least dangerous things about it. We couldn't get a light right into the bottom, where the structure was both narrow and had to be more solid. But we did get lights right up to the top. When Skylon was completed the prop that held it from underneath was removed (you can still see it there in some photos). The structure dropped about two inches. *How did you feel?* Just relief.

The cost set by the competition was £14,000. It came in at £21,000, but was still officially £14,000 because the contractors, Callender's Cables of Hereford, agreed to sponsor the difference on condition that their name appeared on the little plaque that was set into the ground right underneath it. This was where everybody stood to look up inside it. This area was cordoned off when there was a thunderstorm, and there were rather a lot in the dreadful summer of 1951, for the Met Office feared that if there was a lightning strike it might shoot down Skylon and 'jump' to the ground. After climbing ladders up the inside of Skylon all day, a construction worker complained of the danger of tripping over manhole covers on the ground.

The name was chosen in a competition. 'Skylon' was suggested by Mrs Sheppard Fidler, whose husband A.G. Sheppard Fidler was to become the Birmingham City Architect. Nylon was the great new invention, and the name

figure 4
Skylon being dismantled
(The Architectural Press)

seemed to fit the mood of the times. The popular joke was that Skylon was like Britain: 'it had no visible means of support'.

After the exhibition was over there was some talk of Skylon being re-erected elsewhere. The Marquess of Bath (not the present one) tried to get it as a folly for Longleat, to put on a hill there, called Heaven's Gate. He thought you could just winch it up by helicopter, which would have been impossible, and the cost put him off. You couldn't build it on its original site on the South Bank now, for it would be just dwarfed by the Shell Centre. And the Wheel is lovely.

What did you think of the rest of the Festival?

Most international exhibitions are a bit pompous, but the Festival wasn't. That was one of the really specially good things. Some of the pavilions were a bit

strange maybe, but it was very fresh, because of the quality of the spaces in between. I didn't see the 1937 Paris Exhibition, but I was struck by the image of the Nazi and Soviet pavilions facing each other. Later I saw Picasso's *Guernica* at the New Burlington Galleries. The Festival was not spoilt by any such nationalist sentiment, rather the English seemed to be poking gentle fun at themselves, characterised by the Lion and Unicorn Pavilion which was funny and joky. The Festival moved away from the formal, competitive spirit, and saw the whole thing as a single space. The heroes were Peter Shepheard and Jim Cadbury-Brown, but because their work was landscape it was taken for granted.

I didn't spend a lot of time at the Festival because our office just then began to get work, including our first hospital, at Swindon. And Churchill Gardens was at full tilt. The best thing were the cafés, particularly Leonard Manasseh's '51 Bar, the winner of the other open competition, though what was built was very different from the competition entry because the budget was cut. The '51 Bar was good because it did a job but was not swanking with it. Good too was Eric Brown and 'Joe' Chamberlin's 'Seaside', because of the outlook ladders that went out over the river.

The Dome of Discovery was super on the outside. It had a beautiful simplicity, and got away with being just simple and grey. But inside it was just like the Millennium Dome – it was exactly a warning for the present Dome – because you couldn't see it. It was ruined by a reinforced concrete structure that carried the

figure 5
Skylon and the Dome of Discovery (London Metropolitan Archives)

figure 6
Skylon and the Dome of Discovery at night (The Architectural Press)

figure 7
Skylon amidst demolition. (London
Metropolitan Archives)

exhibition stands. There was an exhibition about British science that swallowed the whole place, and because the lighting was concentrated on these exhibits you couldn't even see the lovely roof structure. Circular buildings are particularly confusing as exhibition buildings anyway.

The best thing of all about the Festival was the site itself. It was right in the centre, and what a bit of central London! The layout was aware and respectful of the site, and brought in the river, the Houses of Parliament and Whitehall Court as part of the show. One of the most beautiful things of the exhibition was Whitehall Court – designed for free.

We did one other building for the Festival, which was never built. That was the Newton Einstein Building for Max Born, at the Victoria and Albert Museum, which was to go on the site now occupied by the Ishmaeli Centre. You entered up a lift into a round structure that played with all the forces of gravity. It was a bit like a giant fairground ride – in fact Jacko and I were both made to go on the new ride (The Rotor) at Battersea Park under tarpaulin. We were both sick. That was the difference – it was alright if you could see. Our only other exhibition building was the British Pavilion for Expo '70 in Osaka, Japan. And that too was demolished as soon as the show was over.

09 Films in 1951

DAVID ROBINSON

Films in 1951

DAVID ROBINSON

T HE Festival celebrated, said Herbert Morrison, the veteran London Labour politician who was then Foreign Secretary, nothing less than 'the British contribution to civilisation, past, present and future, in the arts, in science and technology and in industrial design'.

In this grand prospect it was to be expected that the moving image should figure large. The war had launched British cinema upon its finest hour, and in 1951 its outstanding directors – David Lean, Carol Reed, Anthony Asquith, Alexander Mackendrick, Michael Powell and Emeric Pressburger, the Boulting Brothers, Thorold Dickinson, Robert Hamer, Harry Watt, Charles Crichton – were all still in their 30s or 40s, at the peak of their powers. Creative documentary, pioneered in 30s Britain, had triumphantly demonstrated its force for propaganda, instruction and morale-building in the war years, and was still able to excite the public enough for the Festival's Telecinema (also known as 'Telekinema') to boast, rather than excuse, 'First showings of new documentary films in one-hourly programmes.' The future, though, in 1951, was television. Not many British households had a set, and colour was not even a dream, but the universal longing was to possess the little magic box.

Predictably television featured prominently in the Festival's Dome of Discovery, with a comprehensive exhibit on its history and current technology, including a special section showing the production of the BBC's 'newsreel'. Reading between the lines, though, it may have been that cinema proper was something of an afterthought, despite the hindsight assurance of Gerald Barry, the Director-General of the event, that 'those who planned the Festival of Britain recognised from the first the need to include a cinema within the small and jealously-sought space of this Exhibition'. The British establishment is traditionally reluctant to acknowledge a place for film in the national culture, and the presence and prominence of the Telecinema was almost certainly due mainly to the efforts of the dynamic new director of the British Film Institute, Denis (now Sir Denis) Forman. As it was, the Telecinema was not allocated a particularly favoured piece of the 'jealously-sought space', though in the long run its position in York Road, on the perimeter of the Festival site, proved a godsend. During the Festival it was the perfect spot for people with tired feet, and the queues were often enormous. Later, when the building became the first National Film Theatre, the site provided admirable street access.

Designed by Wells Coates, the Telecinema was the first theatre in the world conceived and built to show large-screen television as well as films, with facilities for stereoscopy and stereophonic sound. The plan of the building was a simple rectangle, and the side elevation showed an undulating roof, in the progressive architectural style of the period, rising towards the rear of the auditorium. The walls were rendered and painted in brown, with white and blue detailing. The building was partly underground, so that the public entered more or less on the level of the circle or gallery, descending stairs to reach the stalls. The auditorium held 400, and capacity audiences could be moved out in the space of 5 to 7 minutes, thanks to human skills as well as technology. Leslie Hardcastle,

figure 1
Telecinema and TV, seen from Homes and Gardens pavilion, with Ernest Race 'Antelope' chair and bench.
(The Architectural Press)

who was associated with the building from the start, and was subsequently administrator of successive National Film Theatres and principal creator of the Museum of the Moving Image, remembers that 'Beryl in the box office had a state-of-the-art automatic ticket dispenser but an automatic mind as well: she had the change all ready before the people even proffered their money'.

The theatre was part of the show. Entering the foyer, the public was confronted by glass screens through which they could observe the technical marvels of the projection box – a pair of synchronous drive projectors, two magnetic film sound recorders and reproducers together with two additional tape recorder-reproducers, and the massive equipment for television production and projection. Vaunted as the most highly equipped projection room in the world, it could also be used as a recording studio. The room was manned by three projectionists, neatly clad in blue sports jackets and gray flannels to match the overall interior decorative scheme.

As the public progressed through the foyer, collecting on the way their heavy, visor-form polarised 3-D viewing glasses (manufactured in South Africa), they were caught by television cameras, so that their images were simultaneously projected onto the screen for the amusement and amazement of the spectators already waiting in the auditorium. Grey and grainy as it was, this was probably the world's first regular public demonstration of live projection television. The stairway to the auditorium was enlivened with a large fish-tank and an optional diversion to a pleasant bar, supervised by a convivial barman called Fred who stayed on when the building became the first National Film Theatre, but subsequently left on account of the riotous out-of-hours entertainments he had put on for staff from the British European Airways terminal which took over the Festival's administrative building after closure. The bar was also the base for the first of several cats which guarded the theatre and its successor from waterside pests, and would occasionally startle patrons with the well-meant gift of a gnawed rodent.

The auditorium, designed to achieve the highest projection and viewing standards, was tunnel-shaped, reducing in height from back to front. The projection box was incorporated directly below the front of the circle/gallery, so that it was squarely in front of the screen at a distance of only 50 feet. Below this, the stalls defied tradition by being set on a reverse slope. The decoration was simple, with pale wood walls, brass fittings, bright blue carpet and checked seat upholstery in shades of grey. The grey-blue colour scheme was followed through in the uniforms of the staff: inevitably the usherettes' uniforms (as the press releases boasted) were made of nylon, which washed easily, but rustled in the dark. The mixture of projection media demanded a special screen coated with a metallic spray which did not depolarise the light as normal pigment would have done, and possessed a high reflectance to compensate for the low level of illumination from the television projector and the light losses from the polarising filters used for stereoscopy.

Almost since the birth of the film there had been experiments with stereoscopic cinema, generally using anaglyph systems which required the spectator to view the film through spectacles with one red and one green lens. The coloured lenses appropriately filtered the superimposed red and green images of the same scene, so that each eye perceived only the version appropriate to it. The polarisation system used at the Telecinema had already been pioneered at the New York World's Fair of 1939. In this method, as it was explained by J.D. Ralph, the British Film Institute representative at the Festival, 'The camera equipment employing two interlocked cameras produces two complementary pictures of the object, representing the left and right eye view, and these in turn are projected through polarising filters on to the screen, superimposed, and reflected back to the viewer, who in turn wears spectacles containing filters of the same characteristics as those at the projector ports. The filter has the effect of polarising the light at a given angle. Each one, however, is orientated at right angles to the other, This means that they are mutually exclusive, and the light which has passed through one filter cannot pass through the other, Thus the picture from the right hand projector is excluded from the left eye of the spectator and vice versa'.

Stereophonic sound was not entirely new: already in 1940 the Disney studios had recorded the classical music sound track of *Fantasia* stereophonically, even though at the time no commercial theatre was equipped to demonstrate it. The Telecinema's combination of stereoscopy and stereophony was however another first.

The Telecinema and the stereophonic films set off a heated debate over the conflict of art and technique. Raymond Spottiswoode, the technical genius who principally devised the stereo equipment, naturally defended the technique, predicting that the impact of stereoscopy 'may ultimately be much greater than academic critics assume, who are never tired of lashing at the three-dimensional film for its alleged realism, for aiming at nothing better than an effect of *trompe-l'oeil*. The accurate reproduction of reality is almost impossible to achieve in the cinema by foreseeable stereoscopic means, But instead the director can stretch out a studio scene until it is as long as a football field; he can squeeze it until it is as flat as a postcard; he can turn it inside out so that the nearest object is farthest way, and vice versa; he can even reshuffle at will the order in which things at different distances appear to the eye. An artist with these powers could make Picasso look like an Academician. But he would have to be another Picasso'. Spottiswoode prophesied that the use of the new techniques would be principally confined to the avant-garde, non-theatrical film: 'with its old first-generation pioneers still at the helm', he surmised, Hollywood 'is not likely to welcome any radical solution to its financial worries'. As things turned out, he was wrong. Two years after the Festival of Britain, Hollywood was to seize upon the stereophonic-stereoscopic combination as a defence against the threat of television.

Gerald Barry exulted that 'I can – and I do – say emphatically that there is not a layman alive of any imagination who can fail to be excited by them. Here is something quite new which will amuse and stimulate you in itself and set your mind speculating on the cinema of tomorrow'.

In March 1951, two months before the Festival opened, the British Film Institute's journal *Sight and Sound* concluded, 'Altogether the Telecinema will reflect an admirable balance between art and science: for we shall see not only the mechanical possibilities of a new adjunct to the medium, but also an artist experimenting with it'. That artist was the Scottish-born Norman McLaren (1914–1987), whose inspired stereoscopic abstractions, commissioned for the Telecinema, still amaze after half a century. *Now Is the Time* was drawn directly onto the film: clouds and suns float and dart backwards and forwards in space. In the longer and more ambitious *Around is Around*, animated shapes taken from cathode ray patterns dance and occasionally suggest human forms. Both had synthetic stereophonic sound.

McLaren's films took up less than ten minutes, and the rest of the 3-D programme was made up of more mundane offerings – a visit to the zoo in the black-and-white *A Solid Explanation*, and a pictorial study in colour of *The Distant Thames*. The 3-D films proved so popular that the Riverside Theatre in the Festival Gardens in Battersea, the playground of Festival London, was adapted to show them, though apparently without stereophonic sound. The repertory was hastily extended. A black-and-white tribute to the flourishing British ballet, *The Black Swan*, starring Beryl Grey and David Paltenghi, was respectable, but short documentaries on a Manchester oil refinery, square dancers in action and sports personalities did little to exploit the new techniques, apart from balls twanging out at the startled spectators in the sport film, *On the Ball*. McLaren, however contributed a new 3–minute masterpiece, *Twirligig*, for which he painted synthetic sound directly on to the optical sound track.

Aside from these technical revolutions, a different kind of cinematic experiment was the *Painter and Poet* series commissioned by the British Film Institute and produced by the Hungarian animator John Halas. The most eminent artists of the day donated their services, each providing a visual interpretation of a poem. The drawings were not animated, but were minutely explored by the close-up camera. Each film comprised two poems. Michael Rothenstein illustrated *The Twa Corbies*; Mervyn Peake, Shakespeare's *Spring and Winter* (sung by Peter Pears); Barbara Jones, David Gascoyne's *Winter Garden*; John Minton, Charles Dibdin's *The Sailor's Consolation*; Michael Ayrton, Thomas Nashe's *In Time of Pestilence*; Ronald Searle, Cowper's *John Gilpin*; and Henry Moore, Kathleen Raine's *The Pythoness*. Michael Warre, who originated and devised the series, illustrated Owen Meredith's *Check to Song*.

The Festival documentary films proudly and unashamedly celebrated British life and tradition. Britain's supreme artist-filmmaker, Humphrey Jennings was killed while filming in Greece at the end of 1950, but he had already completed his Festival film, *Family Portrait*. It opens with the pages of a family album, and broadens to a meditation on Britain and the continuities of tradition, culture and spirit. It was a disappointing end to Jennings' career: the incomparable eye for an image or a juxtaposition is still evident, but the film is a speculative literary essay rather than the kind of visual poem that Jennings had achieved in *Listen to Britain* or *Diary for Timothy*. While regretting that *Family Portrait* lacked the 'emotional drive' of Jennings' wartime masterpieces, an appreciative contemporary critic, Gavin Lambert, still noted that 'The fascination of science; the love of landscape, and of the sea; music (... and his superb dramatic use of it ...); a personal sense of the continuity of history and its varied manifestations, which is at the base of many of his analogies and digressions; an affection for simple people and pleasures, and for the ritual and pageantry that symbolise them – the whole rare combination of an artist of highly specialised sensibilities making contact with collective existence is in some ways at its most complete in *Family Portrait*'. This was the stuff of the Festival, 'a tonic for the nation'.

Before the event there had been a lot of gloomy scepticism, and the papers gloated over the difficulties and delays caused by heavy rains that turned the South Bank site into a sea of mud. All that changed once it opened. From today's viewpoint, the public's emotional commitment to the Festival and all it stood for, and the degree of participation and involvement by public and private bodies is astonishing. The ordinarily fragmented British film industry joined forces, under the banner of a company called 'Festival Film Productions', to produce a two-hour feature film, *The Magic Box*, which patriotically, if unhistorically, claimed the motion picture as a British invention. The film was directed by John Boulting and boasted sixty stars, led by Robert Donat as William Friese-Greene and Maria Schell, an Austrian actress then on the eve of international celebrity, as his first wife. Friese-Greene (1855–1921) was a photographer and compulsive inventor, who devised a camera to take images in rapid succession on photographic film. Unfortunately he never succeeded in projecting his pictures, which invalidates the film's climactic and best remembered scene: Laurence Olivier, in a cameo performance, plays a startled London bobby, whom the excited Friese-Greene drags in off the street to marvel wide-eyed at moving pictures on a screen. Sadly, what was generally known as 'the festival film' perpetuated an untruth.

The Port of London Authority presented the Festival with a documentary by Basil Wright, who had made his name, and created a new style of lyrical documentary, with *Song of Ceylon* (1935), but had not directed a film for several years. *Waters of Time* was a personal impression of the lower reaches of the Thames and the trade and traffic of the Port. Critics of the time praised the fine visuals and technical polish, but complained at an excess of aestheticism in Paul Dehn's poetical commentary and Alan Rawsthorne's rich musical score. Excess of aestheticism had become the besetting sin of British documentary; and the film commissioned by the Welsh Committee of the Festival of Britain proved a refreshing antidote. The young Paul Dickson's *David* was the portrait of a Welsh community, which smoothly combined documentary with acted recreation of the life of an elderly miner and poet, the David of the title, now working as a school caretaker. The perceptive Gavin Lambert recognised something new. He found that the film's scenes 'describe ordinary people, infuse life and colour into a background, in a way rare in films of this country. *David* is not only one of the few authentic regional films made here, but reasserts the human values that documentary film-making has lacked for so long'.

The Petroleum Films Bureau sponsored J.B. Napier-Bell's *Forward a Century*, which compared and contrasted the Great Exhibition of 1851 and the Festival of Britain as reflections of the world and society that inspired them. The film retains a historical interest for its pioneering and dynamic use of old printed images.

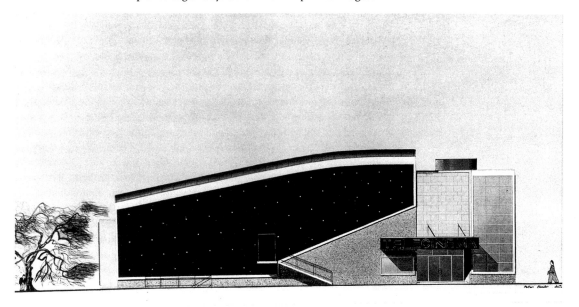

figure 2
Telecinema, as designed in 1949 by Wells Coates. Drawing by Peter Bender. (The Architectural Press)

The Festival itself was recorded in other documentaries. Derek York's charming *Festival* viewed the event through the eyes of a London boy who had landed one of the million free passes sent out attached to balloons. Philip Leacock, a documentary director about to embark on a career as a feature director in Britain and Hollywood made *Festival in London*, in Technicolor and with a specially commissioned Festival March composed by William Alwyn. An anonymous contemporary reviewer in *The Monthly Film Bulletin* thought its patriotic pride excessive, and complained that 'the impression retained is the same as that of actual attendance on a crowded day; one hardly saw anything but people.'

The festival had been significant enough to merit an epilogue in film form, which remains its most touching memorial. *Brief City* was directed by the French emigré film-maker Jacques Brunius, who had worked with the surrealists in the 20s and with Jean Renoir in the 30s. It was produced by Richard Massingham and sponsored by the *Observer* – presumably because Massingham's journalist brother Hugh Massingham was then a pillar of the newspaper. The film opens with shots of the bleak, deserted site, a newspaper blowing through the now empty avenues – Brunius was proud of this, reckoning that anyone else would have ended with this shot, rather than using this as a starting point to look back at the Festival in full swing, commentated by Hugh Casson in conversation with Patrick O'Donovan.

Although the film is in black and white, so that we cannot see how the Festival of Britain 'blazed with bright nursery colours', we still get a vivid impression of its impact from the soberly marvelling faces of the milling crowds – the men with trilbies and ties, the boys in flannel suits, the women with hats and demure summer skirts and blouses – and from Casson's elegantly phrased evaluation. With its 'space and leisured gaiety' it was 'a gigantic toyshop for adults ... light-hearted, sensible, not too serious ... and never boring. An exhibition ought to have an air of gaiety'. The Dome of Discovery was the largest dome that had ever been built, while the sole, beautiful purpose of the Skylon, a skeletal metal pod soaring over the crowd, was 'to hang upright in the air – and astonish'. There is still conviction in Casson's final verdict on the Festival of Britain: 'In a bad year in the world's history it had a spiritual quality that is worth remembering'.

The Telecinema's life was to be prolonged beyond the end of the Festival, and the British Film Institute persuaded the initially reluctant authority to extend the lease to permit the use of the building as a regular cinema. The LCC, who owned the freehold, had no immediate plans for the Downstream site; commercial film exhibitors were openly hostile, but in October 1952 the building reopened as 'Telecinema – The National Film Theatre'. 'Telecinema' was soon dropped. The structure had only been intended to last one summer, and building materials in 1951 left something to be desired; but with some patching-up the roof leaks were stopped and the building functioned pretty well until 1957 when the present, often-altered National Film Theatre was built under Waterloo Bridge. Sadly, as we celebrate the 50th anniversary of the Telecinema, and the NFT approaches its own half century, the greater part of their history is lost. From the first vague proposals in 1949 until 1994, the administration of the two institutions meticulously archived every relevant document, letter or photograph. However in the cause of good management and economy of shelf-space, the British Film Institute precipitately discarded or destroyed the sixty or so box-files that contained it. A few documents may have been retained; a few more were saved by collectors when they found their way into the Covent Garden flea market. But we can now never know the whole story.

The quotations and references are from *Sight and Sound*, *passim*; *The Monthly Film Bulletin*, *passim*; *Films in 1951* (special issue of *Sight and Sound*, 1951) and from conversations with Jacques Brunius (1958) and Leslie Hardcastle (2001).

BRIEF CITY is available on video from the Twentieth Century Society. For further information, see back cover of this book.

10 Modern Sculpture in the South Bank Townscape

ROBERT BURSTOW

Modern Sculpture in the South Bank Townscape

ROBERT BURSTOW

MORE than thirty sculptures[1] and fifty mural paintings by some of the most celebrated British artists of the day were displayed at the Festival of Britain's South Bank Exhibition. Although not a great number by the standards of earlier national or international exhibitions, and only an adjunct to the more spectacular scientific, technological and industrial exhibits, their presence meant that the exhibition rivalled or surpassed other Festival exhibitions in terms of the representation of contemporary British art.[2] Yet the exhibition has tended to be overlooked by writers on the art of the Festival or misleadingly characterised on the basis of a few untypically 'abstract' sculptures and murals (paralleling mis-characterisations of the exhibition's architectural aesthetic based on the untypically futuristic Skylon and Dome). There are several reasons for this neglect or misperception: firstly, since there was no definitive catalogue of the artworks, it has been difficult to establish exactly what was on display; secondly, since the 'abstract' works generated more press attention and were less adversely affected by post-Festival dispersal or destruction, they have become better known. In this essay I will attend only to the sculptures, though many of my observations are applicable to the mural paintings. Having elsewhere detailed the surprising number and heterogeneity of sculptures in the exhibition,[3] I will concentrate here on their relation to the architectural 'townscape' and to the representation of 'New Britain' as an exemplary social democracy.

MODERN SCULPTURE

The better known sculptures on the South Bank – Jacob Epstein's *Youth Advances*, Barbara Hepworth's *Contrapuntal Forms* and Henry Moore's *Reclining Figure* – were commissioned by the fledgling Arts Council. What is less well known is that all of the other sculptures were funded by the Labour government's temporary Festival of Britain Office. While the Arts Council paid out nearly £5,000 to three of Britain's most distinguished, if most controversial, sculptors, the Festival Office distributed no more than twice that sum among more than twenty sculptors, favouring 'young and comparatively untried talent'.[4] The Festival Office's selection was made by the Festival Design Group (a team of architects, urban-planners, and designers), principally Hugh Casson and Misha Black, who had the greatest knowledge of contemporary art. They invited proposals from associations representing both traditionalist and progressive artists, and encouraged the South Bank's architects to commission works from their own budgets. But as Casson explained afterwards, with some apparent exasperation, 'nearly every architect would suggest, first, the name of Mr. Henry Moore, and then his ideas ran out ... nearly every sculptor employed ... had to be proposed by the Festival Office'.[5] Given that many of the sculptors were little known, their fees were comparatively generous; however, perhaps because fees were inclusive of expenses, sculptures were frequently made from inexpensive and unresilient materials, such as terracotta, plaster and concrete, which proved vulnerable when the exhibition was dismantled.

Casson later explained that the Design Group chose artists 'whose work was

figure 1
R. Butler, *Birdcage*, 1950–1, forged & welded iron, h. 162 ins., Thameside Restaurant (Mrs. Rosemary Butler)

The following abbreviations are used in the Notes: ACA: Arts Council Archive, NAL/AAD: National Art Library/Archive of Art and Design, PRO: Public Records Office.

1. I will maintain two distinctions which were generally observed by those who selected, catalogued, reviewed and finally disposed of the South Bank's sculptures: the first is between the sculptures and the vast range of other three-dimensional display material in the exhibition (some of it made by professional sculptors) and the second is between the sculptures and the exhibition's design features, above all, the Skylon, which despite sharing formal affinities with certain modernist sculptures belongs in terms of its genesis and reception to the exhibition's architectural history.

2. Principally, the Arts Council's touring exhibition, *Sixty Paintings for '51*, and the LCC's sculpture exhibition at Battersea Park.

3. Burstow, *Symbols for '51: the Royal Festival Hall, Skylon and Sculptures on the South Bank for the Festival of Britain*, London: Royal Festival Hall, 1996. Since compiling the catalogue, I have identified the presence of other sculptures on the South Bank: Dora Gordine's *Dyak* (1925–30), Maurice Lambert's *Herring and Dogfish* (c.1950–1) and an unidentified wood mobile by Edward Wright.

4. My estimate is extrapolated from the fees which are known, taking into account the size and materials of sculptures. Mitzi Cunliffe, for example, was paid 550 guineas for a large pair of concrete figures but fees could vary from as little as £30 for Lynn Chadwick's mobile to £2,500 for Siegfried Charoux's colossal relief sculpture. It represents less than 0.2% of the total expenditure on the exhibition which is recorded as £5,636,100 (Ministry of Public Building and Works, *Festival of Britain 1951*, London: HMSO, 1953, p.5).

5. H. Casson, 'South Bank Sculpture', *Image*, no. 7, Spring 1952, pp.57–8.

6. Casson, *Image*, Spring 1952, p.58.

7. For example, see C. Wheeler, 'The Royal Society of British Sculptors', *Studio*, vol.CXXXII, September 1946, p.82; C. Lamb, *The Royal Academy: A Short History of its Foundation and Development*, London: Bell, rev. ed. 1951 [1935], p.84.

8. 'Sculptures in the South Bank Exhibition Grounds', 26 May 1951, p.856.

sufficiently varied to be of interest to many different people': 'We did not see why the Exhibition should be either highbrow or lowbrow ... we believed in concertina-brows, high here, low there, the only essential thing being that the work should be sincere, lively and the best of its kind.'[6] However, this eclectic and populist aesthetic resulted in a selection which tended toward moderation and, at times, mediocrity. Senior academicians were excluded, despite the Royal Academy's desire for its members to be involved in post-war reconstruction.[7] There was only one work in the social realist tradition, Peter Peri's *Sunbathers*. And while there were a few neo-constructivist and neo-surrealist works by young and still little-known modernist sculptors such as Reg Butler, Lynn Chadwick and Eduardo Paolozzi, these had often been commissioned directly by architects rather than by the Design Group. As the *Illustrated London News* observed, the sculptures 'for the most part are not of the most advanced modern school.'[8] Rather, the majority belonged to two principal tendencies within the more moderate forms of figurative, modernist sculpture: on one hand, the classicising followers of Maillol, such as Frank Dobson, two of his RCA students, Keith Godwin and John Matthews, and a number of émigré sculptors, including Dora Gordine,

figure 2
J. Epstein, *Youth Advances*, 1950–1, gilded bronze, h. 84 ins., Home & Gardens Pavilion. (Crown copyright. NMR)

figure 3
B. Hepworth, 'Group Symbolizing the Spirit of Discovery' (*Contrapuntal Forms*), 1950–1, Blue Galway limestone, h. c.120 ins., Dome of Discovery. (Sir Alan Bowness, Hepworth Estate)

figure 4
H. Moore, 'Genesis' (*Reclining Figure*), 1950–1, bronze, l. 90 ins., Land of Britain Pavilion. (Crown copyright. NMR)

figure 5
F. Dobson, 'London Pride' (*Leisure*),
1946, plaster (gun-metal finish), h. 84
ins., Royal Festival Hall (Dobson Estate)

Karin Jonzen and Karel Vogel; and, on the other hand, the more expressionist
followers of Lehmbruck, such as Georg Ehrlich and Daphne Hardy Henrion. The
only 'direct' carvers to be included were those who also modelled sculpture, like
Heinz Henghes and Maurice Lambert, or who produced relatively genteel forms
of primitivism, like Anna Mahler and David McFall. Similar caution was exercised in the selection of mural painters who, with few exceptions, practised
forms of Neo-Romanticism, Naturalism or popular illustration. Deviations from
the *juste milieu* were met with extreme anxiety. When a newspaper alleged that
Mitzi Cunliffe's surrealistic sculpture of embracing figures entwined in giant
plant tendrils was obscene, a nervous Herbert Morrison ('Lord Festival') dis-
patched the Festival's Director-General, Gerald Barry, in person to Manchester
to inspect the offending work.[9] But the greatest threat to aesthetic consensus
came from the involvement of the Arts Council, whose officers saw their responsibilities primarily in terms of stimulating public interest in what they regarded
as the best modern art, unlike the Festival authorities who were more sceptical
of the suitability of modernism to 'the People's Show'. Indeed, Casson refused
space in the exhibition for eight further Arts Council sculpture commissions
predominately from younger 'ultra-modernists'.[10]

9. See M. Frayn, 'Festival', in *The Age of
Austerity*, P. French & M. Sissons, eds.,
London, Hodder & Stoughton, 1963, p.326.
10. See Casson, letter to H. Wheldon, 6 June
1950; Casson, letter to James, 22 September
1950; H. Wheldon, minute paper for James,
18 January 1951; ACA (FoB 1951: Sculpture).
Seven of these sculptures were eventually
included in *Sixty Paintings for '51* and an
eighth, by Bernard Meadows, at the LCC's
Battersea Park exhibition (see Sheffield City
Art Galleries, *25 from '51: Paintings from the
Festival of Britain*, 1978, pp.19–20 [though
here it incorrectly states that Meadows's
sculpture was also included in *Sixty Paintings
for '51*]).

SCULPTURE FOR TOWNSCAPE

Rather than have a Palace of Art or Sculpture Court as had been customary at national and international exhibitions, Barry advocated 'the widest possible use of mural decoration and sculpture throughout the South Bank'.[11] Casson described the Design Group's desire for the 'close harmony of sculpture and building, of landscape and mural painting ... ', and Black recalled their wish to show that 'painters and sculptors could work with architects, landscape architects and exhibition designers to produce an aesthetic unity.'[12] Barry later identified 'the marriage of architecture and sculpture' as one of the principal and most influential features of the 'Festival style'.[13] According to Black, an easy and enlightened relationship had ensued between artists and architects:

The architects ... ensured that walls were available for murals and plinths for sculpture. Practically every concourse was designed to contain a major work; each building was a sanctuary for important works of art ... . Associating the artists with the architects presented no problems. Each accepted the authority, wisdom and skills of the other; the task of the co-ordinating architects was the simple one of bringing together those of like mind and intention.[14]

The exhibition offered an opportunity to show that sculpture could be an integral aspect of urban space without being assigned the decorative function typical of architectural sculpture. Sculptures were positioned to achieve a great variety of effect, giving interest and identity to particular areas of the exhibition. Free-standing sculptures were placed on terraces and concourses, in or beside protective reflecting pools, near changes of ground level, and even under the ready-made loggia formed by the arches of Hungerford railway bridge. Relief sculpture was used as a foil to create ornamental contrast: curvaceous forms were set against architectural geometry, smooth plaster or concrete forms against textured brick or concrete, and dark bronze or plaster forms against pale concrete. The emphasis on variety, contrast and surprise was well suited to the South Bank's 'picturesque' architectural layout. In contradistinction to Beaux-Arts classicism or high-modernist formalism, the exhibition had an intimate, asymmetrical layout which exploited contrasts in the pattern, texture, level and colour of 'floorscapes' and 'wallscapes'.[15] The *Architectural Review* hailed the exhibition

11. Black in minutes of Presentation Panel meeting, 3 May 1950, PRO (WORK 25/48/A5/D4).

12. Casson, 'Festival of Britain', MS. of RIBA lecture, 24 March 1950, p.8, PRO (WORK 25/43/A3/7); Black, in *A Tonic to the Nation: the Festival of Britain*, M. Banham & B. Hillier, eds., 1951, London: Thames & Hudson, 1976, p.82.

13. Barry, 'The Festival of Britain', *Builder*, 24 February 1961, p.356.

14. Black, in *A Tonic to the Nation*, p.84.

15. For the fullest analysis of the layout, see the special Festival issue of the *Architectural Review*, vol.110, August 1951. On townscape in general, see especially 'The Editor' [H. de Cronin Hastings], 'Exterior Furnishing or Sharawaggi: the Art of Making Urban Landscape', *Architectural Review*, vol.XCV, January 1944, pp.2–8; 'I. de Wolfe' [H. de Cronin Hastings], 'Townscape: A Plea for an English Philosophy Founded on the Fine Rock of Sir Uvedale Price', *Architectural Review*, vol.106, December 1949, pp.354–62; N. Pevsner, *The Englishness of English Art*, London: Architectural Press, 1956, pp.179–80.

figure 6 · top left
J. Matthews, *The Sisters*, 1950–1, plaster, h. 96 ins., Homes and Gardens Pavilion. (Crown copyright. NMR)

figure 7 · top right
J. Matthews, *Grace*, 1950–1, plaster, h. 58 ins., Homes and Gardens Pavilion. (Crown copyright. NMR)

figure 8 · bottom left
K. Vogel and students of Camberwell School of Arts & Crafts, *The Industries: Heavy, Light, Electricity*, 1950–1, concrete reliefs, h. or l. of each c.144 ins., Power and Production Pavilion. (Crown copyright. NMR)

figure 9 · bottom right
K. Godwin, *Neptune*, 1950–1, plaster, h. 240 ins., Sea and Ships Pavilion. (Crown copyright NMR)

figure 10
F.E. McWilliam, *Spring* from *The Four
Seasons*, 1950–1, plastic wood on metal,
h. *c*.48 ins., Country Pavilion.
(Mrs. Sarah Gretton)

figure 11
S. Charoux, *The Islanders*, 1950–1, plaster,
h. 150 ins., Sea & Ships Pavilion. (Crown
copyright. N M R)

as 'the first modern townscape',[16] a term it reserved for describing the 'urban
picturesque'.

Despite a common perception among historians that the sculptures on the
South Bank bore little or no relation to their place in the exhibition,[17] the Festival Office sculptures were invariably positioned for thematic reasons. Thus,
Godwin's *Neptune* was commissioned for the Sea and Ships Pavilion, Matthews's
The Sisters (personifying domesticity with infant and bird) for Homes and Gar-
dens, F.E. McWilliam's *The Four Seasons* for Country, and Vogel's *The Industries:
Heavy, Light and Electricity* for the façade of Power and Production. Where external, free-standing sculptures were at some remove from their relevant pavilion,
the relation was less apparent; nonetheless, McFall's *Boy and Foal* belonged to
Country, Jonzen's 'Figure Symbolizing Youth, Open Air and Sport' to Sport, and
Cunliffe's 'Group Symbolizing the Origins of the Land and People' jointly to both
the Land of Britain and People of Britain pavilions.[18] While the Design Group admitted a small number of 'decorative' sculptures, even these often carried subtle
allusions to their siting: Mahler's *Woman with Pitcher* was inside a café and Hardy
Henrion's *Youth* outside a bar. Other decorative sculptures transformed that
quintessential feature of the eighteenth-century, picturesque garden, the water
cascade, into a modern form suited to townscape: Richard Huws's 'Water Mobile
Sculpture' flushed water regularly down a stack of pivoting aluminium receptal-
cles, Paolozzi's 'Wall Fountain' emitted a stream of water from a scaffolding of
steel pipes and concrete basins, and Victor Pasmore's shallow-relief mural, *The
Waterfall*, on the side of the Regatta Restaurant represented eddying currents of
water with black spiral motifs on unevenly-laid, white, ceramic tiles.

The Design Group's self-conscious attempt to integrate sculpture into the
formal organization and conceptual meaning of the exhibition followed an approach already championed in the *Architectural Review*. A short article on 'Programme Sculpture' by Andrew Hammer, published on the eve of the Festival, had
stressed its appropriateness to the *Review*'s conception of townscape:

*In a fully realized townscape every street is its own sculpture gallery. Of course that doesn't
mean rows of worthies in bronze, or even personages in iron. Hydrants, pillar-boxes,
bollards, pumps, lamp-posts – these are some of the many things which may be sculpture
in the street. But there is a place for sculptor's [sic] sculpture too, particularly – and this is
the point – if it is strictly ad hoc, purpose-made in relation to its surroundings.*[19]

That members of the Design Group were in sympathy with Hammer's opinions
is suggested not only by their preoccupation with 'street sculpture' – bollards,
lamp-posts, sign-posts, litter-bins, kiosks, planters, and so on – but also by their

16. August 1951, p.77.

17. For example, see A. Causey, *Sculpture Since
1945*, Oxford: Oxford University Press, 1998,
p.22.

18. The relation of Jonzen's and Cunliffe's
sculptures to their respective pavilions has
previously been obscured through being
known by different titles, respectively *Dancing
Girl* or *A Dance Begins*, and *Root Bodied Forth*.

19. *Architectural Review*, vol.109, April 1951,
p.255.

figure 12
D. Paolozzi, 'Wall Fountain', 1951, tubular steel and concrete basins with lighting, h. c.180 ins., Land's End, near Thameside Restaurant. (Crown copyright. NMR)

figure 13
R. Huws, 'Water Mobile Sculpture', 1951, steel & aluminium, h. 552 ins., Sea & Ships Pavilion. (The Architectural Press)

attitude that 'sculptors' sculpture' should remain subservient to architecture and, for the most part, avoid both the traditional and the ultra-modern. Appropriately enough, the *Review*'s idea of 'programme sculpture' revived a practice associated with eighteenth-century, picturesque gardens where complex allegories involving antique gods and goddesses, portrait busts, and so on, were set amid lakes, cascades, garden pavilions, temples and grottoes, alluding to the identity of a garden's owners or to particular themes like Love or Liberty.[20] In such gardens, as at the South Bank, sculptures were sited for thematic reasons – for example, Flora among flowers, Acteon in woods, and Bacchus in vineyards. But just as Georgian sculpture programmes were frequently incomplete, the South Bank's programme was compromised by several sculptures which were purchased, hired or borrowed 'off-the-shelf' and not, despite the official guide's assurances, 'specially commissioned'.[21]

However incomplete the programme, the commitment to art and architectural integration shared by the artists, architects and administrators was a symptom of their democratic aspiration. Barry argued that teamwork 'might bring the artist out from his seclusion, and give him a place in the social order.'[22] Cunliffe longed for a return to the situation 'in medieval France or in Greece when artist and craftsman were one word',[23] thereby 'bringing sculpture into everyone's immediate and accepted environment' and allowing it to 'speak to the community.'[24] Even the supporters and practitioners of the more extreme forms of modernism championed the idea of integration. Herbert Read had recently drawn parallels between the condition of modern and Gothic art which had achieved 'unity and greatness' through its 'alliance with the practical activity of the architect.'[25] Hnery Moore, in the year after the Festival, claimed that an 'integral conception of the arts ... has been characteristic of all the great epochs of art,' though he argued that greater formal integration was ultimately impossible without the social integration borne of wider political change.[26] Behind these aspirations was Ruskin's medievalising hope of cultural and social unity which by re-integrating artist and artisan undid the capitalist division of labour and restored to art its social and moral purpose.

PROGRAMME SCULPTURE AND MODERNISM

Notwithstanding Misha Black's rosy recollections of this collaboration between artists and architects, at the time he and other participants were less confident of their achievement. At a meeting of participating artists and architects held at the ICA in 1952 to discuss 'The Integration of Painting, Sculpture and Architecture at the South Bank Exhibition', the consensus of opinion was that it had

20. See M. Symes, *Garden Sculpture*, Princes Risborough: Shire Garden History, 1996, pp.45–53.

21. I. Cox, *The South Bank Exhibition: A Guide to the Story it Tells*, London: HMSO, 1951, p.90. Sculptures that were hired include Dobson's *Leisure* (renamed 'London Pride' for the exhibition), Ehrlich's *Head of a Cow*, Gordine's *Dyak*, Henghes's *Orpheus*, and Mahler's *Woman with Pitcher* (H.T. Cadbury-Brown in conversations with the author, January 1996).

22. Barry et al, 'Painting, Sculpture and the Architect. Extracts from the speeches at the Symposium organised by the ICA and the MARS group at the RIBA on September 2', *Architect and Building News*, 16 September 1949, p.283.

23. M.S. Cunliffe, 'Sculpture For Architecture', *Progressive Architecture* (US), no.31, December 1950, p.65.

24. M. Cunliffe, 'Sculptures for Architecture', *Architecture and Building*, April 1954, pp.127, 129.

25. 'Epilogue 1947', in H. Read, *Art Now*, London: Faber, 1948 [1934], p.130.

26. 'The Sculptor in Modern Society', an address delivered to an international conference of artists organized by UNESCO, Venice, 1952; in Moore, 'Sculpture in the Open Air' (1955), in *Henry Moore on Sculpture*, ed. P. James, London: Macdonald, 1966, pp.88–9.

failed.[27] This confirmed a perception of the social alienation of modernist artists and the esoteric nature of their art.[28] The *Observer* lamented that 'sculptors do not need to work with other people such as constructional engineers, to seek buyers before they start work, to contend with genuinely functional problems!'[29] To most reviewers of the exhibition, the attempt at integration was either invisible or unsatisfactory: *The Times* was disappointed that the sculptures 'seem to belong to the setting or even melt into the background',[30] while Anthony Chitty, President of the Architectural Association, believed that '[m]any sculptures are spoilt by a fussy background and not enough attention to adjacent materials.'[31] Inevitably, Hepworth's and Moore's sculptures proved highly controversial, attracting criticism for being too 'intellectual' and 'anti-humanistic'.[32] This hostility fuelled conservative criticisms of the allegedly esoteric and elitist policies of the Arts Council which was already under attack for its touring Festival exhibition of contemporary painting, *Sixty Paintings for '51*. When Morrison was invited to give his response to the South Bank, he admitted that there had been surprises, 'especially the sculpture'.[33] The controversy must have been especially galling to the members of the Design Group who had conscientiously avoided the most abstract forms of modernism.

Integrating modern art and architecture had always been problematic, given Modernist antipathy to architectural sculpture. Just as 'programme music' (written to accompany a preconceived narrative or literary idea) had met opposition in the twentieth century from modernist composers who favoured 'absolute' or 'abstract' music, programme sculpture inevitably conflicted with the aspirations of ultra-modernist sculptors who wished to assert the autonomy of their art. Notwithstanding Henry Moore's pronouncements on the desirability of integrating the arts, he later more famously identified himself with architects who wished 'not to have sculpture on a building but outside it, in a spatial relation to it.' As he explained, 'the beauty of this idea ... is that the sculpture must have its own strong separate identity.'[34] The strategy Moore advocated was neither new nor confined to him. A very similar formulation had been arrived at fifteen years earlier by the critic Stanley Casson in his analysis of the siting of two sculptures at New York's Rockefeller Center:

Sculpture can be used to the highest advantage, not on buildings, but in association with them. Thus a statue can stand in a garden or courtyard and be fashioned by its maker to have in itself certain proportions which exist in relation to the buildings around it ... .
So in more subtle ways statues and works of sculpture can be designed and placed in or near buildings so as to bear not only a relation in size and bulk to those buildings, but also a relation in space ... . Both stand in a spatial relationship to the building as a whole and illustrate the wide possibilities of the use of sculpture in modern architecture. [emphasis original][35]

Given the growing acceptance of Modernist polemic for the autonomy of the arts, it was not surprising that some Modernist sympathizers gave ambivalent responses to the application of a programmatic approach to 'public' or 'exhibition' sculpture at the South Bank, believing that such art was inevitably inferior or that, in Philip Hendy's words, 'an exhibition artist is a contradiction in terms'.[36]

Evidently sharing this attitude, the Arts Council had informed Epstein, Hepworth and Moore of the Festival Executive Committee's preferred themes but assured them that 'no restriction is placed on the subject of your group'.[37] Indeed, in an instruction which was fundamentally at odds with the Festival authorities' desire to integrate the exhibition's art and architecture, the Arts Council's Director of Art, Philip James, told Hepworth, 'We want our sculptors ... to do what they are moved to do and not necessarily to accommodate their ideas to the temporary surroundings of the Festival.'[38] The Arts Council's sculptors, however, seem to have been more sympathetic to the Design Group's aims, creating works which all bore some relation to their location in the exhibition, though this has been overlooked by almost all commentators. The relation of

27. See Casson, *Image*, Spring 1952, pp.57–60.

28. See a report on the ICA's meeting in Casson, *Image*, Spring 1952, p.48.

29. 'Profile of Henry Moore', 24 June 1951.

30. 'Festival Painting and Sculpture', 4 May 1951, p.8.

31. 'The South Bank Exhibition Reviewed', *RIBA Journal*, June 1951, p.325.

32. For example, 'Perspex', 'Current Shows and Comment', *Apollo*, vol.LIII, June 1951, p.149.

33. B. Donoughue & G.W. Jones, *Herbert Morrison: Portrait of a Politician*, London, Weidenfeld & Nicolson, 1973, pp.493–4.

34. Moore, 'Sculpture in the Open Air' (1955), in *Henry Moore on Sculpture*, p.99.

35. *Sculpture of To-Day*, London & New York: Studio, 1939, pp.13–14.

36. Hendy, 'Art on the South Bank', *Britain Today*, no.183, July 1951, pp.32–3. See also D. Sylvester, 'Festival Sculpture', *Studio*, vol.CXLII, September 1951, p.77.

37. M. Glasgow, letters of commission to Epstein and Moore, 24 May 1949, ACA (FoB1951: Sculpture).

38. James, letter to Hepworth, 5 September 1949, ACA (FoB1951: Sculpture).

figure 14
H. Henghes, *Orpheus*, 1950–1, concrete, h. 66 ins, People of Britain Pavilion. (H.T. Cadbury-Brown)

Epstein's *Youth Advances* to the exhibition was obscured by the absorption of the section devoted to the 'The Family', for which it was intended, into the Homes and Gardens pavilion.[39] The relation of Hepworth's *Contrapuntal Forms* was always less obvious but her desire to work for a specific site is recorded in a letter to the Arts Council's Director-General.[40] Indeed, she accepted the Festival Committee's brief for a sculpture to stand beside the Dome on the theme of 'Discovery' and worked closely with the concourse architect, H.T. Cadbury-Brown, to ensure the appropriate scale and siting of her anthropomorphic monoliths, respecting the given theme in their uplifted, expectant gaze. Barry, for one, continued to refer to the work as an 'abstract sculpture symbolizing the spirit of

39. Minutes of Presentation Panel meetings,
21 September & 26 October 1949, PRO
(WORK 25/48/A5/D3).

40. Hepworth, letter to M. Glasgow, 13
January 1949, ACA (FoB 1951: Sculpture).

41. Barry, 'The Festival is Britain's', *Picture
Post*, vol.50, January 1951, p.11.

42. Moore, 'Sculpture in the Open Air' (1955),
in *Henry Moore on Sculpture*, p.101.

43. James, Foreword, Arts Council, *Sculpture
and Drawings by Henry Moore*, Tate Gallery,
1951, p.2.

44. Margaret Garlake has previously drawn
attention to the connection between Moore's
sculpture and Hawkes's book but still sees it
as 'a pre-eminently urban image' (Garlake,
'The Construction of National Identity at the
1951 Festival of Britain', *AICARC* [Zurich],
vols.29 & 30, nos.1 & 2, 1991, p.16).

45. Minutes of Presentation Panel meeting,
26 October 1949 PRO (WORK 25/48/A5/D3).

46. As a close friend of Moore, James's
description of its location (see above) would
seem to confirm this suggestion, unless he
mistook the overall name of the pavilion.
Graham Sutherland's mural-sized painting,
The Origins of the Land, was inside the pavilion.

discovery'.[41] Finally, the relation of Moore's *Reclining Figure* to the exhibition has been widely misunderstood, with commentators commonly misappropriating it for the Country pavilion or diverted by his retrospective remark that he 'didn't worry about where it was placed'.[42] The thematic significance of his opened-out, skeletal figure only becomes apparent when we realize that it was placed, as even Philip James noted, 'adjacent to "The Origins of the Land" on the South Bank site',[43] and that Moore had recently illustrated a popular book on British geology, *A Land*, written for the Festival by his friend Jacquetta Hawkes (the Festival's archaeological advisor), which, like the South Bank, represented Britain as a kind of skeletal landscape from which the modern, industrial world had evolved.[44] Indeed, having abandoned the theme of 'The Family' (subsequently taken over by Epstein), Moore had sought the Festival Committee's permission to adopt the theme of 'Genesis',[45] and his figure's position next to the Land of Britain pavilion, with sections devoted to 'The Earth in Labour' and 'The Last Sixty Million Years' suggests that its taut forms were intended to evoke a simultaneously ancient and modern Earth Mother.[46] Analysis of other apparently 'abstract' sculptures on the South Bank suggests that few did not bear some relation to their location in the exhibition, with the rare exception of those commissioned by architects for refreshment buildings, such as Butler's *Birdcage* for Jane Drew's Thames-side Restaurant. The extent to which modernist sculptors of all persuasions were prepared to engage with specified themes and sites at the South Bank has been obscured by alterations to the layout of the exhibition, by post-Festival changes to the titles of sculptures, by artists' retrospective statements, and, more generally, by the difficulty of imagining sculptures in their original settings.

SCULPTURE FOR DEMOCRACY

Describing itself as 'one united act of national reassessment', the Festival presented two particularly dominant ideas about Britain. Firstly, it portrayed a nation which had successfully reconciled the past and future in the present. The South Bank's official guidebook, for example, represented Britain as an ancient land, rich in varieties of landscape and farming, which is peopled by an ancient hard-working, heroic people who have a deep understanding of animals and plants but who, nevertheless, lead the world in scientific discovery, technological invention, and manufacturing capability.[47] It juxtaposed images of rural landscape, agricultural labour and the natural world with those of recent British achievements in industry, engineering, science and telecommunications, leisure and entertainment, and contemporary domestic design. At a less overt level, the Festival asserted Britain's position as an exemplary social democracy which had always avoided political extremism. In the midst of the Korean War, Barry proclaimed that 'The Festival could help to ... assert the strength and value of the democratic way of life at a time when it was being subjected to sharp strains and challenges.'[48] Underlying these perceptions of national identity were those ubiquitous stereotypes of Britishness/Englishness – moderation, tolerance and compromise. A similar account of national identity is found in Sir Ernest Barker's contemporary anthology, *The Character of England* (planned with advice from Attlee), which represented the nation as 'a blended country of compromise' where tradition and modernisation are productively balanced.[49] At the heart, then, of what Festival publications liked to call 'our way of life', was the claim that Britain governed itself democratically, reconciled tradition and modernity, and valued compromise, variety and – one other favourite Festival concept – 'unity in diversity'.[50] Such values corresponded with the social-democratic ideals of Morrison's ascendant, strongly anti-communist wing of the Parliamentary Labour Party which controlled the Festival's gestation during years of deteriorating Cold War.

The popular conception of the national genius for moderation, compromise and diversity was embodied in the style of the South Bank's art and architecture. Barry claimed that '[t]he very architecture and exhibition design were themselves significant statements.'[51] Hugh Casson's appointment as Director of Architecture and first chairman of the Design Group ensured that the Festival would be dominated by a humanistic, moderately-modernist aesthetic.[52] The historical derivation of the principles of townscape and programme sculpture from the picturesque gardens of Whig landowners associated them with indigenous traditions of Liberty and democracy (albeit anomalously with Englishness rather than Britishness), while Beaux-Arts classicism and ultra-modernist formalism were deprecated as 'un-English' and authoritarian. Moreover, the exhibition's moderate and eclectic aesthetic gained further democratic resonances through comparison with the styles favoured by fascist and communist regimes. At the Paris World Fair of 1937, for example, the classicising architecture and sculpture of the German pavilion and the Socialist Realist architecture and sculpture of the Soviet pavilion had confronted one another across the main avenue, demonstrating a shared taste for grandiosity and historicism. Although one member of the Festival Executive Committee had suggested that they 'might learn something from the recent techniques adopted in Eastern Europe',[53] it was inconceivable that the architecture and sculpture of social-democratic Britain should resemble that of 'totalitarian' nations. Revealingly, the only sculpture at the South Bank which attracted adverse ideological criticism was Siegfried Charoux's colossal, overtly nationalistic, relief sculpture of sea-faring 'Islanders' which awoke

figure 17
D. McFall, *Boy and Foal*, 1950–1, Portland stone, h. 62 ins., Country Pavilion. (Mrs. Alexandra McFall)

47. Cox, *The South Bank Exhibition*, p.6.
48. 'The Festival of Britain 1951', *Journal of the Royal Society of Arts*, no.4880, 22 August 1952, p.691.
49. Oxford: Oxford University Press, 1947.
50. An early, confidential Executive Committee report suggested that 'the Festival must give a picture not only of the essential unity of our democracy in action, but also of the diversity within that unity which is an essential ingredient of that democracy ... ' ('Festival of Britain: Purpose and Approach to Theme', August 1948, pp.2–3, NAL/AAD [EL 6/23]).
51. 'After the Ball is Over', *New Statesman & Nation*, vol.XLII, 13 October 1951, p.396.
52. As it would equally have been ensured by Frederick Gibberd's appointment, had he accepted the invitation first offered to him (J. Manser, *Hugh Casson: A Biography*, London, Viking, 2000, pp.120–1).
53. Confidential report, 'Festival of Britain: Purpose and Approach to Theme', August 1948, p.5, NAL/AAD (EL 6/23).

54. F. Watson, 'Art at the South Bank Exhibition', *Listener*, vol.XLV, 10 May 1951, p.766.

55. See the proceedings of the 8th CIAM conference, published as E.N. Rogers, J.L. Sert & J. Tyrwhitt, eds., *The Heart of the City: Towards the Humanisation of Urban Life*, London & New York, Lund Humphries, 1952.

56. Black's phrase appears in the catalogue of the AIA's most important wartime exhibition, *For Liberty* (1943), which excluded works conceived in the constructivist and surrealist traditions.

liberal sensitivities in at least one critic who found it 'a little too close for comfort to the totalitarian style of Exhibitionism.'[54] The example suggests that the presence of a number of sculptors who were refugees from Nazism or Stalinism – including Charoux, Ehrlich, Henghes, Mahler, and Vogel – entailed some threat to the dominant conception of national identity: if artists' styles and/or politics were too extreme, they risked transgressing the mythical national tradition.

That the architectural conception of the South Bank reinforced its meaning as an exemplary site of social-democratic citizenship is evident from ideas discussed at the 1951 Hoddesdon conference of the *Congrès Internationaux d'Architecture Moderne* (attended by many of the South Bank architects). The exhibition's design corresponded with CIAM's call for the reintroduction into the 'urban core' of non-commercialized, public spaces – modelled on the Ancient Greek *agora* – where citizens could meet and debate, supposedly ensuring the survival of democracy and preventing the rise of totalitarianism.[55] The Festival Office's sculptures in these outdoor spaces were the ideal complement to CIAM's vision of the 'humanisation of urban life' since they not only conformed to CIAM's perception of the need to integrate art and architecture but also to its espousal of a moderately-modernist, humanist aesthetic. Moreover, the correlation of a moderately-modernist, figurative styles of sculpture with the values of social democracy had near precedents in the wartime strategies of the War Artists' Advisory Committee and the Artists' International Association which had presented similarly moderate styles of painting as the representative art of democracy. Misha Black, as the wartime chairman of the AIA, had described art as the 'propaganda of the imagination'[56] and his conception was readily transferable to the ideological purposes of the Festival.

figure 18
M.S. Cunliffe, 'Group Symbolizing the Origins of the Land and the People' (*Root Bodied Forth*), 1950–1, concrete, h. 114 ins., Waterloo Station Gate. (Central Office of Information)

EXTANT SCULPTURES (WITH PRESENT WHEREABOUTS)

Reg Butler, *Birdcage*, 1950–1, forged and welded iron, h. 162 ins., Royal Festival Hall, London (coll. English Heritage)

Frank Dobson, 'London Pride' (*Leisure*), 1946, bronze cast (1987), h. 84 ins., Riverside Walk, South Bank, London

Georg Ehrlich, *Head of a Cow*, 1949, bronze, h. 12 ins., coll. Arts Council of England

Georg Ehrlich, *Sick Boy* (*Recumbent Boy*), 1949, bronze, h. 26 ins., Letchworth Museum and Art Gallery

Jacob Epstein, *Youth Advances*, 1950–1, gilded bronze, h. 84 ins., Manchester City Art Gallery

Dora Gordine, *Dyak* (*Head Hunter*), 1925–30, bronze, h. 51 ins., Dorich House, University of Kingston

Daphne Hardy Henrion, *Youth* (*Standing Girl*), 1950–1, Portland cement, h. 108 ins., private coll., London

Heinz Henghes, *Orpheus*, 1950–1, concrete, h. 66 ins., Camden School for Girls, London

Barbara Hepworth, 'Group Symbolizing the Spirit of Discovery' (*Contrapuntal Forms*), 1950–1, Blue Galway limestone, h. c.120 ins., Glebelands, Harlow New Town

Barbara Hepworth, *Turning Forms* (*Dynamic Forms*), 1950–1, reinforced concrete painted white, h. 84 ins., Marlborough School, St Albans

Karin Jonzen, 'Figure Symbolizing Youth, Open Air and Sport' (*A Dance Begins*), 1950–1, terracotta, h. 66 ins., Walker Art Gallery, Liverpool

David McFall, *Boy and Foal*, 1950–1, Portland stone, h. 62 ins., Missenden Abbey, Great Missenden, Bucks.

Anna Mahler, *Woman with Pitcher* (*Sitting*), 1942, English marble, h. 24 ins., present whereabouts unknown

Henry Moore, 'Genesis' (*Reclining Figure*), 1950–1, bronze, l. 90 ins., National Galleries of Scotland, Edinburgh

11 Fat Faces All Around

PAUL RENNIE

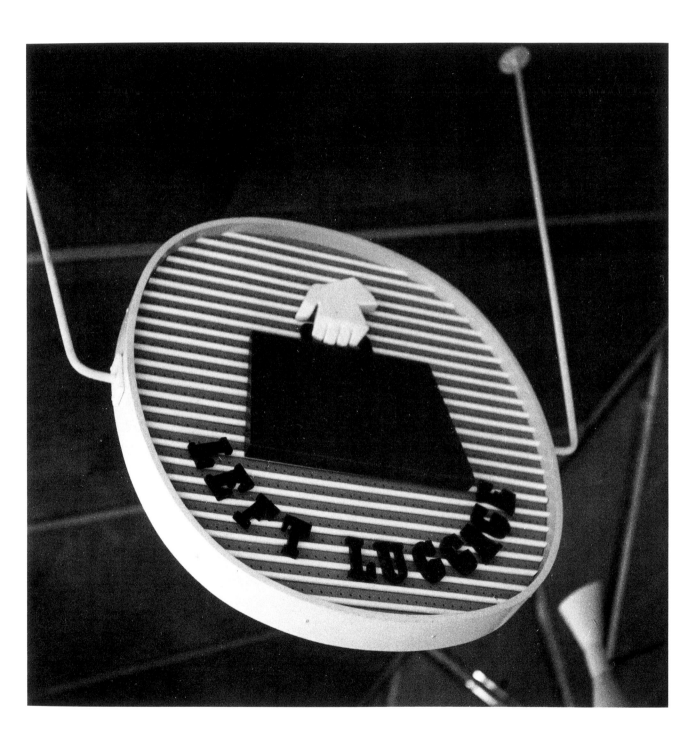

Fat Faces All Around
Lettering and the Festival Style

PAUL RENNIE

T HE Festival architecture was embellished by a wide range of signs and signals in various typefaces. In retrospect that seems one of its most distinctive
features.

Historically, there are two categories of letters on buildings. The first is the
inscriptional letter cut into the fabric of the building, offering the earliest links
between lettering and architecture. The second category is of printed and painted
signs attached to buildings. The ephemeral nature of such signs and the generally mercantile context of their use have prejudiced historians against them. Festival lettering shows the second category at is most active moment, when a
lettering counter-culture came to fruition, leaving an influence that lasted into
the 1970s.

BEFORE THE WAR – SANS EVERYWHERE

The two most famous type faces of the first half of the twentieth century in Britain are Edward Johnston's Railway Type for London Underground of 1916 and
Eric Gill's Gill Sans produced for the Monotype Corporation in 1928. Superfi-
cially, these types appear to be from the same family of functionalist sanserifs.
In reality, their origins point to very different ideas about typographic culture and
its relation to architecture.

Johnston's design is so closely associated with the everyday experience of
London Transport and is so successful within that context that it remains the
most significant contribution of typographic design in relation to architecture in
Britain. However, its influence was limited, partly because of London Transport's copyright of the design and also because Monotype's Gill Sans was so visible and widely used. It quickly became the main Anglo-Saxon alternative to the
Central European sans. Gill's design was based, like Johnston's, on the classical
tradition of Roman inscriptional lettering and its refinement made it suitable for
uses other than signage. Yet it was perhaps the ubiquity of the Gill Sans that pro-
voked the stylistic backlash.

THE *ARCHITECTURAL REVIEW*

The revival of interest in Victorian ornamental types and fat faces began as a self-
consciously antiquarian interest in the fabric of English industrial cities and
market towns. Prominent pioneers of this revival were the poet John Betjeman,
the artist John Piper and the critic and curator Nicolette Gray. They found a platform at the *Architectural Review* in the publishing house of Faber and Faber, and in
Robert Harling's specialist periodical *Typography*.

The pink printed paper-covered boards of Betjeman's *Ghastly Good Taste*, published by Chapman and Hall in 1933, in the pastiche style of Victorian typography, signalled the beginning of a revival of interest in the Victorian style, made
more enjoyable by discovering original Victorian metal type in various printers'
works. The *Shell County Guides*, which he edited from 1934, were another platform
for the spread of these arguments in visual form. The design of the books reflected their interest in buildings of all dates and types. At the same time they

figure 1
Left luggage sign by Milner Gray and
Robin Day.
(The Architectural Press)

figure 2
John Betjeman, *Ghastly Good Taste*,
Chapman and Hall, London, 1933.

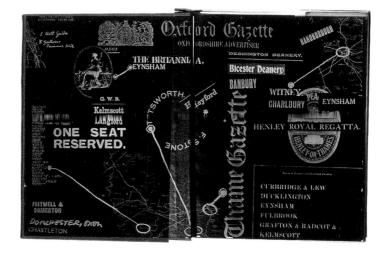

figure 3
John Piper, endpapers for *Oxfordshire*,
(Shell Guide), B.T. Batsford, London,
1938.

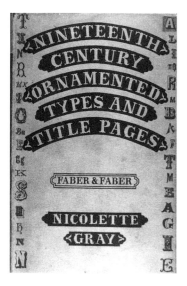

figure 4
Nicolette Gray, *Nineteenth Century
Ornamented Types and Title Pages*, Faber
and Faber, London, 1938.

were in agreement with the consensus in the design community for increased planning control and preservation laws.

In 1938 Nicolette Gray published a book, *Nineteenth Century Ornamented Types* (Faber and Faber), which popularised the English vernacular style. Gray was later one of the originators of the Central School of Art's *Lettering Record*, now the largest documentary collection of lettering in the world. She was a member of the Festival's Typographic Panel and her book, *Lettering on Building* (Architectural Press, 1960) remains the standard work on typographic style in relation to architecture.

Gray organised the pioneering exhibition, Abstract and Concrete, which had toured Britain in 1936, visiting Oxford, Liverpool, Cambridge and London, and included the work of continental artists such as Kandinsky, Miró and Mondrian, and their English colleagues Moore, Piper and Hepworth. Rather surprisingly, she attempted to move the typographic debate within modernism beyond simplistic functionalism. She was adamant that, in most cases at least, the sanserif form was the crudest form of letter and represented a blasted heath of reductionism. Her argument was proved by the war ministries, which favoured the crudest form of sanserif as its exemplar of an unambiguous and easily recognised letterform.

Gray hoped that letterforms would be incorporated into the rhetoric of architectural form, not only as signage for practical purposes but as elements in the surface texture of buildings. This was her argument for the power of suggestion and expression in letters. It was, she thought, especially important given that modern construction and engineering practice were likely to turn the surface of buildings into repetitive and mechanical two-dimensional planes.

She commended the folk art quality of these formerly despised letterforms as 'a communal art as pure as that of any primitive society.'[1]

Gray's publishers, Faber and Faber, were leaders in the revival of nineteenth century typefaces for text setting and display, adopting the German face Walbaum for their modern poets. This crisp letterform, with hairline serifs, was also popular with the Curwen Press, leaders in typography since the 1920s. Faber also used Ultra Bodoni (issued in 1928) and Rockwell (issued in 1930), both variants of early nineteenth century type styles, for display setting, which were promoted by Edward McKnight Kauffer through his design work for the leading modernist printers, Lund Humphries.

Writing in 1939 on 'Victorian Revival', Robert Harling attributed the growth in use of nineteenth century type styles to advertising so that 'types which the more respectable typographical archaeologists had long thought deservedly dead now rear their rather pleasant ugliness before the coveting eyes of lighter-

1. Nicolette Gray, *Nineteenth Century Ornamented Types and Title Pages*, Faber and Faber Ltd., London, 1938, p.16.

hearted authorities.'[2] Harling also remarked on the way that typefounders such as Stephenson Blake in England, Bauer in Germany and Peignot in France all contributed to the revival by making authentic or revivalist faces available.

As an energetic editor and art director, friendly with artists such as Eric Ravilious and Edward Bawden, as well as with Hugh Casson, Harling was an important figure in spreading awareness of lettering and typography both before and after the war. In 1939, he contributed to the Victorian revival himself by designing 'Chisel' for Stephenson Blake, a sparkling 'rimmed' letter form with wedge serifs.

The desire to create a modernist grammar of style that went beyond the functional was at the heart of the *Architectural Review*'s editorial position. This aspect of the project was intellectually distinct from the international style modernism of the 1920s which, whatever its intentions, had found its audience, surprisingly, amongst the aristocracy, country house set and upper bourgeoisie. Later 1930's modernism focused on urban planning and championed the diversity of the crowd rather than the uniformity of the collective as a defining feature of the modern experience and of successful architecture, distinguishing the social reality of towns, cities and buildings rather than just the material presence of buildings. The appeal to English vernacular style to help orchestrate the crowd was rooted in the happy seaside tripper, the market farmer and the shopper. Letters on buildings so clearly contribute to the experience of the building, yet their effect has generally been ignored.

The *Architectural Review* gave visual expression to these ideas through a graphic language involving photography, illustration, typography and different paper stock. An important link between the pre-war magazine and the Festival Typographic Panel was Gordon Cullen, who in 1933 joined the architectural practice of Raymond McGrath. Cullen studied architecture but was soon in demand as a graphic artist, with an attractively loose drawing style that he claimed to have evolved as a synthesis of Paul Nash, Raymond McGrath and Le Corbusier. In 1936 he joined the Tecton partnership formed around the charismatic Russian-born Berthold Lubetkin, and drew the illustrations for the publication *New Architecture* published on the occasion of the MARS Group exhibition, New Homes for Old. These illustrations are the first instance of Cullen's distinctive serial vision, later developed into a major part of the post-war graphic style at the *Architectural Review* and given mature expression in Cullen's own *Townscape* published in 1961. Serial

2. Robert Harling, 'Victorian Revival', in R.B. Fishenden, ed., *Penrose Annual*, volume 41, Lund Humphries, London, 1939, p.73.

figure 5
Gordon Cullen, illustration for 'Waterside New Town, Marlow' in *Architectural Review*, July 1950, special issue by Eric de Maré on 'The Linear National Park', p.61.

vision was also used to great effect in Cullen's articles, 'Westminster Regained' (1947) and 'Bankside Regained' (1949).

Serial vision owes something to the cinematic experience – architectural perspectives are presented from different points of view that describe a trajectory through space and correspond to the experience of how people experience the architectural environment. It was a way of making architectural plans easier to comprehend for the increasingly large numbers of non-architecturally trained committee members involved in the planning and administration of post-war reconstruction. Cullen was always fastidious in including those elements usually read as clutter within the built environment. His interest in supergraphics – signage and advertising – set him apart from many colleagues in planning and prefigured the interests of *Learning from Las Vegas* (1972) by Robert Venturi, Denise Scott-Brown and Steven Rauch, a founding document of post-modernism. Cullen himself was able to accept lettering and advertising as part of a vital urban environment and of a popular and populist tradition. Cullen himself drew the cut-out metal letters, based on Thorne Shaded, for the frontage of the Finsbury Health Centre (1938), and it remains one of the few contemporary examples of lettering in situ.

THE TYPOGRAPHIC PANEL (1951)

Nicolette Gray and Gordon Cullen were among the five members of the Festival Typographic Panel. The chair was Charles Hasler, and the other members were Austin Frazer and Gordon Andrews. The panel was responsible for coordinating the lettering style on printed ephemera, advertising and on the South Bank site itself. Cullen was in charge of external lettering and acted in an advisory capacity.

The panel published a sample book of what it considered suitable letterforms. They chose those types and letterforms, alluded to above, which were already part of the design rhetoric of the age. The sample book is full of Egyptians and Romans, in italics or condensed or extended forms. Some are presented with exaggerated shaded, or blocked, bodies – giving the letters a thrusting three dimensionality intended to project them off the building or page.

The Egyptian form of letter is a letter with an exaggerated, or emphasised, vertical stroke. The first letter within this group was cast by Bower and Bacon in 1810 and was immediately referred to as fat-face. The eponymous Egyptian was cast by Vincent Figgins in 1817 and·is recognised as the first typeface created for the purpose of display in advertising. The progressive exaggeration of the typical characteristics of this type created, throughout the nineteenth century, an extended family of types in condensed, expanded, shaded and decorated forms.

The basic purpose of the fat-face was to make the letter more noticeable by offering a larger printing surface for ink, rather than by making the letters larger

figure 6
Gordon Cullen, illustrations for *A Specimen of Display Letters*, (designed for the Festival of Britain, 1951) reproduced in *Penrose Annual*, 1952, p.29.

figure 7
(left) Gordon Cullen, Italic Egyptian capitals painted on side entrance of Turntable Café, (right) Milner Gray, Condensed Sans serif lettering for direction signs. (*Architectural Review*, August 1950, p.121)

figure 8
Jack Howe, Litterbin, grey with yellow
letter. (The Architectural Press)

– an uneconomic and technically difficult process. The fat-faces and Egyptians
thus combine economy with visual impact and offer a relatively forgiving form
for the jobbing printer. In their most exaggerated forms they are almost impossible to read, but are transformed into powerful symbols that can be understood
beyond their immediate context. The letters also articulate and define the space
on which they are present, understood as negative space, and therefore combine
elements of meaning, symbolic form and abstraction at the same time.

The panel stated explicitly that its purpose was not to confine architects and
designers to a fixed group of types and letters, but to encourage individual expression and visual ingenuity. Perhaps they were helped in this by the fact that
the Festival site was constructed over a relatively short period of time and that the
personnel involved in the project displayed a remarkable unity of purpose, both
in training and temperament. The result, as Nikolaus Pevsner remarked in 1952,
was that the lettering at the Exhibition was both varied and yet of a character.

The sans form was not entirely abandoned either. It was encouraged in its
earlier nineteenth-century forms precisely because, in contrast to the later German sans fonts or the Gill Monotype form, they evince a certain unevenness or
lack of perfection. Writing in the *Penrose Annual* for 1952, Pevsner was unequivo-
cal in this praise of the contribution made by typography to the Festival style. He
identified the Festival as beginning a new phase in the history of modernism that
would be marked by dramatic contrasts between the heavy, robust letters and the
light, transparent architecture of the new technical and engineered structures.
This phase was in contrast to the harmonising tendency identified earlier and
associated with the Johnston and Gill sans letters that characterised 1930s modernism. Pevsner was also encouraged by the variety of more elaborate and decorative scripts used also by the way that many of the letterforms on buildings were
created using teak, perspex and other materials not usually associated with the
traditions of shop signage and external lettering. He attributed the overall success of the Exhibition in giving expression to the new eclectic style to the influ-

ence of Gordon Cullen, by then his colleague on the staff of the *Architectural Review* and praised the successful teamwork between architects, designers, typographers and engineers.

FESTIVAL TITLING

The Panel was instrumental in commissioning a two-dimensional shaded letterform designed by Philip Boydell and launched by the Monotype Corporation in 1951, 'giving the impression of a third dimension without employing perspective or shadow effects'. It graces the cover of this journal and is a letter that alludes to both the cut-letter of classical tradition and the sanserif moderns. It was a perfect complement to the fluttering dazzle effect of bunting that was a feature

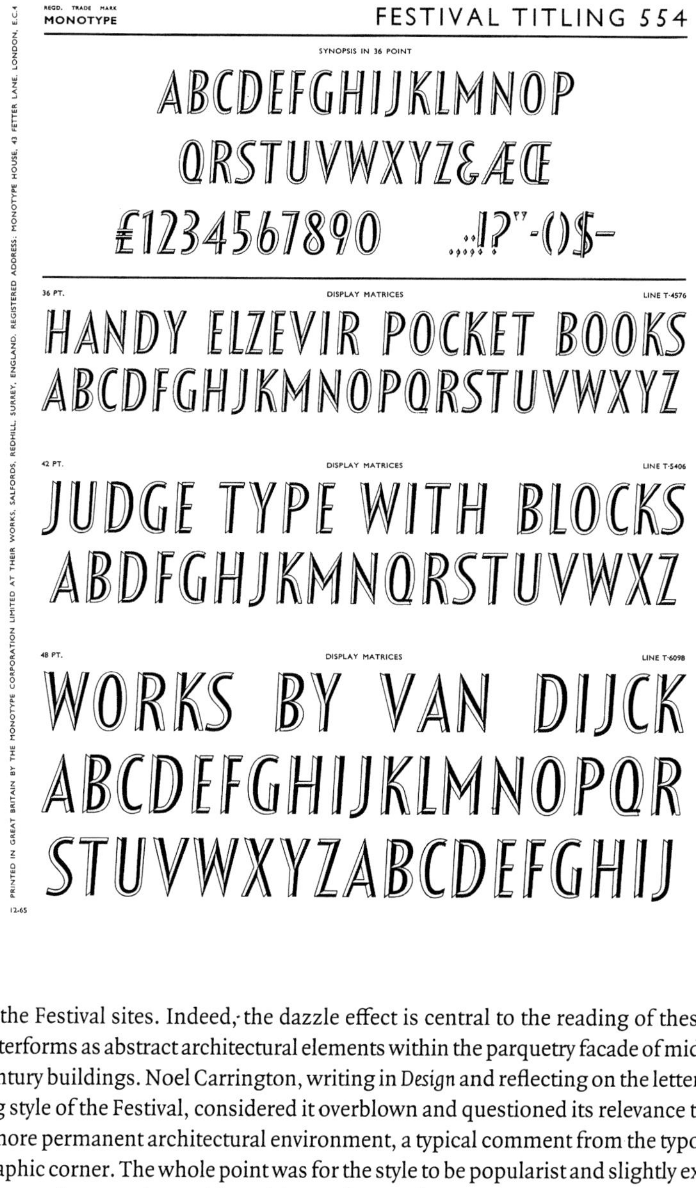
REGD. TRADE MARK
MONOTYPE
FESTIVAL TITLING 554
SYNOPSIS IN 36 POINT
ABCDEFGHIJKLMNOP
QRSTUVWXYZ&ÆŒ
£1234567890 .,:;!?'"-()$-
36 PT. DISPLAY MATRICES LINE T·4576
HANDY ELZEVIR POCKET BOOKS
ABCDFGHJKMNOPQRSTUVWXYZ
42 PT. DISPLAY MATRICES LINE T·5406
JUDGE TYPE WITH BLOCKS
ABDFGHJKMNQRSTUVWXZ
48 PT. DISPLAY MATRICES LINE T·6098
WORKS BY VAN DIJCK
ABCDEFGHIJKLMNOPQR
STUVWXYZABCDEFGHIJ
PRINTED IN GREAT BRITAIN BY THE MONOTYPE CORPORATION LIMITED AT THEIR WORKS, SALFORDS, REDHILL, SURREY, ENGLAND. REGISTERED ADDRESS: MONOTYPE HOUSE, 43 FETTER LANE, LONDON, E.C.4
12-65

figure 9
Specimen sheet for Monotype Festival Titling.

of the Festival sites. Indeed, the dazzle effect is central to the reading of these letterforms as abstract architectural elements within the parquetry facade of mid-century buildings. Noel Carrington, writing in *Design* and reflecting on the lettering style of the Festival, considered it overblown and questioned its relevance to a more permanent architectural environment, a typical comment from the typographic corner. The whole point was for the style to be popularist and slightly exaggerated, even vulgar, without it becoming tawdry or indecent. In any event, his was a lone dissenting voice.

Cullen also illustrated the guide to the Exhibition, and created route maps around the various pavilions that were a simplified form of his serial vision technique perfected at the *Review*. The combination and perfect coincidence in style between the physical reality of the Exhibition and the printed, or graphic, representations of it further enhanced its effect on the public imagination. After the Festival the Clarendon types used in this printed material were rediscovered as a quieter alternative to the fat-faces of 1951.

The Festival signs were dismantled, along with the rest of the Exhibition, in the autumn of 1951. Hardly any examples survive and there are, outside the most specialised publications, very few photographic records of the Exhibition that show those favourable aspects mentioned by Pevsner in the *Penrose Annual* for 1952. The Festival style survived in the important contribution that it made to graphic design and exhibition design in Britain throughout the 1950s and 1960s. The graphic ephemera of the Festival shows the lettering style of the Festival in everything from the emblem, designed by Abram Games, to the multitude of brochures and souvenirs.

VISUAL PLEASURE AND TOWNSCAPE – THE LEGACY OF THE FESTIVAL

Pevsner's comments about the success of the Festival, and its potential contribution to the future development of modernism beyond functionalism, were quickly followed by murmurs that the architectural style was effete and whimsical. Worse still, the architectural style was identified as having been pioneered at the Milan Fair of 1948. The English version was marked down for being flimsy and equivocal in its balance of tradition and modernity. In fact these arguments persist to this day and it remains unclear whether the Festival marked an end or a beginning.

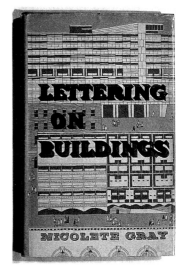

figure 10
Nicolette Gray, *Lettering on Buildings*, Architectural Press, 1960. (cover design by Gordon Cullen)

The Festival was probably both: an end to a first period of modernism associated with unity, functionalism and monumentality, and a beginning of a period of lighter-spirited, more variegated architecture and design. Certainly, it marked the end of a spectacular period of collaboration between artists and technicians. The following years would see changes in design education and management that have tended to separate the activities of architects, planners, typographers and graphic designers.

The brave hope of identifying and creating visual pleasure in the varied vernacular of townscape has become a hostage to, on the one hand, the classicists demanding order and unity; and on the other, those traditionalists who have filled our town centres with faux-Victorian street furniture.

The world has changed enormously since 1951. Lettering and architecture cohabit in ever-closer proximity and in ever more dense layerings. Hardly anyone in 1951 would have predicted the massive impact of road signage on our cities, towns and countryside. This has been made much worse by the extension of the motorway network, and the belief that bigger signs will, necessarily, be clearer. That the Ministry of Transport road letter form is an effective information font has been scientifically established. What a tragedy that it is so artless and so ungracious.

The Festival style became synonymous, for later commentators, with public sector projects for planning and reconstruction. It seems a characteristic of the private sector that no consideration is given to the architectural use of lettering by the developers and architects. It is a concern that is contracted-out to the tenant. Accordingly, some wonderful recent buildings are disfigured by the equivalent of Letraset on their facades. The river front Royal Festival Hall itself at some point lost its original slanted slab-serif Egyptian lettering on the stone-faced upper part, projected forward to give a natural shadow effect, which was replaced by the present sans serif capitals, although the rear retains the authentic style.

It is perhaps a happy coincidence that, fifty years on, Alsop and Störmer's award-winning Peckham Library should remind us of the Festival. Firstly, it echoes the progressive and socially articulated spirit of modernism from 1930–51;

secondly, it has reminded us that the public sector and architecture can combine in fruitful partnership, and, lastly, it signals itself to the world by the letters LIBRARY thrusting from the roofline. This acts as both a physical sign and semiotic portal in reading the building. The public response to the library and especially to the sign, both overwhelmingly positive, are testimony to the prescience of Nicolette Gray and Gordon Cullen and the spirit of 1951.

BIBLIOGRAPHY

'The Exhibition as a Town Builder's Pattern Book', in *Architectural Review*, August 1951.

Alan Bartram, *The English Lettering Tradition – from 1700 to the Present*, London, Lund Humphries, 1986.

Mary Banham and Bevis Hillier, eds., *A Tonic to the Nation*, London, Thames and Hudson, 1976.

John Betjeman, 'A Shell Guide to Typography', in *Typography*, no.2, London, Shenval Press, Spring 1937.

Noel Carrington, 'Legibility – South Bank Lettering', in *Design* (COID), no.32, August 1951.

Barry Curtis, 'One Continuous Interwoven Story', in *Block*, University of Middlesex, 1985.

Nicolette Gray, *Nineteenth Century Ornamented Types and Title Pages*, London, Faber and Faber, 1938.

Nicolette Gray, *Lettering on Buildings*, London, Architectural Press, 1960.

David Gosling, *Gordon Cullen – Visions of Urban Design*, London, Academy Editions, 1996.

Richard Hollis, 'Building a Graphic Language – The Architectural Review', in *eye*, vol.7, no.28, Summer 1998.

Justin Howes, *Johnston's Underground Type*, Harrow Weald, Capital Transport, 2000.

A.F. Johnson, 'Fat Faces – their History, Forms and Use', in *Alphabet and Image*, no.5, September 1947.

Ruari McLean, 'An Examination of Egyptians', in *Alphabet and Image*, no.1, Spring 1946.

Denis Megaw, 'Twentieth Century Sans Serif Types', in *Typography*, no.7, Winter 1938.

James Mosley, 'English Vernacular', in Ruari McLean, ed., *Motif*, Winter 1963.

Nikolaus Pevsner, 'Lettering and the Festival on the South Bank', in *Penrose Annual*, vol.46, London, Lund Humphries, 1952.

John Piper, *Oxfordshire – A Shell Guide*, London, B.T. Batsford, 1938.

Frances Spalding, 'Nicolette Gray's Promotion of Modern Art', in *Typography Papers*, no.3, University of Reading, 1998.

James Sutton and Alan Bartram, *An Atlas of Typeforms*, London, Lund Humphries, 1968.

Michael Twyman, 'Nicolette Gray – a Personal View', in *Typography Papers*, no.3, University of Reading, 1998.

12 The Appliance of Science

MARY SCHOESER

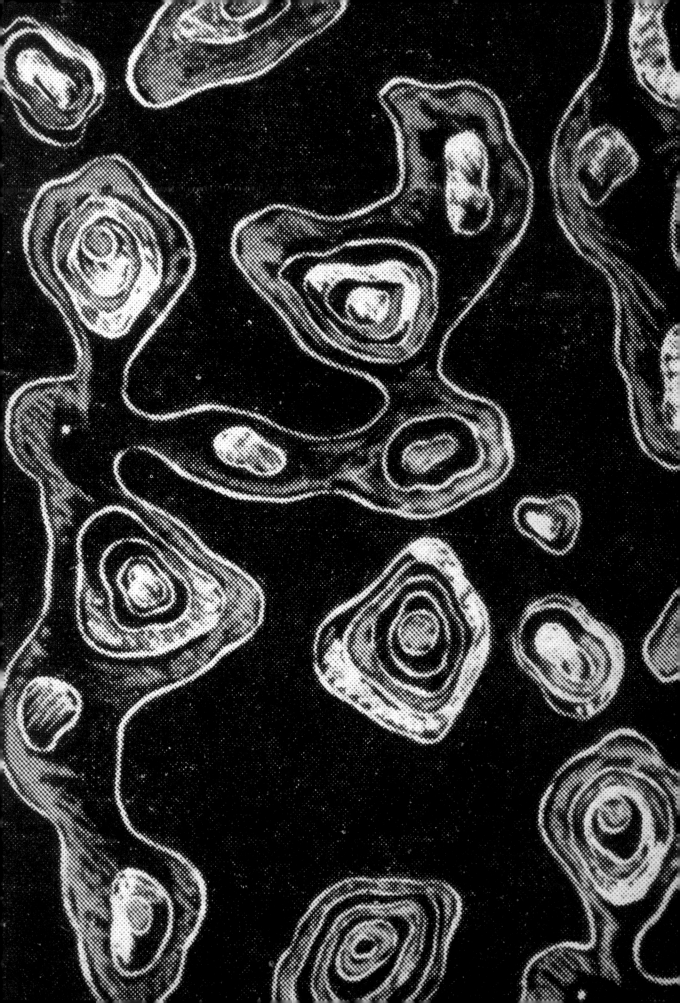

The Appliance of Science[1]

MARY SCHOESER

T HERE are two sides to textile design at the Festival of Britain. Lucienne Day's 'Calyx' won awards in Milan and in California, and is one of the best-known designs from the era. My theme, however, is better represented by the *Festival of Britain Souvenir Book of Crystal Designs*,[2] which demonstrates the influence of science and its implication in the development of patterns. I'm going to extend the discussion from the Festival Pattern Group (FPG) project to the way in which science and scientific thought can be tracked through the textiles and wallpapers that one can find in the 1950s.

The FPG project began in 1949 with Mark Hartland Thomas attending a conference of the Society of Industrial Arts (SIA), as it was then, and hearing a paper by Kathleen Lonsdale on crystallography. She herself had already identified that crystal patterns were particularly appropriate for textiles, and when Hartland Thomas spoke to her afterwards hoping to pursue this as a Council of Industrial Design (COID) project for the Festival, she referred him to Dr Helen Megaw, who had produced Lonsdale's diagrams. In the end, out of 28 manufacturers who took part in the FPG project 11 were involved in textiles. This is for two reasons, I believe. The first is because textiles had, before the war, been the most important exports in the British manufacturing sector. The second was a more personal reason, for the chairman and owner of Barlow and Jones, a major cotton manufacturer whose own Festival pattern was a very subdued little cotton print, was Sir Thomas Barlow, Chairman of COID at the time.

It was a project that was served up to the manufacturers complete, created not by designers but by committee. Hartland Thomas was himself in charge of the engineering complement of the Festival. All the FPG designers got a complete pack of dyelines, and they were asked by their managing directors to come up with a pattern to contribute to the group. There was tolerance for the project in the textile industry because the Festival, like *Britain Can Make It* (1946), and like all the great world fairs and festivals that have happened before and since, was seen by the major manufacturers as an opportunity to sell their exports. And the textile industry indeed had a great deal to sell. For example, they had in 1941, at the Calico Printers Association works, created polyester, but because of the war it was first produced in America by du Pont in 1946. Among the crystal patterns was one of Terylene, then the British trademark for polyester; it is a nice British characteristic to find amusement in producing designs from a diagram of the molecular structure of a synthetic fibre they wished to sell. Variety in this and all crystals was derived from their structures in three ways: they were shown in plan, in section, and in what was the equivalent of the axonometric view. Thus, depending on how one looked at the crystals, a different sort of pattern was produced.

The crystal patterns look very simple but they are illustrating at enormous magnification what crystal structures look like, which is not unlike the sort of crystals that you can see forming on a frozen window pane or on a large leaf in the winter time, but minute. Among the many photographic studies of visible crystals were those made by Dr Wolfe Strache, a German using a Leica camera,

figure 1
A John Line hand printed wallpaper designed by William Odell from the afwillite crystal structure, was from the same source as 'Surrey' (fig.2). Both were produced in two colourways – a background colour of oak-leaf green or deep red.

1. This text is taken from a paper presented at the Twentieth Century Society conference 'Refashioning the Fifties', October 1992. Transcribed by Elaine Worrell.
2. Mark Hartland Thomas, *Festival of Britain Souvenir Book of Crystal Designs*, London Typographical Designers, London, 1951 (reprinted with additions from *Design* magazine).

figure 2
'Frost Crystals on a Window', photographed by Dr Wolfe Strache for *Forms and Patterns in Nature* (London: Peter Owen) 1959; the caption explains how water vapour forms different crystal shapes depending on the rate of cooling, humidity and purity of air and that they have a structural system like that of quartz.

and published as *Forms and Patterns in Nature*, which was translated into English in 1959. It and other volumes like it inspired numerous designs during the 1950s and first half of the 1960s. Photography as a complement to the crystal pattern structures is important for other reasons. One can say glibly off-hand and passing over it, that it was important, of course, in the development of graphic design, in advertising, in the way that it suggests to us the development of television – the first public television broadcast took place in America in the year of the Festival of Britain. But it was also important for other reasons. In 1948 Edwin Land produced a camera known as the Polaroid today; in 1950 Cecil Powell, an Englishman, won the Nobel Prize in physics for his photographic study of atomic nuclei; in the year before, X-rays were used for the first time for medical diagnosis and treatment; these are things we're very familiar with. And today we're very familiar with the laser, but the work by the Alsatian physicist Alfred Kastler on article pumping, as it was then called, was intended to (and did) reveal the atomic structure; started in 1950, it was from article pumping that the laser shows we now enjoy stem. This great interest in vision, in the way we look at the world, is also in a more trivial way represented by the introduction of 3-D motion pictures in 1951. And while we're on the subject of trivia, it's important I think to remember that Velcro, for example, was invented by a Swiss *engineer* in 1948, the first LP also in the same year by a *physicist*, the transistor by three *physicists*, and on an even more pedestrian level, one might say perhaps on a more annoying level, in 1950 the first Diners Club card was introduced – the prototype credit card – and the first cyclamate was put on to the market.

What I see in all this is that photography and the interest in looking deeply into things is the representation of several key themes that run through science and as a result through popular imagery in the 1950s. That is an interest either in revealing the miniature or in miniaturization itself, in replacement (of money or of sugar in the case of the cyclamates) or in penetration, and I use that word advisedly because there are many people today who would say that the rape of the landscape, of the environment, really begins with the faith in science that we see in the 1940s and 1950s. Aside from the specific agenda given to the FPG itself, many other patterns were derived from the celebration of scientific technology. This was a topic widely reported – and illustrated photographically – in the popular press, in part because British prowess in engineering, chemistry and physics was one of the country's most important exports through the 1950s. I mentioned penetration, and just to bring it home to you, in 1950 there was the first embryo transplant for cattle. In 1952 the UK perfected the first amniocentesis. So they were really messing about with the old 'natural' order in the late 1940s and early 1950s, as others were with the old political order; during the same period came the division of Germany in 1949 and the creation of NATO.

In the year of the Festival of Britain there were great many developments in science, and there were many that I've mentioned that didn't reach the popular level until much later. But some did. There was vaccine for yellow fever, there was the heart-lung machine and not long afterwards there was Salk's vaccine for polio. While in many such developments it may be hard to grasp the link between experiential pattern-making by designers and systematic pattern-study by scientists, in some cases it is evident. For example, in 1949 D.H.R. Barton started work on complex molecules, the most famous of which is now the steroid, and he showed that shape is important to the properties of a molecule and that even the smallest alteration of the actual shape will change the behaviour of that molecule. So here we have a direct link between the scientist's interest in shape as a way of modifying the world and the design interest in science as a way of producing an interesting shape. Also in 1949, the English biochemist Dorothy Hodgkin was the first to use the electronic computer to work out the structure (meaning shape) of an organic chemical and that was penicillin, and that of course had great ramifications for all of us, not only in medical terms, but in proving the value of high-speed mechanical 'data crunching': the first commercially available computer, the Univac, was launched in 1951.

There are lots of reasons for looking at the FPG closely, but the main one is that it has very little meaning but great significance if you like; it's one of the few projects in relation to surface pattern of the period that's extraordinarily well documented, and that's because of the COID's involvement in it and its liking for linking its visual material with a lot of written explanations. So let's look a little closer at the FPG and see whether it was a successful project. We can see if it was successful through the eyes of Hartland Thomas because it was he who wrote the souvenir brochure.

The centrepiece of the FPG project was the Regatta Restaurant, designed by Misha Black, with curtains called 'Surrey' by Marianne Straub and produced by Warners. The same source for 'Surrey', afwillite, led to a wallpaper designed by William Odell and produced by John Line. They tried to match the wallpaper with 'Surrey' the cloth; Hartland Thomas noted that it was very difficult to get wallpaper colour to match, but that it was a promising field, and this I think was absolutely correct. One sees a better expression of this promise of colour matching with a GEC light fixture, which combined A.C. Gill lace as the cover of the light with a Wearite plastic back plate. This was the first time in Britain that a concerted effort was made to coordinate design across product areas. And this together with the developments in dyestuffs is a reminder that the plastics industry is essentially at this time, indeed today still is, the textile industry, in that the base product out of which they come in manufactured by the same unit. This meant that great strides were being made in colour chemistry through this period to allow the plastics, textiles and wallpapers to match more accurately. There had been matching wallpapers and textiles prior to this for over fifty, well in fact you could say 300 years; but they didn't actually match in terms of colour, they matched in pattern but not in tone. Plastics, as I've indicated, were really the most important area of innovation in the FPG, that is the solid plastics or what we know better now as Formica, as well as the plastic-coated fabrics. It's revealing that with regard to the latter Hartland Thomas commented on FPG patterns used on Dunlop PVC sheeting or ICI Leathercloth, saying what pretty colours they are, and that this was the big surprise for most people.

On colour, however, the real breakthrough can be seen in the more traditional products such as Templeton carpets designed by R. Anderson. Here we see the characteristic and brand new colours of the 1950s, including deep bright orange and a very distinctive slightly battleship turquoise blue. These were to become the colours of the 1950s for the textile industry at least. We can also stop here and consider what Hartland Thomas wrote about the designs themselves; he described a strongly marked out lattice-like carpet pattern as measuring out the space in a room and giving it scale. This to me has a lingering sort of Design and Industries Association quality to it, still trying to justify design in terms of its function, its performance in the room. But at the same time he also described patterns very carefully in relation to how much alteration has taken place between

figure 3
A display case in the foyer of the Regatta Restaurant housed the products that were not used in furnishing the restaurant itself. Among these are Wedgwood ceramics by Peter Wood (right among the ceramics); wall tiles by Reginald Till for Carter and Co., showing the now classic 'ball and rod' molecular schemata; and two patterns based on afwillite (upper left, see also figs.1 & 2) between which is the Arnold Lever London Ltd design for a fashion fabric based on haemoglobin.

figure 4
The Regatta Restaurant, designed by Misha Black; everything – from menus and cutlery to upholstery and carpeting – was a Festival Pattern Group product. Marianne Straub's 'Surrey' curtaining was the most widely associated with the project, which she believed was because it was on such a large scale (see fig.9).

figure 5
ICI Leathercloth designs by C. Garnier tried out several differently scaled designs, and it was the tiny repeats that became the standard.

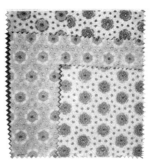

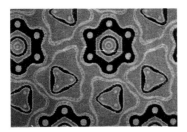

figure 6
Designed by G. Brown and based on insulin, this Templeton carpet was described by Hartland Thomas as having a lattice-like pattern that would measure out the space in the room.

the dyeline that has been provided to the designer and the end result. He's clearly in a quandary and presumably expresses something that was discussed around board room tables at the time. He commented that it was clear that more rich-ness and style in decoration was wanted, but where, he asked, was it going to come from? Remember that Raymond Loewy in America had already condemned functionalism and had introduced the idea of pro-consumerist design, design created to tempt the buyer to buy, but Loewy also insisted on high standards of design or engineering perfection. And what exactly was perfection? Well, it's pretty hard to believe that designs developed from myoglobin for ICI Leathercloth represents perfection, but then it's difficult to look at these things from the viewpoint of the 1950s. An Oxvar decorative finish from Vernon Indus-tries, which was patterned via an offset process, was described as 'witty' because it has a pattern within a pattern. These are quite different interpretations within the same project and it's very difficult to know which of these were meant to be perfect. From insulin, a John Line wallpaper was described in this way: 'despite bold treatment the character is not lost'. Again one has the sense that Hartland Thomas had to justify what the designers were doing: Templeton's darkly col-oured carpet was described as Turkey carpet colours but not an imitation – truth to materials one might say. A lace pattern by A.C. Gill, and also from insulin, is described as a 'free adaptation' (there is a sense of confession when you read this booklet really) and the haemoglobin design by Arnold Lever London Ltd admit-tedly 'goes furthest from the original'.

The departure from the crystallography dyelines that were provided is, I think, the key point to understanding what was going on in the industry at the time. The important thing about this departure is that it is most evident in dress fabrics, which then as now represents something like 60% of the entire sales in the tex-tile industry. And it's a quixotic industry, it has to follow fashion, it can't be pinned down and therefore many designers weren't having these rigid crystal patterns at all. Ceramics designs, like those by Hazel Thrumpston for R.H. and S.L. Plant Ltd, also tended to be general essays on a theme; their manufacturers really didn't participate in it at all. Most FPG ceramics conformed to the appear-ance of a fashion fabric design based on afwillite, like 'Surrey' and the John Line wallpaper in the Regatta Restaurant but very different in effect; it was justified or rather advertised as 'like the free shape outline of current fashion.' One only needs to think of Asher's production of the Henry Moore patterns, for example, to see the kind of reference they were making, and the Henry Moore designs were produced five years before this. So there is a great deal of light-stepping around the issue; it's not clear who's committed to what or indeed what direction they're going in. Most revealing to me is that the giant, 'exploded' pattern on wall tiles by Reginald Till for Carter and Co., which to my mind is the most striking of all the FPG products, passes completely without comment at all. And yet clearly it's in the right place at the right time, so similar in colour and shape is it to Charles and Ray Eames's 'Little Toys' of exactly the same year.

Now this brings me to a point about the more general use of scientific imagery

figure 7
The text in the FPG souvenir brochure often justified the decisions taken by the designers, as in the case of the Elkington flatware designed by H.G. Bowring (right).

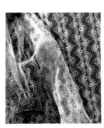

POLYTHENE   POLYTHENE

Embroidered cotton lace: A. C. Gill (H. Webster): repeat 1 x 1½in. Right, cutlery and flatware: Elkington and Co (H. G. Bowring). It is easier to spoil silverware by decoration than to improve it. Here the designer has graduated the pattern in sympathy with the pro-file and made a decorated handle that is as good as, if not better than, the plain one (p. 13)

and it is that it did in the 1950s have a great element of fun about it, it wasn't all serious and there were different types of fun. There was fun for all, represented by machine produced textiles such as those of Turnbull and Stockdale, and fun for some, with more expensive products such as hand-painted aluminum figurines on a cast-iron base, then called 'Golliwogs' by their manufacturers, Laverne Originals, which had been founded in New York in 1937. The images in both examples come from the distillation glass that was produced en masse for the scientific industry at the time. The production of this glass depended on developments that were made during the war, the improvement of the fine gearing of moulding machinery, and of extruding machinery. These also relate to the textile industry, its ability to produce polyesters, acrylics, monoacrylics and all the

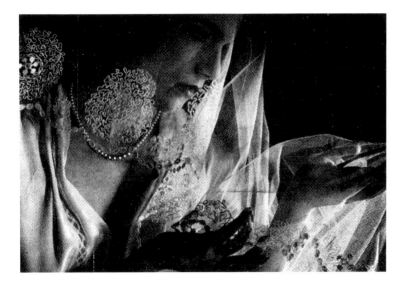

figure 8
This A.C. Gill machine-embroidered lace, by H. Webster from insulin, is 'admitted' by Hartland Thomas to be a free adaptation: compare to Figure 5, which is faithful to the crystal's structure.

figure 9
These ICI Leathercloth designs, by C. Garnier from myoglobin, are described by Hartland Thomas as representing little alteration from the crystal's pattern itself.

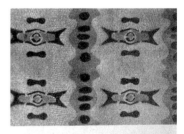

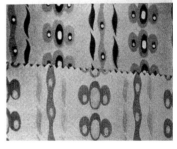

new fibres such as nylon, that came through the war and afterwards; all have to do with the control of extruding and moulding machinery. One can see such developments explored in other well-known products: the 'Tulip Chair' by Knoll, the great Saarinen design of 1956; and also, more widely, in pottery.

Aside from the technology of the form-making machines themselves, there are other important technical and scientific developments that one has to take on board in relation to interiors and the textile industry. The first is Scotchguarding, which is something that comes out of the war, out of the need to produce waterproof, rot-proof textiles for the use, particularly in the Pacific arena, by the army, navy and the marines. This is the first time when it really becomes practicable to put printed fabrics on furniture. It therefore means it was the first time that one could have furniture that was both fashionable and inexpensive; weaves were always much more expensive. In the arena of weaves an example of established usage is the Arflex (by Marcio Zanuso) 'Lady Chair' of 1951, with tubular steel and rubber webbing; the upholstery here is baize, one of those wonderful woollen fabrics, with a natural 'give' that a good upholster could make move around this sculpted shape. The innovation was soon to come with the development of stretch jersey, which was imported from Hungary by refugees, and taken up particularly in Britain and America. That was the second important technical development, really providing the furniture designer with a cloth that moves like clay around the outside of the sculpted shapes of furniture. And the third development occurred within the textile industry, in relation to the rollers used for printing. At the outbreak of war, machine production of printed cloth had depended almost entirely on copper engraved rollers. These had been very badly hit by the needs for this particular metal in the war; huge numbers of them had been requisitioned and one of the benefits of the subsequent peace was that manufacturers had to retool. One of the down sides of all this was that copper was so much more expensive; this was one of the factors that crippled the Lancashire cotton industry, and indeed the British industry never recovered in terms of its worldwide dominance. Some 250 mills closed in Lancashire alone through late 1954 and through 1955.

Coming up behind established and often entrenched firms were new, young, innovative companies or older companies that had new, young, innovative designers. One of these, perhaps the most important in retrospect, was David Whitehead. John Murray, the architect who came in to Whiteheads, pioneered and broadcast his view that cheap need not be cheap and nasty, and it was Whitehead who really pushed forward modern design in textiles using mass production techniques. All of the other companies we associate with good design in wallpapers and textiles were still using hand techniques. If we look at these Whitehead cloths more closely we can see a lot of the elements that are typical of the 1950s: designs composed from cross-sections (a simpler variant of the FPG principle) and the use of texture. Printed texture is a very important element because it disguises cheap cloth and it was something that was done in the 1940s, when chevrons, herringbones, tweeds and so on were printed on to completely plain rayons just to give them a look of quality, and we see this continuing through the 1950s.

But let's look more carefully at this wide range of popular images and relate them to science. Hartland Thomas had written that crystal patterns were modern, the most up-to-date, scientific technology and yet they still came from nature. This was very, very close to the British heart, deriving pattern from nature and coincided neatly with the seemingly universal 'exploratory' zeitgeist of the postwar period. There was a widespread interest in looking into, somehow exposing, or exploring in closer detail the fundamental elements of nature. This trend is represented by 'Coalface', by Nigel Henderson and Eduardo Paolozzi for Hull Traders (1957). Its pattern-source is suggested by its title; even so, the design also bears a striking resemblance to photographic studies of crystals formed by flourspar, a chemical used in etching glass. Yet we see a similar trend in avant garde American textiles. Those woven by Ed Rossbach, using black-out and pattern paper together with silk and reed, show us in a very large and crude scale what a textile looks like, how it's constructed, as does a blind by Dorothy Liebes, another Californian who became very well known in America, using bamboo and lurex, the latter another new product from the 1950s that was expensive and luxurious. If we look at this idea of exploding, of looking closer, of being a scientist examining reality, we can find a range of witty examples, all making reference to textiles themselves. In 'Interlace', a handscreen printed paper by Ben Rose (1952), the pattern is a vastly enlarged depiction of a lace structure; in 'Fibra', a handscreen printed furnishing fabric by Esther Haratsy for Knoll (1954) it is a blown-up detail from the centre of an old hand loom. By the 1960s such large patterns were commonplace, but their origins lay in the 1950s, among such high quality, hand made products.

Now the whole point about expense and luxury brings us back to the contradiction between the desire to produce modern designs for everyone, and in Britain, in the textile industry at least, the slow take-up of new rotary screen printing which is today's process of machine printing. It had been invented in the 1930s but because of the financial restraint was only very slowly introduced into Britain in the mid-1950s. Quality therefore remained something that was extremely important in the marketplace. The beauty of hand-printing by any method is that you can overlay one colour over another and create a watercolour-like impression. This quality has largely been lost in the industry now, but it is still true that without any exceptions the innovative textiles and wallpapers of today are produced by a method that allows the overlapping of colours. Machine printing still

figure 10
Strache's *Forms and Patterns in Nature* also included aerial photography, including this creek system, channels formed by the flow of the tides in shallow portions of the sea, but always remaining under water. His introduction highlights its resemblance to a tree as evidence of a 'system' of pattern-making in nature.

requires 'clean' printing with no overlap of colours because you end up with a grey smudge at the end of the process if you risk it. Thus many effects could not be found in both hand and machine prints. There was one, nevertheless, that could be: the incorporation of fine lines and crisp textural effects.

Line is extremely important, as I've said, as one way in which to add texture to a fabric and suggest quality. However, during the 1950s line took on a new visual role, alluding to science. It suggested cartography, very important in the 1950s not only an important earth science but particularly when directed specifically towards the lunar system. Space generally was a very important theme, particularly the moon, stars and so on. Line was used in a completely different way in the more high-brow designs, as they were called at the time, as represented by Angelo Testa's work in America. Testa was the most important speaker on behalf of modern textile design in America, and interestingly enough convinced – I'm sure he was right – that architects and furniture designers did not want to see nature parading across windows, furniture, carpets and so on, and deliberately set out to produce designs that did not have that suggestion. They nevertheless tend now to fall into the more scientific category if for no other reason that you can't see flowers on them. He also worked to the rule that a great deal of blank cloth should be exposed; this was not because of the restrictions in colours left over from the war, which is why it happened in Britain; this was because he felt that a good quality cloth should be allowed to show through, that it should not be covered entirely with printed colour. A Testa pattern like 'Fun to Run' by Laverne Originals depicts the vectors of scientific notation. You might say it resembles a detail from a Matisse, or something primitive, but nevertheless in this and similar patterns line is being used to add a sense of modernity, a sense of science.

But of course the most typical use of line is that with the blob at the end, and this takes us directly back to the Festival Pattern Group. The blob is the atom at the end of the typical scientific schematic of a molecular structure and sometimes in popular designs it's a diamond, or in the much more up-market printed furnishing cotton 'Graphica', by Lucienne Day for Heals (1954), we see it in its square form. Richard Hamilton, looking back at this in 1961 (*Design* no.149), called this 'mass produced contemporary with knobs on' and indeed there was a great deal of it. This is the point at which the scientific imagery becomes simply style. And there are lots and lots of examples of these, including Turnbull's expensive design called 'Electronic' (1954) just to help consumers feel they really are partaking in something new and scientific. The winner for 'contemporary with knobs on' has to be George Nelson with his famous Howard Miller 'Atom' clock and bubble lamps, the latter taking the idea of the visible molecule and blowing it up even larger.

What is interesting about all of this to me is how intellectual so much of this design was. One can see this simply by looking at the language of the period, the language the designers placed around these designs. For example, a pattern by Sven Markelius based on triangles, screen printed in 1952 by the Swedish firm Nordiska Kompaniet, is called 'Pythagoras'. And in England one can see also the effect of the different nationalities who were living here after the war, bringing in all kinds of different attitudes, all kinds of different intellectual sets. Hans Tisdall, German by birth but trained and influenced by the French, made three designs which were purchased by Marianne Straub for Helios in the 1940s but never produced, sadly. Let's just look at some of the names for these simple, non-pictorial designs: 'Dangerous Flirtation', 'The Lodger Unbuttoned' and 'The Eclipse of the Neckline'. Now let's compare two very similar 'block' designs, one 'Eclipse' by Tisdall and the other by Angelo Testa of about 1957. Testa calls his in a very straightforward, down-the-line, no nonsense American way, 'Square Deal': a pun – or is it a jibe? – referring to Roosevelt's 'New Deal' of the prewar period. Lucienne Day's title 'Spectators' is a pun too, but in the light-hearted

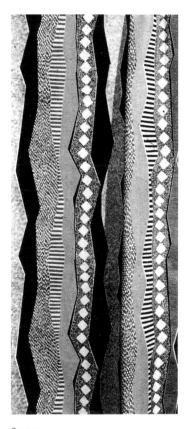

figure 11
Semi-automatic-screen printed by Turnbull & Stockdale, Bury, in 1951, this three-colour design illustrates the rich tonal effects created by the use of line and texture.

figure 12
Typifying the numerous designs
produced in the 'contemporary with
knobs on' style is 'Graphica' by
Lucienne Day. Handscreen printed on
cotton for Heal's, it was one of four
designs that jointly won the *Gran Primo*
award at the tenth Milan Triennale in
1954, and in the following year a
variation was issued as a wallpaper by
Rasch, Germany.

English mode: it makes you look a bit more carefully, to spot the glasses sported
by some of her abstracted figures. Summing up the forthright cleverness demonstrated by many designers and artists of the 1950s is Berthold Wolpe's brilliant
example of calligraphy, in which he actually dared to use Latin scripts with City
and Guild students. This was a level of erudition that could be taken on board in
the 1950s because no one was frightened to be known as an intellectual; indeed,
many who weren't pretended to be. The widespread celebration of empirical
science ensured this was the case.

An abstract Warner handscreen print of 1954 that resembles a diagram of
stars going around the earth, and called 'Departure', seems scientific as well. But
the designer, Hilda Dirkin, told me it was taken from a line in Omar Khayyám,
referring to a nut in a bowl. The intellectualism quite often leads off into different arenas. But both the literal and visual languages of the period, as clearly expressed in textiles, for the most part exposes a great faith in science. A final
example from the Festival Pattern Group makes this point in a way that is both
telling and, today, rather poignant. It is a small pattern woven by Warners. Designed by Alex Hunter, who was very actively involved in the SIA through the
1950s until his death in 1958, it was developed from the china clay crystal pattern.
Its name is 'Harwell'. It's hard to believe, now that we are so jaundiced, that his
choice celebrated in all innocence what was deemed the most important, the
most magnificent scientific technology developed to that date.

13 Fun and Fantasy, Escape and Edification: The Battersea Pleasure Grounds

BECKY CONEKIN

Fun and Fantasy, Escape and Edification:
The Battersea Pleasure Grounds

BECKY CONEKIN

WHEN asked by Bevis Hillier twenty-five years after the 1951 events if he had been 'particularly involved in the Festival Gardens', James Gardner, its co-ordinating designer, replied:

Oh completely, that's when my hair turned white. Barry, the inspiration behind it all, was finding the South Bank rather too clinical for his tastes. Architects and scientists seemed to be running away with it. He wanted a place where people could relax and have fun – elegant fun. Remembering the old pleasure gardens at Vauxhall, he decided we'd have a Festival Gardens. Battersea Park, then given over to allotments and a cricket pitch, was to be the site.[1]

For the Director-General of the Festival, Gerald Barry, 'elegant fun' were the key words – he wanted to provide the war-weary British people with 'elegant fun'. And, although the Battersea Pleasure Gardens were to be a kind of antidote to the serious and more overtly educational exhibitions on the South Bank, this did not mean that they missed their chance to be edifying. Even with American fun fair rides, commercial sponsorship – banned on the South Bank – and the consumption which logically followed, improving agendas were prominent at the Battersea site. These seeming contradictions and their sources are the subject of this article.

The Pleasure Gardens shared a climate of controversy and contention with the entire Festival, and yet were unique in allowing corporate sponsorship. Like the Festival as a whole, the Gardens were a political football, with the Beaverbrook press and most Conservative MPs vociferously against the idea. One newspaper, for example, proclaimed on its front page: 'Spend the money on St. Thomas's Hospital', which had been bombed. After initial discussions, the Gardens project was shelved for almost a year, but then given the go ahead with about half the budget originally estimated as necessary by the planners.[2]

CORPORATE SPONSORSHIP & CONSUMPTION

With such a small budget, it was obvious to Gardner that they had to ' ... get the major features sponsored'.[3] Such sponsorship had been barred on the South Bank. Gerald Barry, in his unpublished memoirs, linked this decision to the wider purpose of the Festival.

By contrast, Battersea's Pleasure Gardens included the Lewitt-Him Guinness Clock,[4] the Lockhead Hydraulic Brake Company-sponsored bronze sculpture of a mermaid,[5] the Leichner Cosmetics' Ladies Powder Room,[6] the Schweppes Grotto, the Sharp's Kreemy Toffee Punch and Judy Show, and three beer gardens sponsored by the Worshipful Company of Brewers.[7] As a place of fun and fantasy, the Battersea site was seen as more appropriate for sponsorship, advertising and overt commercialism, than the more educative exhibitions created on the South Bank or in the Science Museum at South Kensington where science was presented as fun and fantastic. Battersea offered the hedonistic pleasures of an amusement park, dancing, shopping and eating, in addition to improvement.

In the Ladies' Powder Room and the shops along the Parade, one could 'buy almost anything from perfume to tobacco, from toys to jewelry.'[8] 'Half-a-dozen

figure 1
The Guinness Clock tinkled out *Three Blind Mice* every quarter of an hour to accompany an automaton display of spinning acrobats, a town crier with a bell, and the Mad Hatter, who popped out of a tower and fished out fish from a well. (Crown copyright. NMR)

1. James Gardner, 'Pleasure Gardens Battersea Park, Battersea Pleasures: Interview with James Gardner', in Bevis Hillier and Mary Banham, editors, *A Tonic to the Nation: The Festival of Britain 1951*, London, Thames and Hudson with the cooperation of the V&A Museum, 1976, p.118.

2. ibid., p.120.

3. ibid.

4. William Feaver, 'Festival Star,' in *A Tonic to the Nation*, pp.40–55: 53.

5. *Festival Pleasure Gardens Battersea Park Guide*, Festival of Britain 1951, PRO, Kew, Work 25/233/E1/D3/6.

6. *Festival Pleasure Gardens Battersea Park Guide*, pp.16 & 38.

7. 'Confidential, FG Ltd. (50) 8th meeting, Festival Gardens Limited, Minutes of the 8th Board Meeting held at 2 Savoy Court, London, WC2 on Thurs. April 27, 1950 at 2: 30 PM,' p.7, Work 25/21/A2/A6, PRO, Kew. For one planning discussion of the merits and appropriate types of sponsorship, please see: 'Confidential FG Ltd. (50) 9th meeting, Festival Gardens Limited, Minutes of the 9th Board Meeting held at 2 Savoy Court, London, WC2 on Thurs. May 25, 1950 at 3 p.m., p.5, '7. Sponsorship of Individual Attractions and Features', Work 25/21.

8. *Festival Pleasure Gardens Battersea Park Guide*, p.16.

expert assistants', were centrally located in the Ladies' Powder Room. 'In the dove-grey salon with its twelve mirrored dressing-table [sponsored by Leichner Cosmetics] the ladies, in their pause for beauty, find a full range of powders, lipsticks … , eye-shadows in all the colours of the spectrum.' Also available were 'cleansing creams and lotions.' The brochure further states that: 'there are special trays of make-up for blondes and brunettes.'[9] This passage reminds us not only of the almost complete absence of cosmetics and creams in wartime Britain, but also of the perceived homogeneity of white Britain with its assumption that British women come in two colours: 'blonde or brunette'!

The further gendered assumptions revealed in the descriptions of the 'small blue-and-white shops designed in the Regency style' are also striking to today's sensibilities. 'Practically everything you can find in Bond Street, and a good many places beside, is here on sale.'[10] The souvenir brochure further informed the visitor that:

Along the Parade is to be found … shops whose very names spell quality and luxury. Here you can find exquisite antiques, figures in porcelain and ivory … Here, too, are bright adornments for my lady – earrings and necklaces of pearl and brilliants, costume jewellery of every description. And while madam yearns over gems and fine perfumes, elegant slippers and diaphanous underwear, the mere male can comfort himself with the contemplation (and purchase) of pipes, snuff, fountain pens, cameras, watches or electric razors – while younger members of the family gape at miraculous toys, stamps (including the special Festival issue), and other wonders,[11]

If one ignores the gender assumptions, what strikes one most is the descriptive language in this brochure: the visitor 'yearns' and 'gapes' for things characterized as 'quality,' 'luxury,' 'elegant,' 'miraculous,' 'wonders.' Such language seems extreme today, yet in a period which produced tales of men resorting to shaving with the same razor blade for six weeks, women creatively employing burnt match sticks to blacken their eyebrows, and everyone rolling their own low-quality, smelly cigarettes, the variety of such goods for sale in such charming shops must have been a welcome relief indeed.[12] It was an age of austerity so severe that the post-war national industrial design exhibition of 1946, named 'Britain Can Make It,' was re-dubbed by the press 'Britain Can't Have It'.[13] This shopping parade must have felt like the height of extravagance in such circumstances. It must also have been a good advertisement that Britain could both 'make it' and 'have it' in 1951. Luxury consumption signalled recovery to people at home and abroad – an important message the Labour government and the Festival aimed to relay.

Add the 'luxury restaurant' to this picture and the place must have seemed the epitome of opulence for many British visitors. This most elegant of the Gardens' restaurant offerings was housed in the Riverside Rooms, 'a long low restaurant of West End standard with a Wine Garden … consisting of little umbrella-ed alcoves of Vandyke brown-and-white behind a white trellis fence, webbed above with fairy lights suspended from a central mast.'[14] The terrace overlooked the Thames and you could eat inside or out, accompanied by 'music from a small orchestra.'[15] For those less willing or able to indulge in such extravagance, there were six other restaurants, half of which were buffet style, a tea shop, two snack bars, three pubs, a wine garden, a refreshment stand, and two 'refreshment bars'.[16] Catering for all classes – or 'all tastes, all ages and all pockets', in the Festival's language – was on offer, and in the evenings 'the most spectacular and unusual' fireworks and illuminations lit the skies for all to enjoy.

BATTERSEA AS NOSTALGIA

In addition to offering an arena for sponsorship and consumption, the Pleasure Gardens were also seen as a place more appropriate than the South Bank for nostalgic representations of the past. The South Bank exhibitions overwhelmingly stressed progress and modernity, projecting 'the belief that Britain will

9. ibid., p.38.

10. ibid., p.16. The publication is revealing some class prejudice here, in its reference to the exclusive Bond Street.

11. ibid., p.38.

12. See for example: Paul Fussell, *Wartime: Understanding and Behaviour in the Second World War*, Oxford & New York, Oxford University Press, 1989, pp.195–228, or Robert Harris' *Enigma*, London, Arrow Books, 1996, first published by Hutchinson, 1995, p.113.

13. S. MacDonald and J. Porter, 'Mid-Century Modern: The Campaign for Good Design', in *Putting on the Style: Setting up Home in the 1950s*, London, The Geffrye Museum, 1990, n.p. and Patrick J Maguire and Jonathan M. Woodham, eds., *Design and Cultural Politics in Postwar Britain: The Britain Can Make It Exhibition of 1946*, London & Washington, Leicester University Press, 1997.

14. *Festival Pleasure Gardens Battersea Park Guide*, p.15.

15. ibid.

16. Gardner in *A Tonic to the Nation*, p.121, and 'Architectural Preview: Festival Pleasure Gardens Battersea Park,' *Architectural Review*, April 1951, p.231.

have contributions to make in the future.'[17] 'The contemporary style', so important to the South Bank's identity, 'had been deliberately eschewed' at Battersea, according to a planning document.[18] In the Battersea Gardens one found oneself in a beautiful setting far from the realities of post-war Britain – a setting incorporating many architectural styles including that of Regency Brighton and eighteenth and nineteenth century London.[19]

Laid out on thirty-seven acres, the Gardens offered visitors from Britain and beyond a six-acre amusement park, a children's zoo and pet corner, two theatres, one dedicated to music hall performances, the other to ballets, revues and marionettes, a fanciful tree-top walk, a Mississippi Showboat, and a huge tented

figure 2
The Tree Walk. (Crown copyright. N M R)

dance pavilion.[20] A respectable mixture of 'high' and 'low' culture was on offer, furthering the illusion of a classless society which was the goal of many of the South Bank's displays. One major aim of the Festival organisers was to diffuse education, ideas and tastes, generally the preserve of elites, to the people of Britain. Selected visions of the past supplied the backdrop at Battersea for this place of fun and fantasy.

One of the most popular attractions offered a nostalgic, child-like pleasure in the form of the enchanting Emett railway designed by the cartoonist, Rowland Emett. His 'Far Twittering and Oyster Creek Railway' appeared regularly in contemporary issues of *Punch*.[21] Battersea's version, a complete miniature 500 yard-long railway, was described in the souvenir brochure as containing 'all his characteristic fantasy.'[22] According to Emett himself:

The main station, at the western end of the line, was Far Tottering ... There were many nice railway touches about this station: a luggage-crane ... from which hung a wealth of Gladstone bags, leather silk-hat boxes ... A wicker bird-cage containing a depressed seagull, was consigned to Oyster Creek ... the railway teemed with forbidding notices – 'Do NOT tease the Engines' ... 'Do NOT feed the Bats' ... 'Passengers must NOT cross HERE, so there!' And, of course, the one that stated quite simply: IT IS FORBIDDEN.' All of these strictures carried the normal penalty of forty shillings.[23]

Between these two stations ran the three cartoon-inspired versions of the train, led by locomotives 'Nellie,' 'Neptune,' and 'Wild Goose,' each pulling three or four coaches and conveying passengers from one station to the other. The trains were a favourite amongst Gardens visitors and ran continuously throughout the summer.[24]

17. Ian Cox, *The South Bank Exhibition, A Guide to the Story it tells*, London, H M S O, 1951, p.8. Becky Conekin, 'Here is the Modern World Itself: The Festival of Britain's Representations of the Future', in *Moments of Modernity: Reconstructing Britain 1945–1964*, Becky Conekin, Frank Mort, Chris Waters, eds., London, Rivers Oram Press, 1999, pp.228–46, or Becky Conekin, *'The Autobiography of a Nation': The 1951 Festival of Britain, Representing Britain in the Post-War Era*, Manchester, Manchester University Press, 2002.

18. 'Confidential, FG Ltd. (50) 9th meeting, Festival Gardens Limited, Minutes of the 9th Board Meeting held at 2 Savoy Court, London, WC2 on Thurs. May 25, 1950 at 3 p.m.', p.3, Work 25/21/A2/A6, PRO, Kew.

19. Sue Harper's work on the great popularity of the 1940's Gainsborough melodramas, historical romance films, primarily set in the Regency period, may offer some explanation of why particular centuries were seen as more popular, fanciful and elegant than others. See Sue Harper, *Picturing the Past: The Rise and Fall of the British Costume Film*, London, BFI Publishing, 1994.

20. *Festival Pleasure Gardens Battersea Park Guide*, Festival of Britain 1951. See also: *The Official Book of the Festival of Britain*, 1951, and Inyang Isola Ime Ebong, 'The Origins and Significance of The Festival of Britain, 1951,' unpublished Ph.D. Thesis, University of Edinburgh, Department of History, 1986, p.390.

21. Rowland Emett, 'The Far Tottering and Oyster Creek Railway,' in *A Tonic to the Nation*, p.125.

22. *Festival Pleasure Gardens Battersea Park Guide*, p.16.

23. Emett, op. cit., p.126.

24. Emett, op. cit., pp.125–7. Also, see Ebong, op. cit., p.396.

figure 3
Nellie, Far Twittering and Oyster Creek
Railway, by Rowland Emett. (Crown
copyright. NMR)

The Pleasure Gardens' dance pavilion by James Gardner, modelled after a similar one in Copenhagen's Tivoli, was deemed impressive, the Battersea version having the biggest single pole tent ever erected in the world at the time. Gardner claimed that, 'it turned out that the English are too shy to dance in public, so we had to engage tame dancers to start the ball rolling. Then it worked.'[25]

BATTERSEA'S FUNFAIR WITH ITS AMERICAN RIDES

Thrilling American fun fair attractions were on offer at the Pleasure Gardens as well. The British people and their visitors were treated to an impressive fair, featuring a Waterfall 'twenty-five feet high, 65 feet wide, pouring up to 7,000 gallons a minute ... an exact replica of Niagara Falls, down to the smallest details,'[26] the Skywheel, the Bubble-Bounce, and the Flyo Plane. There was also a Water Splash ride, resembling those present-day versions in which cars ascend a steel ramp and then descend ' ... a slope at ever-increasing speed to splash down in a large pool of water!,' and other new American rides developed while the British were understandably too preoccupied with the war effort to spend money and talented labour on fair rides.[27]

The Board of the Battersea Pleasure Gardens had decided that for the funfair to be as attractive and appealing as they desired, it was necessary to purchase new features from America. Under post-war conditions this was a bold step. The Festival of Britain Council Meeting Minutes from October, 1950 state:

While plans for entertainment were proceeding well, the provision of amusements was causing some anxiety. This was primarily due to the fact that no novelty of the type sought had been introduced into this country during the past 10 years, owing to lack of dollars. The prospect of having any unique and new amusement feature in the Gardens was therefore remote, even though there was now in progress a search which might extend to the United States.[28]

They agreed to apply to the Treasury for £30,000 (at that time the equivalent of approximately $84,000) to facilitate these purchases. This is £500,000 in 1990s terms, but its significance was still greater, given the acute shortage of dollars in Britain. Surprisingly, the Treasury agreed, and a date was set for a trip to the States. In an attempt to make this journey seem more practical, the Board recommended that a number of large British funfair operators should accompany the Battersea representatives, and that if these operators decided to purchase new attractions for their own fairs, then the Battersea Company would buy those chosen. The individual operators could then purchase them from the Battersea Com-

25. Gardner, op. cit., pp.121–22.

26. *Festival Pleasure Gardens Battersea Park Guide*, p.24.

27. Quotation from Gwendoline Willis, 'An incident in the Grotto,' published in *A Tonic to the Nation*, p.181. Also, Ebong, op. cit., p.402. On issues surrounding purchasing American fun fair equipment, please see: 'FBC (50) 4th Meeting October 4, 1950,' 8. Festival Pleasure Gardens, Work 25/21/A2/A6, (Festival Gardens), in PRO, Kew, and Undated Document on Funfair Equipment, in CAB 124/1302, PRO, Kew. See also Ebong's discussion of this in op. cit., pp.399–402.

28. 'FBC (50) 4th Meeting October 4, 1950,' 8. Festival Pleasure Gardens, Work 25/21/A2/A6, (Festival Gardens), in PRO, Kew.

pany at cost, plus transport costs, eschewing the import duties or purchase tax.[29] Thus, on the 16th of November, 1950, Major Joseph, as the representative of the Battersea Pleasure Gardens, a Board member and the Chairman of the National Amusements Council, along with four large funfair operators, set off for America. Not surprisingly, the Pleasure Gardens Company wished to keep all of this quiet, as Lidderdale told Nicholson:

All concerned should be given a special warning not to make it public. It would be very unfortunate, just when we are at last beginning to get across the serious purpose of the Festival, to have attention focused on this side line.[30]

However, the money spent on American rides did not go unnoticed by the Beaverbrook press, Conservative backbenchers or the increasingly vocal Nottingham Housewives' Association. There followed questions in Parliament, *Daily Mail* headlines asking why the Government was about to spend $100,000 on a new roundabout, and a telegram from Nottinghamshire housewives to the Ministry of Food which read: 'if no dollars available for purchasing eggs and other food, why use same for funfair equipment – should be all British – we protest strongly.'[31] The *Daily Graphic* featured an article which quoted William Burke Teeling, Conservative MP for Brighton, asking Morrison in the Commons why if 'the Festival is supposed to show people from overseas what Britain can do, ... it seems we are spending a great deal of money to show what America ... can do?'[32]

WHICH FANTASIES ON OFFER?: ENGLISHNESS AND OTHERNESS

It is a valid question. 'British contributions to civilisation' was the overarching theme of the Festival of Britain. And the range of those on show at the Battersea Pleasure Gardens was certainly rather modest. This is especially striking when one notes that Britishness was so explicitly emphasised on the South Bank that there was even a rule that foreign food should not be served there. Versions of an English past were evoked in the Gardens' early Regency architecture, the rendition of the popular elite fashion for the 18th century grotto, the traditional Punch and Judy show, the music hall performances, and the Nell Gwynn-like orange girls. Raphael Samuel explained how follies, 'one of the commonest eighteenth-century forms of holiday architecture, contrived to be both experimental and atavistic, playing on the appeal of antiquities and reproducing them in replica, while at the same time cultivating an appetite for the exotic.'[33] In addition, according to the souvenir brochure, the Battersea Pleasure Gardens strove above all to

29. Undated Document on Funfair Equipment, in CAB 124/1302, PRO, Kew. See also Ebong, op. cit., pp.399–402.

30. Letter from Lidderdale to Nicholson, dated 7 October, 1950, in CAB 124/1302, PRO, Kew. See also Ebong, op. cit., p.400.

31. Ebong, op. cit., p.401. Sources listed are: the *Daily Express*, 13 November, 1950; the *Daily Graphic*, 13 November, 1950 and 'Telegram to Minister of Food from Nottingham Housewives,' dated 14 November, 1950 and filed in CAB 124/1302, PRO, Kew.

32. Ebong, op. cit., p.401. Quote from William Burke Teeling, MP, as published in the *Daily Graphic*, 13 November, 1950 and as cited by Ebong, op. cit., p.401.

33. Raphael Samuel, *Island Stories: Unravelling Britain. Theatres of Memory Vol.II.*, edited by Alison Light, with Sally Alexander and Gareth Stedman Jones, London and New York, Verso, 1998, p.358.

figure 4
Girl selling flowers, dressed in Victorian style. (Crown copyright. NMR)

figure 5
Candelabra entrance to the Grand Vista, by Osbert Lancaster.

34. Dr. Johnson on the Vauxhall Pleasure Gardens, as quoted by Anthony Hippisley Coxe, 'It Sprang from Spring Gardens,' in *Festival Pleasure Gardens Battersea Park Guide*, op. cit., p.44.

35. ibid., p.44.

36. Making a virtue of necessity, Gardner designed this feature when a sponsor withdrew leaving him with an unused scaffolding pier (Gardner, op. cit., p.121.)

37. *Festival Pleasure Gardens Battersea Park Guide*, op. cit., p.14.

38. Michael Frayn, 'Festival', in Michael Sissons and Philip French, eds. *Age of Austerity*, 1945–1951, Harmondsworth, Middlesex, Penguin Books, 1963 p.344.

39. *Festival Pleasure Gardens Battersea Park Guide*, op. cit., p.15.

figure 6
The Grand Vista designed by John Piper and Osbert Lancaster. The arcades to either side are by Piper, the obelisks in the water by Lancaster. Note the model of the Crystal Palace behind the firework platform at the end of the vista.
(Crown copyright. N M R)

create a place evocative of the Belvedere Gardens, which existed on the South Bank from 1781 to 1785, and the Vauxhall Gardens which flourished even earlier, and of which Dr. Johnson wrote the following description:

That excellent place of amusement … is particularly adapted to the taste of the English nation, there being a mixture of curious show, gay exhibition, music, vocal and instrumental, not too refined for the general ear … and though last, not least, good eating and drinking for those who chose to purchase that regale.[34]

Johnson's demotic evocation of the 18th century pleasure gardens was quoted in the Battersea souvenir brochure as an appropriate description of 'the Festival Gardens today.'[35]

Yet, however English these representations, many other nations and styles were on display at Battersea as well. There were the American fun fair rides, as well as the Mississippi Showboat at the end of a pier,[36] but there was much more. For example, the popular Tree-Walk sported a Chinese-style dragon. The bronze sculpture of a mermaid, sponsored by the Lockhead Hydraulic Brake Company, was inspired by its creator's time on Bali.[37] The 'Piazza', although not specifically named or written about as Mediterranean beyond that evocative word 'piazza', featured 'shadows painted and the flooring so designed that … [it] looks half as long again as it really is.' 'Reds and yellows on the facade of the building fade in the distance into pinkish greys and blues,' giving the impression that one is in 'The Land of Always Afternoon' with 'deep shadows cut[ting] down the faces of the buildings on the right-hand side.' And, as if this was not exotic enough for the British, rain-soaked visitor ('the first five months of 1951 were the wettest since 1815 … '[38]), the 'skyline, especially at the end, is an oriental wonderworld of minarets and turrets,' and on the roof to the right were 'two mighty Centaurs.'[39] When you came out of the Grotto and turned left towards the Grand

figure 7
Centaur by Hans Tisdall.
(The Architectual Press)

figure 8
Lockhead Fountain 'Miranda', by Arthur
Fleischmann (now at Leamington Spa)

Vista, you walked under 'a curving row of hanging chandeliers in the Chinese taste'[40] and both arcades were 'in the Chinese Gothic style, built of timber and cane with golden roofs.'[41] Finally, although English antecedents were emphasised in the official Pleasure Gardens' souvenir brochure, the planners and designers repeatedly remarked that their Gardens were modelled after those of Tivoli in Copenhagen.[42]

THE BATTERSEA PLEASURE GARDENS AS A SITE OF IMPROVEMENT

James Gardner declared that the Pleasure Gardens 'put a moment of dreamworld into a lot of peoples' lives', and the critic William Feaver, called the Gardens a place where 'fantasy was the rule'.[43] As we have seen, these statements seem apt. Improving agendas, like those found in the more overtly educational exhibitions on the South Bank and in South Kensington's Science Exhibition, were also in evidence.[44]   The regulation of 'leisure in socially beneficial directions' and the education of the (female) citizen consumer were both acknowledged goals of the post-war settlement led by Labour and featured at the Battersea Gardens.[45] A Tribune correspondent wrote after Labour's victory in 1945 that: 'the time has now arrived when culture should cease to be the hallmark of the leisured classes and should be available to all.'[46] At the 1949 Labour Party conference 'Lord Festival', Deputy Prime Minister, Herbert Morrison, declared that: 'Part of our work in politics and in industry must be to improve human nature ... we should set ourselves more than materialistic aims'.[47] And *Labour Believes in Britain*, published in the same year, asserted that there was a need to stimulate leisure and the arts, as

40. ibid. p.19.

41. ibid., p.21.

42. John Piper, 'A Painter's Funfair: Interview with John Piper,' conducted by Bevis Hillier, and published in *A Tonic to the Nation*, p.124; 'Memo: Festival Gardens, Battersea Park,' from E.W. Swaine and G.A. Campbell, dated March 30, 1949, located in Work 25/21/A2/A6, PRO, Kew.

43. *A Tonic to the Nation*, p.118 & 53.

44. On the improving agendas of the South Bank and the Science Exhibition, see Becky Conekin, 'Here is the Modern World Itself ... ', op. cit.

45. Peter Hennessy, *Never Again: Britain 1945– 1951*, London, Vintage Books, 1993, p 310: 'Inevitably in the afterglow of the 'People's War' there were attempts by those in authority to regulate leisure in socially beneficial directions especially where it spilled over into culture.'

46. *Tribune*, 17 August, 1945, as quoted by Steven Fielding, Peter Thompson, and Nick Tiratsoo, 'England Arise!': *The Labour Party and Popular Politics in 1940s Britain*, Manchester, Manchester University Press, 1995, pp.136–7.

47. H. Morrison, in M. Francis, *Ideas and Policies Under Labour, 1945–1951: Building a New Britain*, Manchester, Manchester University Press, 1997, pp.56–7.

figure 9
John Piper and Osbert Lancaster
working on their model of the main
vista. (The Architectural Press)

48. Labour Party, *Labour Believes in Britain*, p.3;
Francis, op. cit., p.57.

49. Francis, op. cit., p.57.

50. Ellipsis in the original. Labour Party,
Womanfare, London: Labour Party, 1951, pp.6–8.
On clothing, consumer knowledge and
working-class women in the post-war period,
please see A. Partington, 'Popular Fashion and
Working-Class Affluence', in J. Ash and E.
Wilson, editors, *Chic Thrills*, London, Pandora
Press, 1992, pp.145–161, and 'The Days of the
New Look: Working-Class Affluence and the
Consumer Culture' in J. Fyrth, ed., *Labour's
Promised Land?: Culture and Society in Labour Britain
1945–51*, London, Lawrence and Wishart, 1995,
pp.247–63.

51. Labour Party, *Festival*, London: Labour Party,
1951.

52. Elizabeth Wilson, *Only Halfway to Paradise:
Women in Postwar Britain: 1945–1968*, London
and New York, Tavistock Publications, 1980,
p.36.

53. Newsom, 1948, p.103, as quoted by Wilson,
op. cit., p.36.

54. *Labour Believes in Britain*, op. cit., p.3.

55. There is a huge literature on 19th century
'rational recreation'. See for example, Robert D.
Storch, 'Introduction: Persistence and Change
in Nineteenth-Century Popular Culture', in his
*Popular Culture and Custom in Nineteenth-Century
England*; Gareth Stedman Jones, 'Class
Expression versus Social Control?: A Critique of
Recent Trends in the Social History of Leisure'
in his *Languages of Class*, Cambridge and New
York, Cambridge University Press, 1983, pp.76–
89; Eileen Yeo and Stephen Yeo, *Popular Culture
and Class Conflict, 1590–1914* and James Walvin,
Leisure and Society 1830–1950, London, Longman,
1978.

56. Labour Party Archive, Research Department
Files, RDR 284/March, 1945, P.J. Noel-Baker,
'Facilities for Popular Entertainment and
Culture', RD 35/November, 1946, Anon., 'A
Policy for Leisure', and RD 43/February 1947,
Anon., 'The Enjoyment of Leisure', as cited by
Fielding, et. al., op. cit., p.137.

well as for a state-funded holiday council, providing cheap holidays for the British people.[48] The historian Martin Francis has argued that Labour's policies during the period point up the ways in which the party's policy-makers were committed, however modestly, to a version of socialism 'concerned with ... an improvement of the "quality of life" in its widest sense, and not merely with questions of economic power and material improvement'.[49]

Rational consumption was, furthermore, essential in the imagined New Jerusalem led by Labour. For example, an official Labour publication, Womanfare, published in the Festival year, celebrated 'Joan':

*the most important woman in Britain today. She is the shop girl ... the factory worker ...
the girl who works in the mill, the local store. She is business girl, housewife, teenager and
mother. The wise girl knows that she can have a smart wardrobe through wise planning –
she knows, too, that some Tories have threatened to do away with the Utility scheme.*[50]

The Labour Party's special 1951 magazine, Festival, celebrated rationing as the only way to control price increases, which had been exacerbated by the Korean War, and compared the situation in Britain favourably to that in France where 'prices have increased fivefold since 1945' and the United States where 'housewives find that prices are driven up so high that the ordinary family can't afford to buy'.[51] In John Newsom's The Education of Girls (1948), he included a chapter on 'Woman as Purchaser' in which he 'envisaged education as guiding working-class girls towards middle-class standards of taste'.[52] He wrote:

*Our standards of design, and therefore our continuance as a great commercial nation, will
depend on our education of the consumer to the point where she rejects the functionally
futile and aesthetically inept and demands what is fitting and beautiful ... Woman as
purchaser holds the future standard of living of this country in her hands ... If she buys in
ignorance then our national standards will degenerate.*[53]

And if women were to consume in a restrained, aesthetically pleasing, and by implication, middle-class, fashion, all British citizens were to spend their leisure time in similarly defined pursuits. The Labour agendas outlined above acknowledged the need for leisure and holidays in the same breath as 'the evolution of a people more ... intelligent and rich in culture.'[54] Raphael Samuel identified that the post-war Labour leaders shared the concerns held one hundred years before by Methodist teetotallers and working-class radicals, who desired 'rational recreation' for the people, involving no violence, no alcohol and activities more 'improving'.[55] Labour had identified a 'leisure problem' in 1946 and 1947, the result of which was 'the failure of the majority of Britain's citizens to enjoy a full life through their leisure pursuits'.[56] Due to their narrowly defined pastimes, like pub- and cinema-going, their recreational activities were 'passive', superficial and only temporarily exciting. Labour's leisure policy, according to M.P. Philip Noel-Baker, wished to help 'the citizens of Britain to live full and varied lives' and facilitate 'a great extension in the horizon of mind and spirit for the men and women of Britain.'[57] 'The love of beauty can be inculcated in the mass of people', declared a *Tribune* correspondent. 'Guidance' in the form of 'a consciously edu- cative' Labour cultural programme would lead to more fulfilled and discriminat- ing citizens of all classes.[58]

Gerald Barry wished to provide the British people and their visitors with not just fun, but 'elegant fun.' As Tony Bennett has written, fairs have commonly been conceived of as diametrically opposed to museums. Since the late nineteenth cen- tury, museums' advocates have furthered this dichotomy by claiming that the fair not only occupied time and space differently, but also 'confronted' and 'affronted' 'the museum as a still extant embodiment of the 'irrational' and 'chaotic' disor- der that had characterized the museum's precursors', including fairs.[59] But, Bennett challenges this appraisal, arguing that the fixed-site amusement park occupies 'a point somewhere between ... the museum and the travelling fair.'[60] Amusement parks are, according to Bennett, 'modern' and committed 'like the museum, to an accumulating time, to the unstoppable momentum of progress which ... [they] claimed both to represent and to harness to the cause of popular pleasure' through their stress on 'the new', and their inclusion of the latest me- chanical rides.[61] As we have seen, the latest American rides were a priority for Battersea's planners. The stationary amusement park also represents a negotia- tion of the perceived dichotomy between museums and fairs by producing regu- lated and orderly crowds, 'unlike their itinerant predecessors'.[62]

Nevertheless, the traditional view of the fair as the definitive unruly and dan- gerous place of crowds, disorder and distasteful (working class) pleasures haunted the middle-class planners of the Festival Gardens who repeatedly stressed that they did not want this place to be known as a fair. As such, they in- troduced the word 'Pleasure' into its name as an attempt to get 'away from the idea of a fun fair.'[63] Concerns about 'Americanisation' – that shorthand for commer- cial, crass, cultureless culture – lurked behind most critiques of popular culture, at least from the inter-war period onwards. F. R. Leavis wrote in 1933, that, 'mass media', disseminated from America, was uniform and standard, offering 'satis- faction at the lowest level' which taught people to want only 'the most immediate pleasures, got with the least effort'.[64] Such people's 'natural urges' or desires needed to be suppressed and re-channelled into worthwhile, respectable pur- suits. Or in the words of Lord Reith's motto for the BBC, those who knew best should 'give the public slightly better than it now thinks it likes.'[65] The Pleasure Gardens did incorporate an amusement park, featuring all the latest rides, many imported from America. But, it was only one of many options and, in the end, the Pleasure Gardens were in fact so elegant that one Gardens Board member, Sir Arthur Elvin, 'questioned whether the general treatment was not too high-class for the tripper element,' while another responded that he 'thought that it was appropriate to preserve a reasonably high tone in view of the expectation that a number of Continental and other high-class visitors would attend.'[66]

But, these class anxieties were suppressed by the time the Gardens finally opened.[67] The 1950 press release contained only a broad hint: 'The Festival Pleas- ure Gardens ... will provide facilities for entertainment, refreshment and relaxa- tion to suit all tastes, all ages and all pockets.'[68] By the time one actually entered the Gardens in the summer of 1951, the illusion of equality dominated this fanci- ful land. The same press release may have explained that 'the pavilions will be an echo of the 'follies' and temples that gentlemen built in their parks at the end of the 18th century,' but one of the fantasies encouraged by the Pleasure Gardens was that in post-war Labour Britain access to such 'gentlemanly' pleasures was available to everyone.[69]

57. P.J. Noel-Baker, 'Facilities for Popular Entertainment and Culture', RD 35/ November, 1946, Anon., 'A Policy for Leisure', as cited by Fielding, et. al., op. cit., p.137.

58. *Tribune*, 17 August and 7 September, 1945, as quoted by Fielding, et. al, op. cit., p.138

59. Tony Bennett, *The Birth of the Museum: History, Theory, Politics*, London & New York, Routledge, 1995, pp.1–4.

60. Bennett, op. cit., p.4.

61. ibid.

62. ibid.

63. Sir Henry French alerted the Council to the insertion of the word 'Pleasure' into its name for this reason, 'FBC (50) 4th Meeting October 4, 1950, 8 Festival Pleasure Gardens' (part of a document, some of which is missing), Work 25/21/A2/A6, PRO, Kew.

64. F.R. Leavis and Denys Thompson, *Culture and Environment: The Training of Critical Awareness*, London, Chatto and Windus, 1933, p.3. See also D.L. LeMahieu, *A Culture for Democracy: Mass Communication and the Cultivated Mind in Britain Between the Wars*, Oxford, Clarendon Press, 1988, p.299.

65. Lord Reith, as quoted by McKibbin, *Classes and Cultures*, op. cit., p.460.

66. Ibid.

67. On the opening of the Pleasure Gardens, see, Gardner, in *A Tonic to the Nation*, p.122.

68. 'Gerrard 2842, Release date: Immediate, FG/Press/4/50, Festival Gardens Limited, 5, Sidney Place, New Coventry Street, London, W1, Festival Pleasure Gardens in Battersea Park' (n.d., April, 1950?), Work 25/21/A2/A6, PRO, Kew.

69. ibid.

figure 10
The Schweppes Grotto by Guy
Sheppard. A series of caves set behind a
waterfall, popular with children.
(Crown copyright. N M R)

70. Gardner, op. cit., p.122.

71. Gerald Barry, as quoted by Frayn, op. cit.,
p.337.

72. Adrian Forty, 'Festival Politics,' in *A Tonic to
the Nation*, p.37.

73. Beatrice Webb on Beveridge, as quoted by
Gareth Stedman Jones, 'Why is the Labour
Party in a Mess?' in his *Languages of Class: Studies
in English Working Class History, 1832–1982*.
Cambridge and New York: Cambridge
University Press, 1983, p.245.

74. Ebong, p.59. There was also an official
Festival Council. The Official Committee seems
to have played much less of a role in creating
and actualizing the Festival than did the two
committees. The most interesting thing about
the Official Committee is that General Lord
Ismay was appointed the Chair of the Festival
Council. Although Ismay described himself as
'a complete ignoramus about the arts,' his
appointment was an extremely intelligent
move. As a dear friend of Churchill's he was
able to stop criticism from the Festival's most
persuasive and respected critic. (Quote from
General Lord Ismay, *The Memoirs of General Lord
Ismay*, p.448.)

75. On the role of the Council of Industrial
Design in the official Festival exhibitions, see
my chapter, '"Here is the Modern World Itself:
... "', op. cit., or 'The Autobiography of a
Nation', op. cit.

76. For their helpful suggestions pertaining to
this article I would like to thank: Adam Tooze,
James Vernon, Christopher Breward, Caroline
Evans, Sonya Rose and Geoff Eley. I would also
like to acknowledge the support of the London
College of Fashion in the form of a part-time
Research Fellowship. The initial research for
the larger project of which this is a part was
funded by the (American) Social Science
Research Council.

CONCLUSION: WHOSE FANTASIES ON OFFER?

One may ask what sort of men, for they were almost exclusively men, created this
fantasy world? Gardner remarked in 1976 that the Festival Gardens 'did put a
moment of dreamworld into a lot of people's lives.'[70] But, whose dreams were
represented at Battersea? The Gardens were the actualisation of a dream created
by artists, architects, designers, and planners – a particular package of 'fun, fantasy and colour' which Gerald Barry wanted to give the British people.[71]

The planners were overwhelmingly middle-class men in their forties who
would have been students in the early 1930s. These 'radical, middle-class do-
gooders' could also be characterized as representatives of the new post-war public sphere dominated by experts and professionals, members of a 'technocracy'.[72]
Like William Beveridge they were 'obstinately convinced' that their class would
have to do the job; 'there must be a revolution; but it must be guided by persons
with training and knowledge.'[73] They were 'officers and gentlemen,' who were
'steeped in paternalistic philosophy ... determined not only to protect and care
for the ordinary man [sic], but ... to make his drab existence worthwhile.'[74]

The vast majority of written historical evidence relating to the Battersea Pleasure Gardens tells us more about the fantasies of escape, pleasure and extravagance of its middle-class planners than about the average British visitor. And
encouraging aesthetically orientated consumption was something the Battersea
planners shared with those middle-class arbiters of taste, the B B C and the Council of Industrial Design.[75] The planners of the Battersea Pleasure Gardens offered
an alternative classless world constructed of a curious combination of architectural styles eclectically borrowed from 17th, 18th and 19th-century England, with
a cartoon-inspired, whimsical railroad, a Mediterranean piazza, Chinese Gothic
arcades, an American fun-fair and paddle-boat, as well as 'Bond Street'-stand-
ard luxurious restaurants and shops. Yet, the fact that eight million people (many
of whom must have been counted more than once) attended the Gardens in the
summer of 1951 implies that the planners got something right. This seems especially true since anecdotal evidence suggests that Battersea is the best-remem-
bered and most-loved memory of the London Festival for many people. One
London black cab driver told me he had proposed to his wife on their visit to the
Festival Gardens. Democratic or not, a 'real' world of dreams, however ephemeral, must have been worth quite a lot to the British who had had almost nothing
but dreams since the late thirties.[76]

14 Lansbury

ELAIN HARWOOD

Lansbury

ELAIN HARWOOD

WRITING in 1964, Ian Nairn felt that Lansbury 'seems much further away than the war. It was as much of a confused but worthwhile melting pot as the Festival itself. The bits which looked likely to fade have faded ... ; the bits which had some real understanding of Cockneys have mellowed and grown into the life of the East End'.[1] What was hard to grasp in 1964 and is almost impossible now, is that in 1951 there was nowhere else in England with a contiguous group of modern buildings to demonstrate any of the ideas of modern architecture and town planning that had been so fervently discussed for ten years – since Donald Gibson had first expounded his plan for rebuilding Coventry in late 1940.[2] We may question what Lansbury achieved, but the real issue is why so little was done anywhere else: tracts of housing around London's fringes; a few pretty terraces in south Norfolk. The Festival's architecture awards show how little was built in the late 1940s.

THE CONCEPT OF A 'LIVE ARCHITECTURE' EXHIBITION

Proposals for the organisation of an Exhibition of Architecture, Town Planning and Building Science were worked out by the Ministry of Town and Country Planning with the Royal Institute of British Architects and Town Planning Institute, and were approved on 27 February 1948. The Festival's Council for Architecture had overall control of the form of the exhibition, supported by editorial and technical committees. The main themes were to be reconstruction and redevelopment, and first plans were for a general exhibition in London and provincial shows focussing on specific towns and cities.[3]

Frederick Gibberd later admitted that he was sounded out for the job of co-ordinating achitect eventually awarded to Casson, but that 'it was not my forté.'[4] Nevertheless, the offer gave him cause to think what an exhibition on architecture might be. In July 1948 he wrote to the Council for Architecture, suggesting that there was only one sure method of explaining architecture and town planning. 'The only way architecture can be exhibited is as architecture.'

Gibberd proposed a 'live' architecture exhibition: 'to take a bombed or cleared site of four to six acres, as near as possible to the site of the main Exhibition; to develop it as a cross section of a Neighbourhood ... The buildings would be loaned to the Exhibition and they and open spaces between them would then be treated as full-sized exhibits. The cost of the usual Exhibition would be devoted to explaining, by exhibition technique, the environment which had been made; and creating such additional amenities that may be necessary, such as cafés and gardens.' He proposed that a range of housing types be built, from old people's bungalows to flats and family houses, perhaps with a community hall, small shopping centre and industrial units. Some buildings could be left partially completed as exhibits of building construction, and finished after the show was over. Save that churches and schools were preferred to factories, this is pretty much what happened.

In Europe there had been numerous building exhibitions. Between 1927 and 1933 no less than thirteen housing exhibitions had been held in Czechoslovakia,

figure 1
Visit of the Mayor of Kettering, 8 September 1953. The delegation is admiring the sign to the Festival Inn, based on Skylon, with the tower of Chrisp Street Market behind. (London Metropolitan Archives)

1. Ian Nairn, *Modern Buildings in London*, London Transport, 1964, p.24. The essential introduction to Lansbury is Stephen Porter, ed., *The Survey of London*, vol.XLIII, *Poplar, Blackwall and the Isle of Dogs: the Parish of All Saints*, 1994, pp.212–43.
2. D.E. Gibson, 'Problems of Reconstruction', in *Architect and Building News*, vol.164, 6 December 1940, pp.141, 148.
3. AI/B2, PRO WORK 25/7.
4. Frederick Gibberd, 'Lansbury', in Mary Banham and Bevis Hillier, *A Tonic to the Nation*, London, Thames and Hudson, 1976, p.138.

figure 2
The Lansbury area prior to its
rebuilding. (London Metropolitan
Archives)

5. Stephan Templ, *Baba, The Werkbund Housing Estate, Prague*, Basle, Birkhäuser, 1999, p.12; Roderick Gradidge and David Prout, *World's Apart, a tour of Gidea Park*, Thirties Society 1989; Maurice de Soissons, *Welwyn Garden City, a Town Designed for Healthy Living*, Welwyn Hatfield, 1988, pp.47–8.

6. Frank Schaffer, *The New Town Story*, London, Paladin edition 1972, p.71; Gordon E. Cherry, *The Evolution of British Town Planning*, Leighton Buzzard, Royal Town Planning Institute, 1974, p.144.

7. Forshaw and Abercrombie, op. cit., p.9; Frederick Gibberd et al, *Harlow: the Story of a Town*, Stevenage, Publications for Companies, 1980, p.43.

8. F.B. Architecture (50) 2, 16 March 1950, in PRO WORK 25/49.

9. *Architectural Review*, vol.110, no.657, September 1951, p.192.

10. London Metropolitan Archives, LCC Housing Committee Presented Papers, LCC/MIN/7638, report October 1949. Additionally, 7,865 prefabs had been erected.

Switzerland, Germany, Italy, Austria and Sweden. The best known and most radical was the Weissenhofsiedlung Exhibition in Stuttgart, one of six organised by the Deutscher Werkbund to demonstrate industrialised building techniques, and noted for the involvement of Le Corbusier, Walter Gropius, Mies van der Rohe and other names from the top drawer of modern architecture. Model housing was a prominent component of the Stockholm Exhibition of 1930, and even the New York World's Fair of 1939–40 had grown out of an idea for a housing exhibition. But in Britain public housing programmes had been preferred to private exhibitions; closest perhaps were the model homes competitions held in Gidea Park, outside Romford, in 1911 and 1934. The Ideal Home Exhibitions organised by the *Daily Mail* had also sponsored a few model houses, among them the small estate built at Welwyn Garden City in 1922.[5]

Gibberd's idea differed from the European exhibitions in that he did not propose a new residential suburb, but the rebuilding of a real piece of the city, with a greater variety of buildings. In developing the idea of a neighbourhood he was assuming a concept already adopted by planners in London and the New Towns. Ebenezer Howard had in 1898 subdivided his garden city into 'wards' of some 5,000 people, with its own school and shops, and this idea was developed more formally in 1929 in America by Clarence Perry, who advocated traffic-free neighbourhoods large enough to support a primary school. This idea was supported by the Dudley Report (*The Design of Dwellings*) in 1944 and by Lord Reith's New Towns Committee in 1945. The influence of neighbourhood planning came to the fore in the *County of London Plan* of 1943 and the 1944 *Housing Manual*, and it dominated the planning of the New Towns, including Gibberd's own work at Harlow.[6] The 'neighbourhood unit', for between 6,000 and 10,000 people, was based around the catchment of a junior school, and designed so that no child should have to cross a main road to attend it. For Forshaw and Abercrombie it was a means of bringing order to the East End, whose comprehensive redevelopment in eleven neighbourhoods was declared in 1948. 'New opportunities are now presented for the development or provision of groups of public and other buildings to form nodal points around which the general interest and life of the communities would centre', while the boundaries of the neighbourhood would be defined by open spaces.[7] The exhibition was to be one of these nodal points.

Gibberd's proposal was well received, and was formally approved by the Festival Council in August 1948. Originally it was proposed that a small exhibition on town planning should also be included in the Combined Exhibition on the South Bank, but eventually this too was erected at Lansbury. It was also proposed to hold an architecture exhibition in Edinburgh and a 'live' architecture show at East Kilbride, but both schemes were abandoned when budgets were cut in March 1950.[8] A show on modern architecture was, however, held in Belfast.[9]

THE CHOICE OF SITE

In London, the difficulty was to find a suitable site, a decision ironically made less easy by having Robert Matthew, Chief Architect to the London County Council, on the Council for Architecture. For in 1945 responsibility for housing construction had been passed from the Architect's Department to that of the Chief Valuer, Cyril Walker, to concentrate production under one head. Matthew had arrived at the LCC the next year determined to win it back. While the valuers could rightly claim efficiency and productivity, with over 18,000 permanent houses built in the post-war years to September 1949, doubts were raised about the quality of their designs.[10] Many of their flats still relied heavily on models approved as long ago as 1934. The dispute came to a head in 1947–8 over the Minerva Estate, rows of four-storey walk-up flats built of concrete next to the railway line in Bethnal Green. 'Every defect of pre-war planning practised in municipal flats seems to have been repeated in contradiction to all experience and to every hope for the improvements so lavishly promised during the war years', wrote the young architects Kenneth Campbell and Kenneth Easton in a letter to the *Architects' Journal*.[11] Correspondence followed for several months with the tacit connivance of the LCC Architect's Department. It led to an exhibition promoting recent LCC housing in 1949, that was so lambasted by the press that Matthew won back responsibility for housing the next year. Lansbury remained under the control of the Valuer, but nevertheless gave architects an opportunity to revert to the concept of the 'neighbourhood' and show what could be done.

No site was readily available near the South Bank. The Council was thus forced to consider areas already designated for comprehensive redevelopment by the LCC, and to look specifically at sites where Matthew and his team 'have so far withstood pressure from the Valuer's Department to develop high-density flats in isolation.'[12] Their search led them to the largest of the LCC's designated redevelopment areas, Stepney/Poplar. The Festival's choice fell upon 'Neighbourhood no.9', subsequently named Lansbury after George Lansbury (1859–1940), former Mayor of Poplar and leader of the Labour Party between 1931 and 1935. Lansbury was chosen despite the difficulty that much of the land had still to be purchased, because the layout was still sufficiently fluid that the Festival could have an input. Jack Godfrey-Gilbert of the Festival Office recalled 'open derelict landscape, formerly occupied by terraced houses which had been completely devastated by the bombing and cleared away. There were the remains of a church on the corner of East India Dock Road and Upper North Street with some of the Gothic arches still intact ... The whole area had an atmosphere of foreboding, gloom and despondency'.[13] One attraction, however, was that the site was a short bus ride from the river boat services, which provided a connection from the South Bank, another that part of the site had already been proposed for a nodal shopping centre to serve three neighbourhoods.[14] On 14 December 1948, with Cyril Walker's support, a formal request was made for the site.

The exhibition was to be 'a cross-section of a residential neighbourhood' with about 400 new houses. Some buildings would be completed, while others would be left as 'cut aways', under construction until the exhibition was over. The LCC gave its support in January 1949. But when the Valuer's Department determined that it was going to design 70% of the area itself the Festival Council was appalled. It resolved that 'the Live Architecture Exhibition should be planned not by accident of site ownership as just another housing site, but as a National Exhibition of Architecture in which every building and group must earn its place by attaining the highest possible visual and technical standards', a strong stance

11. *Architects' Journal*, vol.105, no.2734, 7 April 1947, p.315.
12. F.B. Architecture (48) 2, 20 August 1948, in PRO WORK 25/28.
13. Jack Godfrey-Gilbert, 'Joining the Team', in *A Tonic to the Nation*, op. cit., p.160.
14. F.B. Architecture (48) 2, 20 August 1948, in PRO WORK 25/28.

figures 3 & 4
The plan and model of the Festival of Britain site. The plan shows the suggested route through the estate, beginning and ending at the temporary exhibition site, bottom left. This is not shown on the model, which differs from what was built only at this point.
(London Metropolitan Archives)

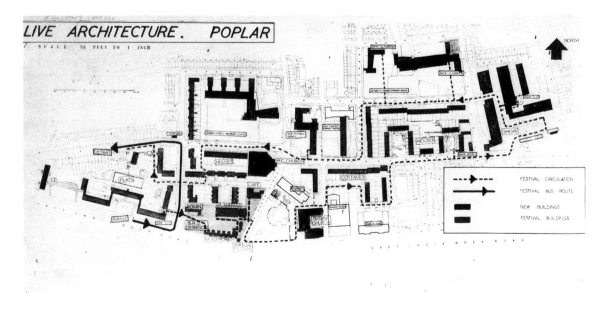

expressed publicly with the support of Patrick Abercrombie. In February 1949 it was determined that the choice of architects for the permanent buildings should be agreed by all parties, while the Festival of Britain would be responsible for the temporary structures and the interiors of show homes to be open during the Exhibition, and Poplar M B would be responsible for street furniture and planting.

By this agreement, 80% of the area was designed by private architects, with only 20% left to be built up with Valuers' housing. The central housing area was divided between Geoffrey Jellicoe, Peter Shepheard of Bridgwater and Shepheard, Graham Dawbarn of Norman and Dawbarn, and Edward Armstrong. This list appears to have been drawn up by the Valuer's Department in close collaboration with the Festival authorities; Geoffrey Jellicoe and Graham Dawbarn were not on the LCC's list of approved private architects but were recommended as having 'considerable experience in the planning and design of varying types of buildings and are well known in the Profession.'[15] When Armstrong pulled out, Jellicoe took over his section too. Judith Ledeboer designed an old people's home. Yorke, Rosenberg and Mardall were commissioned to design a primary school, and Frederick Gibberd was given control of the shopping centre. Other commissions were awarded by private clients. Trinity Congregational Church, destroyed by a V2 rocket, was rebuilt by Cecil Handisyde and T. Rogers Stark. David Stokes was appointed by the Roman Catholic authorities to build a boys' secondary school, and Adrian Gilbert Scott was commissioned to rebuild the bombed Church of Our Lady and St Joseph at the heart of the site. Plans for a health centre had to be abandoned when the National Health Service refused to fund new construction, and its site on East India Dock Road was given over to the temporary exhibition. For the LCC a Reconstruction Group led by Percy Johnson-Marshall led a multi-disciplinary team of architects, planners, landscape architects, and surveyors; and a sociologist, Margaret Willis, was the first to be appointed to a planning team in the United Kingdom.[16]

THE TEMPORARY EXHIBITION

The centrepiece of the accompanying temporary display was to be 'Lilliput', a massive model of the completed site intended at one third scale and to be built by designers from the film industry. It was to be even larger than the futuristic 'Democracity' model which filled the Perisphere at the New York World's Fair. It was a victim of the cuts made in the budget late in 1949, which hit the architectural projects in England and Scotland particularly hard, but in any case there was no sufficiently large open space to put it once the LCC had ruled out the use of its school playgrounds. In its place a tall crane leased from MacAlpine's provided a vertical feature, and was regarded as a genuine novelty.

The main exhibition was held in a large tent at the corner of East India Dock Road and Upper North Street, with the theme of 'New Towns for Old' scripted by Jaqueline Tyrwhitt. The Council for Architecture felt that 'New Towns and Redevelopment were a feature in which this country was leading the world and the main point to be driven home in the Exhibition was the necessity for planning, because of conflicting claims for land.'[17] Tyrwhitt's text began with 'The Battle for Land', and continued through 'the Heart of the Town' to feature the winners of the Festival of Britain Special Architectural Awards. 'The Heart of the Town' was dominated by a mural by Tom Mellor to a very particular brief, for 'a diorama of buildings, trees, sculpture and water ... it should not be treated with nostalgic sharrawaggy'; and after sketches by Bryan Winter and Carel Weight had been rejected, a mural depicting 'The Battle for Land' was commissioned from Stephen Bone. The principal designer was Ronald Avery, working with John Ratcliff, Deputy Architect to the Festival, and Hening and Chitty, the site architects responsible for the layout and coordination of the scheme.[18] John Wright was responsible for the crane and its decoration – it was effectively a

15. London Metropolitan Archives, LCC Housing Committee Presented Papers, LCC/ MIN/7635, 9 March 1949.

16. Survey of London, op.cit., p.219.

17. F.B. Architecture (50) 1, 19 January 1950, in PRO WORK 25/49.

18. Town Planning and Research Sub-Committee meetings, 13 January and 3 March 1950, in A5/E3, PRO WORK 25/49.

19. F.B. Architecture (50), paper 9 March 1950, in PRO WORK 25/49.

20. Conversation with Leonard Manasseh, 2 November 2000.

21. Official Diary, Exhibition of Architecture, Poplar. A2/F5/1, in PRO WORK 25/31.

constructivist 'ready made'. The Building Research Station had its own pavilion, designed as a series of tableaux devoted to problems of rain penetration, heating, lighting, maintenance and noise set in brilliantly painted red and pink boxes.[19] Alongside, Gremlin Grange was a three-quarter scale mock-Tudor house displaying all the structural failures, smoking chimneys and damp problems commonly found in gimcrack suburban houses. Leonard Manasseh took over Sadie Speight's rough sketches for the Rosie Lee tea bar, and developed a jaunty design with a yellow and green canopy, surmounted by an 8' high teapot.[20]

The Festival's landscape architect, Frank Clark, worked with the LCC and Poplar MB on the landscaping and the three authorities collaborated on street furniture (much of it supplied free from manufacturers) and signage. The Central Office of Information and the Festival staff furnished a show house, show flat, and a room in the old people's home, but the LCC's requirement that the Festival pay rent for these precluded their being more than one of each. Visitors to Lansbury paid 1/6d to see the exhibition, which was open until 8pm every night and included admission to the showhouse and flats.

The Official Diary for the exhibition paints a miserable picture of cold, dank weather described as 'December conditions', leaking roofs, and a night-time theft of the souvenir spoons. On Opening Day, 3 May, the construction staff should have worked all night and all morning to complete the Town Planning Pavilion. Instead it was left 25% unfinished, while the Building Research annex was completed only in early June, by which time the low number of visitors had led to London Transport withdrawing its special bus service and to six attendants being made redundant. A large proportion of the visitors were special groups with an interest in housing and planning, and school parties. Yet the final tally of 86,646 visitors now seems remarkable for so small and specialised a show, and more people wandered freely through the neighbourhood itself, particularly at weekends.[21]

THE PERMANENT EXHIBITION – HOUSING

Visitors by bus or river bus were expected to first visit the Town Planning and Building Research Pavilions. There was then a suggested route through the neighbourhood passing behind Trinity Church to the shopping centre, past the schools and back through the housing, dropping in at the show homes, and returning back to the bus stop outside the pavilion enclosure. Yet, in truth, how much was there to see? Much of the housing was being completed only as the Festival itself came to an end, and of the most prominent landmarks, the Clock

22. *Architectural Review*, vol.110, no.660, December 1951, p.361.

23. John Summerson, 'Lansbury', in *New Statesman and Nation*, vol.XLI, no.1058, 16 June 1951, p.679.

24. LCC Housing Committee Presented Papers, London Metropolitan Archives, LCC/MIN/7639, 30 November 1949.

figure 9 · top left
Mr Albert Snoddy and family, including their pet tortoise, Tommy, were the first residents of Lansbury. They moved into a three-bedroom flat in Gladstone House on 14 February 1951. Mrs Snoddy was still living there in 1984. (London Metropolitan Archives)

figure 10 · right
Pekin Close, Bridgwater and Shepheard. (London Metropolitan Archives)

figure 11 · bottom left
Inside one of the show homes. At about £365 the cost of its furnishing was considered rather high. The picture is Edwin LaDell's *Tower of London*, a lithograph published by School Prints Ltd. (London Metropolitan Archives)

Tower was built only in 1952, while only the foundations could be seen of the Roman Catholic church, not completed until 1954. With the built elements so raw and only a model to give an indication of the completed whole, Lansbury seems to have been unfairly condemned.

For while other elements of the Festival of Britain were admired, if sometimes reluctantly by the more serious critics, Lansbury received little save admonishment. J.M. Richards, who was a member of the Festival's Architecture Council, considered the best housing to be the surviving 1860s' terrace in New North Street, while castigating the small-scale and restless detailing of the new work, and asking why 'no large-scale industrially produced components or scientifically devised structural systems' had been experimented with.[22]

There are some rather ordinary blocks of flats and rows of houses, a clever but too emaciated church with a toy tower, a good school, and an experiment in the way of a shopping centre which has pedestrian access only. It is not exciting but it is important, ... because here is the first realisation of a formula for urban re-development which appears to have great merit. Here, conceivably, may be the first step towards the redemption of our disgusting cities. Lansbury is unimposing but not unpromising.[23]

Lansbury's 'formula', however, was to be a model not for London, but for the New Towns such as Stevenage and, particularly, Harlow. This was in part because there was a remit to build at much higher densities in most of the LCC area than were achieved at Lansbury. With the LCC effectively a vacuum for innovation while housing remained within the purlieu of the Valuer, and the small London metropolitan boroughs reliant on private architects for small schemes of flats, no matter how well done, who was to bring Richards's vision to fruition? Richards's opinion, no matter how we may decry it with hindsight, reflected a popular will among young architects anxious to develop the ideas of Le Corbusier's Unité d'Habitation on London soil. And their chance was coming, following the appointment of a principal housing architect and a team of six architects in early 1950 to work under Robert Matthew, initially on the superlatively landscaped sites at Roehampton.[24] But when Lansbury was commissioned in 1949 the architects with experience of designing public housing were those working in the New Towns: Gibberd at Harlow, Shepheard and Judith Ledeboer at Stevenage, Jellicoe at Hemel Hempstead; and many of these same architects had undertaken projects for small provincial towns: Gibberd at Nuneaton, Jellicoe at Mablethorpe in Lincolnshire. It was disillusion with bureaucracy and the slow pace of building in the New Towns that had prompted Peter Shepheard,

figure 12
One of Geoffrey Jellicoe's houses,
no.14 Grundy Street, was decorated as a
'show home' during the exhibition.
A uniformed Festival attendant outside.
(London Metropolitan Archives)

figure 13
Another view of the Jellicoe housing.
(The Architectural Press)

Leonard Manasseh and others into private practice – but they brought with them a New Town aesthetic that was well established in design terms, even if Lansbury was to become the first example to be built.[25] Summerson seems to have recognised this, while Richards aligned himself with the younger generation to whom so much suburban planning was entirely anathema. It must be remembered, too, that most of the East End had traditionally been built up with tiny terraced houses of only two or three storeys, and the LCC were not yet ready to abandon this scale.

The layout for Lansbury was set out and approved in October 1949, with Jellicoe's detailed designs accepted in November, Shepheard's in January 1950 and Dawbarn's in March. All the architects were asked to use London stock bricks and purple grey slates, though some paler Uxbridge bricks and clay tiles were later substituted to bring down costs, notably of Shepheard's scheme.[26] Robert Matthew explained to a LCC Housing Committee suspicious of rising costs that 'stock bricks and slates were chosen for the whole of the Festival area because they are the traditional materials, have excellent weathering qualities and form a good background for the smaller areas of brighter colours on doors, windows, balconies etc., and for planting. It is vitally important to preserve the visual unity of the scheme.'[27] None of the work was technically innovative, save for Dawbarn's terrace of flats set over two-storey maisonettes, where the crosswalls of the flats did not rest logically above those of the maisonettes. The difference between the public and private architects was rather in the complex mixture of house types the latter introduced in an attempt to create a modern form of the three- and four-storey Georgian terraced house, whether set close to the street or in small squares. 'The dregs of classical tradition embody a principle to which, in a revolutionised context, we justly return', commented Summerson.[28] Hence Dawbarn's complex scheme of twelve two-storey maisonettes with nine flats over, the flats served by external staircases to the rear and each with their own canted balcony. More complex still is the larger scheme by Geoffrey Jellicoe along Grundy Street, where three-storey houses, maisonettes and ground-floor bedsits are gathered around two small squares. Pitched roofs and broad stacks are contrasted with spindly steel balustrades and an exposed concrete beam over the set-back, partly tiled ground floor.[29] Most impressive is the relationship between the different-sized elements and the threading of a pedestrian route between them. Sir Peter Shepheard claims that he could have done all his scheme as houses, rather than the mix of two-storey houses and three-storey flats eventually agreed upon; nevertheless his section around Pekin Street has the lowest density, at 87 persons per acre instead of the 136 p.p.a designated for the area.[30]

The area developed by the LCC Housing Division, by contrast, comprised blocks of walk-up, balcony accessed flats varying from three to six storeys, set around the perimeter of the triangular site and enclosing a grassed area and sandpit, now a fenced rose garden and a children's playground. Externally the zig-zag line of blocks formed three sides of a square set-back from the East India Dock Road behind grassed plots; to the rear, along Canton Street, the later

figures 14 &15
Two views of the LCC flats, taken in the 1970s when the original landscaping survived. (Architectural Press)

25. Conversations with Sir Peter Shepheard and Leonard Manasseh, Oct-Nov 2000.

26. *Architect and Building News*, vol.197, no.4251, 9 June 1950, p.591. LCC Housing Minutes, London Metropolitan Archives, LCC/MIN/7305.

27. LCC Presented Papers, Housing Committee 11 October 1950, in London Metropolitan Archives, LCC/MIN/7644.

28. John Summerson, *The Listener*, op. cit., p.679.

29. This can be seen still better at Jellicoe's terrace of old people's flats in Walsall, completed in 1954.

30. Conversation with Peter Shepheard, 6 October 2000.

phase of linking blocks was never completed. The idea of linked perimeter blocks, forming a series of semi-enclosures without and a quiet courtyard within, was popular with the LCC for its post-war flats. It was first demonstrated at the colossal White City development, begun in 1938 and completed after the war, and was followed by many post-war schemes, such as the first phases of the Gascoyne Estate in Hackney, begun in 1947. Only at Woodberry Down was the continental zeilenbau system of parallel blocks introduced, and issues of traffic noise and daylighting fully addressed.[31] At Lansbury the stripped neo-Georgian blocks were given pleasant modern touches with glass bricks to their balcony fronts and thick trellises to their entrances, details that led J.M. Richards to describe them as 'coarse and heavy, but much less offensive than the housing lately put up elsewhere by the same department'.[32] The blocks were named after Commissioners of the 1851 exhibition, as too were those by Peter Shepheard.[33]

'Rest homes for the aged' had been invented during the war for those who had been bombed out of their own homes, and the National Assistance Act of 1948 authorised local authorities to build old people's homes for the first time.[34] London's first purpose-built home was Lansbury Lodge, by Judith Ledeboer of Booth, Ledeboer and Pinkheard, built in 1950–1 and demolished in 1995 after a serious fire. A site was carefully selected opposite two schools and the Roman Catholic church so that there would be plenty of passers by for the residents to watch.[35] Although the southern part of the building was completed by the time of the Festival, and one room was open to visitors as a sort of show home, it was only in December 1951 that the Lodge was formally opened. The accommodation comprised 33 single rooms and eight double bedrooms (for married couples, sisters, brothers or two friends of the same sex to share), with five sitting rooms including a library, and a dining hall that could also be used for religious services, concerts and film shows. With its oversized stacks and – inside – a large, double-height entrance hall wrapped around on three sides by a wide, shallow staircase, Lansbury Lodge had a grandeur disproportionate to its modest two

31. I am grateful to Andrew Saint's research on the Woodbury Down Estate for highlighting this development in LCC planning.

32. *Architectural Review*, vol.110, no.660, December 1951, p.363.

33. *Survey of London*, op. cit., p.224.

34. W. Eric Jackson, *Achievement, A Short History of the London County Council*, London, Longman Green and Co., 1965, p.178.

35. London Metropolitan Archives, LCC/MIN/7365, presented papers February 1949.

figure 16
Lansbury Lodge, the old-people's home by Booth, Ledeboer and Pinkheard, now demolished. (Architectural Press)

storeys, and Ian Nairn appreciated that 'these buildings must somewhere be larger than life as well as being cosy and humane, that the greatest problem of old age is to keep the tensions going.'[36]

THE PERMANENT EXHIBITION – THE SHOPPING CENTRE

The LCC was committed to the preservation of London's street markets, but also to the development of Chrisp Street as a north-south through road following the closure of the adjoining railway line to passenger traffic in 1944. A new market place fulfilled both ambitions. Gibberd designed 38 shops, with two- and three-bedroomed maisonettes over, two pubs, a covered market for the sale of meat

and fish (demolished in 1993 with his adjoining lavatories) and the clock tower. Building began in May 1950 and was completed in November 1951 save for the clock tower, which was begun only in June 1951 and opened on 16 May 1952.

The first pedestrianised shopping centre to be planned – perhaps in Europe – was at Coventry, but Lansbury was the first to be built. It was designed by Frederick Gibberd in 1949, the same year that he produced a similar scheme for The Stow, Harlow's first neighbourhood centre and not originally car-free. Lansbury was tiled in blue and The Stow in yellow. The shops themselves are small by today's standards, particularly the three-storey shop at the corner of the market, which was first intended as a British restaurant, became a furniture store, and is now a neighbourhood housing office. The shops in the northern part of the arcade furthest from the market were always the hardest to let. What works at Lansbury, and looked much better before it was remodelled in 1994–6, is the relationship between the shops and the market, this last a mixture of permanent covered stalls and open street market. The market buildings were commissioned by Poplar M BC, the shops from the LCC; Gibberd seems to have had no difficulty in working for two clients – even when the LCC paid for the clock tower and Poplar for the clock.

The clock tower was intended to provide a vertical feature in a very horizontal scheme, and was seen by Poplar councillors as a statement of civic pride. Gibberd himself determined that it should also be an outlook tower, and designed two scissor stairs that start together but which meet only at the top, in the manner of

figure 17
Perspective by Myerscough Walker of Frederick Gibberd's scheme.
(Gerald Barry archive)

figure 18
Chrisp Street Market as it was in April 1950, before redevelopment.
(Gerald Barry archive)

36. Ian Nairn, op. cit., p.24.

those at Chambord. 'It was a practical folly that gave pleasure, but only for a short time. The fear was suicides; the base was surrounded with spiked railings and the viewing platform enclosed in wire mesh.'[37]

Gibberd also designed a public house at each end of the Market Square. The Festive Briton, now Callaghans, was completed only in July 1952, with interiors by Stewart and Hendry for the brewers Mann, Crossman and Paulin. But at the western end, the Festival Inn was officially opened by Truman, Hanbury, Buxton and Company on 2 May 1951. Its interior, originally by their architect R.W. Stoddart, retains a mirror bearing Abram Games's Festival logo. What has gone is the extraordinary freestanding pub 'sign', a lampstandard with a seat round it, on top of which was a ring of carved figures representing 'typical' Londoners dancing round a 'shaft of light', a streetlight designed as a model of Skylon.[38]

37. Gibberd, op. cit., p.140.

38. *Architects' Journal*, vol.114, no.2949, 6 September 1951, p.293.

figure 19
The Festival Inn in 1974.
(Architectural Press)

figure 20
Chrisp Street Market at the opening of the Clock Tower in May 1952.
(Architectural Press)

figure 21
Chrisp Street Market today.
(English Heritage)

At the northern end of the shopping centre is Susan Lawrence School, for infants and juniors.[39] This was the first building in Lansbury to be begun, in December 1949, and it was not only completed but had been open for a term by May 1951. The architects were Yorke, Rosenberg and Mardall. They had already designed one secondary school, Barclay School in Stevenage, opened in 1950, where they had adapted the light steel-framed Hills' 8'3" system refined by Hertfordshire County Council to two-storey use and clad it in a mixture of brick and natural stone. The use of materials is reminiscent of Denis Clarke Hall's winning design in the *News Chronicle*'s competition of 1937 for an ideal school, a version of which was built at Richmond a year later. Yorke, Rosenberg and Mardall justified their use of mixed materials by the fact that, as a private firm, each of their schools was a one-off.[40] At Susan Lawrence they repeated the Stevenage formula to still greater effect because the school is smaller and more compact. The similarities extend even to the plan of the classroom wing with its upper classrooms for juniors set apart from the corridor, each pair reached from spurs so that the more centrally placed corridor on the floor below serving the infants could get natural daylighting from skylights.

The Elizabeth Lansbury Nursery School, opened in 1952, was a single-storey building to a more informal design. It was the first post-war nursery school built by the LCC, allowed only as a 'special case' with Festival funding, and it made a feature of its toddler-sized furniture and fittings, curly bargeboards and protective canopies. Both schools featured tiles by Peggy Angus, a noted ceramicist and briefly the wife of J.M. Richards. The tiles hard surfaces and bright, repetitive patterns combining a cleanliness, simplicity and gaiety that consummately expressed the architectural ideals of the time, and repeated the Hertfordshire policy of introducing art into schools. Of all the buildings in the Lansbury Exhibition, the Susan Lawrence School was the most admired. 'It seems to have passed its searching test with dazzling success', wrote *Building*, regarding this as a great refinement of ideas explored only tentatively at Barclay School. 'It has urbanity, it has an elegant unity of planning, it is something new in London's East End', which had an interest in child-sized practical spaces.[41] Formally opening the school in April 1951 Gerald Barry considered the importance of an architectural environment for learning, and the way its light, air, colour and equipment were enjoyed by the children attending it. He also singled out the lack of a high perimeter wall as important to the new friendly image for schools.[42] For Ian Nairn it was 'one of the best things the firm has done, large-scaled and relaxed'.[43]

39. Susan Lawrence (1871–1947) was a Municipal Reform (Conservative) member of the LCC who had turned to Labour on seeing conditions in the East End, and had served Poplar and East Ham on the LCC and in parliament, taking a particular interest in education. Elizabeth Lansbury was the wife of the Labour leader, and the nursery was opened by their elder daughter, Dorothy Thurtle. The actress Angela Lansbury was their younger daughter.

40. *Architects' Journal*, vol.114, no.2958, 8 November 1951, p.563.

41. *Building*, vol.26, no.7, July 1951, p.264.

42. Gerald Barry Papers, notes for his speech at the opening of the Ricardo Street School, Poplar, on 26 April 1951.

43. *Architectural Review*, vol.110, no.660, December 1951, op. cit., p.364; Ian Nairn, op. cit, p.25.

figure 22
Susan Lawrence School, by Yorke, Rosenberg and Mardall, from the playground. (London Metropolitan Archives)

The St Philip Howard Secondary School was originally named Cardinal Griffin School after the then Archbishop of Westminster, who laid the foundation stone on 11 July 1950. The school received its first pupils in September 1951, but the dining hall fronting Upper North Street was not completed until September 1952, after the Congregational church had left its mission hall on the site. Originally a relatively small school, with just ten classrooms for 11–15 year-old boys and girls, it was much extended to the north in the 1970s. To the rear, however, the spurs to the main classroom range can be seen, containing arts, crafts and science rooms, as well as the mixture of brick and concrete slabs with which the concrete frame was clad. Of all the Festival buildings it has the least street presence, set back behind dense planting. Closer examination reveals the original parts to be relatively unaltered, but so austere in their detailing as to appear quite dull.

Across Upper North Street from the exhibition site was an open space, landscaped by Handisyde and Stark with a small pool, long filled in. Next to it is the former Trinity Congregational Church, which has been a Methodist church since 1974. The original Trinity Congregational Church got a direct hit from a rocket, and was totally demolished, but the bell survived and this the congregation was keen to reuse. Among the congregation of local shopkeepers and some middle-class 'do-gooders' from further afield was J.R. Stark, an LCC architect nearing retirement, who passed the commission on to his son, Douglas, also an architect with the LCC.[44] Lacking the spare time to carry out the commission himself Stark brought in Cecil Handisyde, an architect at the Building Research Station (BRS) who specialised in research into building materials and services. This was their only collaboration. Handisyde prepared most of the sketch designs, introduced technical innovations, particularly to the roof, and was responsible for the top of the tall tower (necessitated by the bell) resembling Stockholm Town Hall, which he thought magnificent. Stark did a lot of the detailing, including a pulpit of Hopton Wood stone and an etched glass panel in the side wall of the church,

44. This section is based on an interview between Andrew Saint and Cecil Handisyde, 7 August 1991.

figure 23
Cardinal Griffin School, by David Stokes. (Architectural Press)

then a new thing and which Handisyde liked to think inspired Spence's choice of the medium at Coventry. The fact that Stark worked for the LCC helped them to bring their commission within the Lansbury project and to co-ordinate their building programme with the others. The community buildings were ready by May 1951; the church itself was completed a month or so later.

The minister, Balding, Handisyde remembered as very good client, 'educated, a good listener and prepared to work', though initially conservative. He wanted an appreciably smaller church than the old one but one which could accommodate plenty of extra people on special occasions. The galleries, which followed traditional non-conformist lines, were for such occasions. Balding having agreed the plans, Handisyde invited him to see a model of the design, but only after first showing him some still more radical student schemes then on display at the Architectural Association. Balding was at first 'thunderstruck', but then acquiesced to it. The Treasurer of the church council, a City gent, saw the model an hour later and agreed to it because Balding had done so. The architects then attended an open meeting of the church council at which the scheme was unanimously agreed and prayers were said for the architects.

The design incorporated a number of technical ideas Handisyde had been interested in at the BRS, perhaps too many, he subsequently felt. Acoustics were an important factor, for in both the church and the hall the canted and baffled walls reflected Hope Bagenal's ideas that non-parallel surfaces reduced echo. The absolutely flat church ceiling, suspended from structural beams above them, was for the same reason. Balding wanted a well-lit church, and to reduce noise from the road Handisyde and Stark put lights into the roof and reduced the number of windows on the sides. Hidden lighting in the chancel, with tinted glass on one side, was carefully calculated to avoid glare, which was also why there is no east window. The underflow heating was a BRS idea also. The design was considered in terms of the problems to be solved rather than previous church architecture, with Handisyde egged on by the engineer Felix Samuely. Hence the exposed concrete frame from which the roof is hung, made as thin as possible and bush hammered. In 1972–4 Edward Mills restored the church for the local Methodist community, and adapted many of the community facilities as a hostel for Vietnamese refugees.[45]

The Roman Catholic Church, now known as SS Mary and Joseph, was built to replace a bombed church on the site now occupied by the Cardinal Griffin School. As part of the Festival scheme it became one of the first churches to be funded by the War Damages Commission, and Adrian Gilbert Scott was commissioned in 1948 to build a new church. A condition of the licence, reflecting a policy of the War Damages Commission, was that the new church should be the same size as the old, with 800 seats, although much of the population of the area had been dispersed.[46] The result is that the church is the most monumental building in the exhibition area and a stronger focus for the western part of the site than is Gibberd's clock tower to the east.

The site was an awkward one, being almost square. The presbytery sits on the opposite side of Pekin Street from the church, and was to have been linked by a covered way. In the church's Greek cross plan one can see echoes of the work of Scott's older brother Giles at Ampleforth (1922–61), and particularly of his 1943–5 scheme for the rebuilding of Coventry Cathedral. Sir Giles Scott's Coventry was not only liturgically inventive in its 'T'-shaped plan, but it was there that the parabolic arch construction that is a feature of both brothers' post-war work first appears. This last is also a feature of the conventionally-planned St Leonard's, St Leonards-on-Sea, Sussex, rebuilt to Adrian's design from 1953 onwards after that of 1945–6 by Giles was rejected as too expensive.[47] SS Mary and Joseph is thus the closest built expression of Giles's scheme for Coventry. It is extremely early in the development of liturgically-influenced planning in Britain, and its four equal and very broad arms have enabled the altar under its baldacchino to

figure 24
Trinity Congregational Church, by Handisyde and Stark, now Trinity Methodist Church. (Elain Harwood)

figure 25
The Roman Catholic Church of SS Mary and Joseph, by Adrian Gilbert Scott, towering behind Pekin Close in the mid-1950s. (London Metropolitan Archives)

45. Letter from Edward Mills, 16 January 1996.
46. Public Record Office, IR 34658.
47. *The Builder*, vol.170, 26 April 1946. Louise Campbell, *Coventry Cathedral, Art and Architecture in post-war Britain*, Oxford, Clarendon Press, 1996, pp.22–31.

be brought forward in accordance with modern practice entirely successfully. The church's yellow Leicestershire brick and brown 'Lombardic' tile roof, also reminiscent of the Coventry scheme, fits gracefully amid the surrounding housing in what Gavin Stamp describes as a Jazz-moderne Byzantine style and reminiscent of Clemens Holzmeister's Vienna crematorium of 1922.[48] Scott designed all the interior furnishings, from the large marble baldacchino down to the hymn boards. The interior features an eight feet high dado of blue Hornton stone, into which the Stations of the Cross by Peter Watts are set. The soaring upper parts of the church were covered in acoustic tiles which soon discoloured black, but which were painted in the mid-1990s. The incumbent, Canon John Wright, was an amateur architect who seems to have personally supervised the works; the weekday chapel formed from the priest's sacristy in 1979 is dedicated to his memory.

This was the most derided of all the buildings at Lansbury. Condemnation began when it was but a hole in the ground, and when it opened in 1954 Ian Nairn brutally condemned its 'sprawling, lumpish mass' with no understanding of the underlying novelty of its plan or attention to detail. 'Here is a building that is both aggressive *and* flaccid, vulgar *and* genteel, pretentious *and* timid.'[49] A generation later it is possible to accept the building on its own terms, Esher in 1981 recognising that 'the fortress-like Catholic church that once seemed so old-fashioned ... is now so functional.'[50] There was a satisfying irony when it became the first building in Lansbury to be listed, in 1998.

CONCLUSION

Lansbury is special precisely because, as Gibberd planned, it was permanent. 'It did not go to the breakers; even the vertical feature, the tower crane, went on to move many thousands of tons of building materials.'[51] It was bright, cheerful and human in scale at a time when nothing else had been built. Yet it occupies a pioneering place in the New Towns movement, rather than serving as a model for the rebuilding of London. The best summary of its significance was provided by Clough Williams Ellis, writing as the New Towns were finally getting underway, in 1954. 'One welcomed this brave new baby townlet, peeping hopefully out, as it were like a little kangaroo from the pouch of its old mother borough of Poplar. The child of her shabby old age, there was something poignantly inspiriting about its own fresh vigour, its well-articulated little minimal body with all its parts properly proportioned and promising to function as they should.'[52] Nairn recognised it as something more, that 'this is the one neighbourhood where a genuine attempt has been made to reinterpret the old pattern and not superimpose a new one. It is not entirely successful – few first attempts are – but it is a brave try.'[53] While we may disdain the window replacement and individual personalisation which has destroyed its homogeneity, it can equally be claimed that it is its small-scale and populist raggedness which still makes Lansbury an identifiable place, with a bit of a buzz. 'Lansbury's architecture may be bland but its staying power has been proved.'[54] It was declared a Conservation Area in 1998, and though promised improvements to the environment have yet to be seen, the buzz that this is a special place is spreading.

48. Gavin Stamp, in *Catalogue of the Drawings Collection of the RIBA, The Scott Family*, London, Gregg International, 1981, p.185.

49. Ian Nairn, 'Lansbury Centrepiece', in *Architectural Review*, vol.116, no.694, October 1954, p.263.

50. Lionel Esher, *A Broken Wave*, London, Allen Lane, 1981, p.120.

51. Frederick Gibberd, in *A Tonic to the Nation*, op. cit., p.141.

52. Clough Williams Ellis, 'The Lansbury Exemplar', in *Architecture and Building*, vol.29, no.10, October 1954, p.367.

53. Ian Nairn, *Architectural Review*, vol.116, no.694, October 1954, op. cit., p.264.

54. Lionel Esher, op. cit., p.120.

15 'Restive rather than festive': Coventry and the Festival of Britain

ROBERT GILL

'Restive rather than festive':
Coventry and the Festival of Britain

ROBERT GILL

figure 1
The Godiva Pageant. Lady Godiva.
(*Coventry Evening Telegraph*)

THE Festival is nation-wide ... Britain was regularly assured, and to prove it Arts festivals were staged in the right sort of towns – Stratford-upon-Avon, Bath, York, etc. – not to mention the widespread fêtes, flower shows, Morris Dancing and so on, thought to represent the national character and dubbed 'The Merrie Effort' by *Punch*.

Even Coventry, a place of industry, lacking cultural amenities and with a war-devastated centre, pressed its claims early, and, if the Corporation's news-sheet can be trusted, was rather put out not to be chosen as one of the provincial centres.[1] After that initial disappointment the Labour-controlled council appointed a Festival of Britain sub-committee which reported back early in 1950[2] with ideas under three headings: Reconstruction; Development of Mechanical Transport; Drama and Pageantry. From these, on a limited budget and with rather less than universal enthusiasm, a programme of events was devised that did attract some national attention.

Reconstruction, not surprisingly, came first in Coventry, symbol of Blitz devastation. But in 1950 Donald Gibson's ambitious redevelopment plan had practically stalled in the face of Government emphasis on industrial production before all else; with little to show but the Godiva Statue and the beginnings of Broadgate House. So it was proposed that the foundation stones of a civic theatre and art gallery could be laid in 1951 – a symbolic act with no prospect that a start could be made on either building. It was also recommended that a Planning and Redevelopment Exhibition be held during the festival period. Secondly, Coventry was the birthplace of mass car production in Britain, with a central role in the early days of cycles and motor-cycles. And finally, Coventry possessed a unique bit of pageantry, the Godiva Procession, staged infrequently enough for each revival to be a notable local event.

The sub-committee had recommended a grant of £25,000, but this was a time of continuing economic difficulties and shortages. Following a rate rise of 14% in April 1950, it was hardly surprising that in August, when the Mayor, Alderman J Howat, moved a General Purposes Committee resolution that the Council approve finance for Coventry's Festival of Britain, the sum had been reduced to £5,000. There was even an unsuccessful Conservative amendment to reduce this further to £1,000, though the proposer was at pains to stress that he did not oppose the principle of the celebration.[3] The local (Conservative) weekly, the *Coventry Standard*, had applauded the reduction to £5,000, describing the mood of the people as 'restive rather than festive'.[4] Even so it was prepared to concede that in the climate of 'dark foreboding' some diversion might be welcome, and that there would be support for a revival of the Godiva Pageant.

Responding to the drastic cut in budget, the Festival sub-committee looked to voluntary organisations and local firms to underwrite the events. A Pageant Master was appointed, Leonard Turner, deputy principal of Coventry Technical College, and best-qualified having run two previous Godiva Pageants in 1929 and 1936. During the early months of 1951 he became a familiar figure to readers of the *Coventry Evening Telegraph* with PR stories aimed to build interest: that 1,500

1. *Coventry Civic Affairs, the Monthly News-Sheet of the Corporation of Coventry*, August 1949.
2. *Coventry Civic Affairs*, February 1950.
3. *Coventry Evening Telegraph*, 2 August 1950.
4. *Coventry Standard*, 21 July 1950.

costumes had been hired from two London theatrical costumiers; that the procession might be more than 2½ miles long; that 'Sauce', the circus elephant chosen to represent Coventry's elephant and castle coat of arms, might have to be accompanied by her inseparable companion 'Salt', thus duplicating the civic symbol ...

However, two months before the event, in a surprisingly frank speech to the Coventry Publicity Association, the Pageant Master referred to some of the problems. Limited finance had meant abandoning plans for 12,000 capacity stands in the War Memorial Park, and the staging there of a large industrial exhibition. The onus had been placed on local voluntary organisations and industrialists, but these initially had proved difficult to mobilise. He described the spirit for the pageant as less than in previous times.[5] The experience of Coventry Guild of Citizens, as reported in their newsletter, illustrates this: 'we volunteered to take part and ... the Guild was given the opportunity of depicting the opening of Coventry Railway Station approximately one hundred years ago. As this was not considered a particularly suitable subject and as British Railways did not show any great interest, members preferred to give assistance individually'.[6]

Even so, a substantial 'Festival of Britain Official Programme' – 80 pages including advertisements and priced at one shilling – was published by the Corporation's Public Relations Department, and the entire edition of 15,000 sold out.[7] There was to be a Festival Week, beginning on Saturday 17 June with the Bishop of Coventry preaching in Holy Trinity and ending with a mass church rally in Broadgate. Apart from the main event, the Godiva Procession on Saturday afternoon, it was thin stuff – some sporting events, a fair, circus, and the final of the 'Miss Coventry' competition. These were austere and egalitarian times, reflected in the condition of the beauty contest. 'In order to remove any unfair advantage which the possession of an exclusive or expensive dress might give, candidates are required to appear before the judges in a jumper and skirt'.[8]

The Godiva Pageant and Procession was divided into two parts, historical and industrial. The first part consisted of twelve 'episodes' – significant moments in Coventry's history from the 1951 Corporation back to Lady Godiva, played by Ann Wrigg, a London repertory actress with some TV and radio experience, notably in Wilfred Pickles productions. The second part covered the development of Coventry's major industries – textiles; watches and clocks; cycles and motor-cycles; machine tools; motor cars and aeroplanes – in a series of tableaux with motor transport predominant. Drama groups, silver bands, NALGO and other organisations were involved in the historical section; Daimler, Humber and other well-known car firms, Courtaulds, and some smaller businesses were responsible for the industrial section.

Naturally there were fears about the weather, but on the day the rain just held off. The Festival of Britain flag flew on Broadgate House, heralding not just the

5. *Coventry Standard*, 4 May 1951.
6. *The Coventry Watchman*, December 1951.
7. *Coventry Evening Telegraph*, 21 June 1951.
8. Official Programme.

figure 2
The Godiva Pageant. The Coventry Martyrs' float with Broadgate House behind. (*Coventry Evening Telegraph*)

figure 3
The Godiva Pageant. The Motor Cycle Float with the festival symbol and showing the bridge of Broadgate House. (A.H. Lealand)

pageant but the completion of the top floor of this first block of the new city centre. The procession, over 2,000 strong, left the War Memorial Park at 3pm and followed a long route round the city for 2½ hours before returning to the park. A giant phoenix made by Art students was to the fore in the 'Spirit of Coventry – 1940' episode, and there were indeed two elephants, though only one bore a castle. On foot were bands of peasants, bowmen, eighteenth-century citizens and the like; with some unscripted drama supplied by Godiva's horse which gave her a rough ride, spooked by the crowds, perhaps, or the elephants. The crowds were very large, even if an official estimate of 500,000 – about double the city's population – sounds incredible.[9]

The burden of being regarded as Coventry's main contribution to an important national event seems to have engendered a seriousness noticeably different from previous processions, and rather at odds with the playful spirit usually associated with the Festival of Britain. The tone was set, for one local reporter, by the phoenix rising from the ashes and the tableau of the cathedral ruins:

Perhaps because it was a pageant, and not the carnival of former years, this note of dignity was struck, and maintained a respectful reverence as centuries of the city's magnificent history trundled by ,[10]

Elsewhere it was felt to be 'half gay, half solemn',[11] and, while letters published in the local press were mostly positive, one did take up this theme:

Sir, in my opinion the Godiva Pageant was too serious and "far above" the heads of the thousands of children in Coventry … the "set" costumes and scenes were too morbid and dull and not in keeping with our great "Festival Year".[12]

The Pageant Master was unrepentant:

It was our intention to have a pageant and not a carnival. That was what we had. I did not want baloney, big heads or balloons.[13]

The Public Relations Department had claimed it as a success in advance –

'*probably the most attractive provincial contribution to the general national festivities*'[14]

with publicity 'world-wide' by press, radio, cinema and television. And it was duly summed up in characteristic upbeat local authority PR style:

'*The pictures and stories which have appeared everywhere as a result and the publicity for the city is most valuable in many ways not directly connected with this particular occasion. Coventry is very much "on the map".*'[15]

Extending beyond Coventry's Festival Week, other events received the Festival imprimatur. The Mystery Plays were staged in the Cathedral ruins throughout June, with a Festival concert featuring suitable composers – Elgar, Walton, Ireland and Vaughan Williams – at the Hippodrome in September. More interesting, reflecting the national dimension to Coventry's reconstruction, two architecture exhibitions achieved 'official' status by virtue of attracting some Arts Council funding.

The original idea of a Planning and Redevelopment Exhibition was realised by the expanding of an already proposed show of the work of the Coventry Society of Architects. It was staged at the Herbert Temporary Art Gallery – the basement of the never completed pre-war gallery – from June 4th to the 30th, and consisted of 49 perspective drawings, 15 models and 40 photographs. Donald Gibson, City Architect and Planning Officer; W.S. Hattrell and Partners; Hellberg and Harris; and C.F. Redgrave and Partners were strongly represented. Gibson showed drawings of Broadgate House, Council offices, shopping precinct blocks, old people's bungalows and a three-bedroom house; and models of Broadgate House, the Broadgate hotel, a secondary school and a one-bedroom flat; but with Broadgate House not completed and little else built there were no photographs.

W.S. Hattrell had a model of Coundon Court Primary School, and a number of photographs, chiefly industrial and commercial buildings, but including three private houses, whose scarcity in this exhibition the local paper noted as 'a sign of the bureaucratic times'.[16] Hellberg and Harris's drawings included a training

figure 4
The Godiva Pageant. The Electrical Home float. (BTH Ltd)

9. *Coventry Civic Affairs*, July 1951.

10. *Coventry Standard*, 29 June 1951.

11. Quoted, unattributed, in E.B. Newbold, *Portrait of Coventry*, 1972, p.195.

12. *Coventry Evening Telegraph*, 27 June 1951.

13. *Coventry Evening Telegraph*, 28 June 1951.

14. Quoted, unattributed, in *Coventry Civic Affairs*, June 1951.

15. *Coventry Civic Affairs*, July 1951.

16. *Coventry Evening Telegraph*, 2 June 1951.

college hostel, two schools and the Broadgate department store; with models of the department store and a Roman Catholic secondary school; and photographs of a factory, a school and two houses, one in Birmingham. C.F. Redgrave had models of a Methodist church, neighbourhood flats and a community centre; with photographs of junior and infant schools, an orthopaedic centre, a church and hall, and a weaving mill in Stoke-on-Trent.

The local paper was impressed – 'Coventry for its enterprise in reconstruction and Coventry architects for the excellence of their designs have gained a national reputation ... ' [17] and a few days later ran a picture of the model of Redgrave's Methodist church, due to be built in suburban Macdonald Road, with the comment:

Like all the other models that are featured in the Festival Exhibition of Coventry architects ... it reveals a striking modernity of design. [18]

Such perceived modernity was not to everyone's taste – the Conservative Mayor, Harry Weston, confessed at the opening to 'a certain amount of fear and anxiety' [19] – though to us now this small brick church surely looks to be a typically modest product of post-war austerity. This had indeed been acknowledged in the foreword to the exhibition catalogue (presumably written by the Society's chairman, Rolf Hellberg):

... the qualities good buildings should possess are sincerity, simplicity and good manners. We believe that in assessing the qualities of buildings in this country today, some consideration should be given to the post-war difficulties of high cost, shortage of building labour and fluctuations in supply and scarcity of materials. These difficulties cause contemporary design to lay stress on simplicity and economy. [20]

The recorded attendance at the exhibition was 6,714, an average of 280 people a day. [21]

At the very end of June the other exhibition to receive Arts Council funding was held in St Mary's Hall, the medieval guildhall. Running for one week only, it was advertised as the 'International Theatre Institute Exhibition of Theatrical Architecture', with plans, models and photographs of modern theatres in 22 countries. From its opening in Paris the year before, in conjunction with a conference, it went to Germany, with Coventry the only appearance in this country before the return to Paris. Richard Southern, a London theatre consultant who arranged the exhibition in Coventry, said that the city was chosen 'partly' due to the major reconstruction programme, which might eventually include a civic theatre. [22]

All in all, it would be fair to say that Coventry had taken the Festival of Britain seriously, perhaps too seriously in some ways. But neither Donald Gibson nor the influential members of the Council had been closely involved, and it all evaporated rather quickly, leaving no mark on the city. The Mayor, Harry Weston, announced in July that he would be commissioning local artists to execute murals ' ... to commemorate the Festival of Britain and pay permanent tribute to the city's craftsmen of the past ... ' [23] but it seems that nothing ever came of this. Weston, a wealthy industrialist, did commission a stained glass window depicting a Coventry craftsman for the West Orchard Congregational church then under construction in the suburb of Cheylesmore, but the inscription at the base commemorates his mayoralty with no mention that it was Festival of Britain year.

At the planning stage the intention had regularly been expressed that projects of lasting value to the community would result from the Festival. There had been talk at the sub-committee of laying foundation stones, even that there might be monies remaining and profits to establish 'as a permanent symbol of the Festival of Britain, a Civic Theatre.' [24] The aftermath was pure bathos. It was resolved that some of what remained of the £5,000 grant be spent on providing two seats for elderly people in both the War Memorial and Naul's Mill parks. The seats were to bear plaques, not commemorating the Festival of Britain but two former Mayors of Coventry. [25] Any money still left over would be used to provide TV sets for old people's homes.

17. Coventry Evening Telegraph, 2 June 1951.

18. Coventry Evening Telegraph, 8 June 1951.

19. Coventry Evening Telegraph, 4 June 1951.

20. Festival Exhibition of Architecture, catalogue, Herbert Art Gallery collection.

21. Coventry Standard, 6 July 1951.

22. Coventry Evening Telegraph, 28 June 1951.

23. Coventry Evening Telegraph, 27 June 1951.

24. Coventry Standard, 15 September 1950.

25. Coventry Evening Telegraph, 9 October 1951.

16 Trowell, Festival Village

ELAIN HARWOOD

Granite

CONSTRUCTION

DESIGNED TO BUILD

0332 - 340113

A member of the **Birch** *group of companies*

Trowell, Festival Village

ELAIN HARWOOD

IN 1951 2,000 towns and villages staged events connected with the Festival of Britain. Glasgow mounted an exhibition of heavy engineering, and Belfast one on agriculture. Around the country special events were arranged at the established arts festivals, from the historic Three Choirs Festival to the International Eisteddfod founded at Llangollen only in 1947. At Stonehenge the Festival was celebrated on Sunday, 8 July by the service of the Golden Dawn, and a noonday Crowning and Holy Union.[1] Tours were arranged round the building site that was Stevenage New Town, while the picturesque Cotswold village of Stanton built model cottages 'in a traditional style'.[2] The National Association of Parish Councils promoted a tidy village scheme and the building of rural bus stops, while the Gardening Association sponsored a 'best kept garden' competition. Rural councils pushed programmes of new sewers and electric street lights, along with dances and sporting events. But one village put together a more extensive programme than any other, and in doing so earned itself the title 'Festival Village'. In the Festival Committee's final report its location is given as Northamptonshire, in *A Tonic to the Nation* as Buckinghamshire. In fact Trowell sits forlornly on the Nottinghamshire/Derbyshire border, loveless and unlovely; today few local people know the reason why its pub is called the Festival Inn. If Trowell is known at all, it is because it has given its name to a service station on the M1.

Trowell was chosen from over a thousand submissions to appear in the Festival of Britain Souvenir Programme as 'an example of what a small community has done to celebrate the Festival and make itself a better place in which to live.'[3] It was also said to be close to the exact centre of Britain. There was no suggestion that Trowell could begin to match the beautiful villages of Dorset or the Cotswolds. 'They represent the Britain of 1851, but in many places like our own, the hundred years have almost destroyed the old conditions and Trowell represents 1951.'[4] Herbert Morrison considered that the object of the selection was to encourage villages, which were not conventionally beautiful to 'have a go'.[5] In a parody of the bar room talk of D.H. Lawrence's *Sons and Lovers*, the *New Statesman* questioned the choice of 'some obscure village in the Sheers, name o'Trowel. One and all disclaimed knowledge of the place while agreeing that, since it was in the Sheers, it could not be worth knowing.'[6] Gerald Barry recorded in February 1951 that not all the members of the Festival Council and its administration supported the selection. 'My own view is that this was an unfortunate, indeed a rather thoughtless choice, but we must see it through now.'[7]

There is a medieval church, much restored, a few farms, and a canal. But by 1951 Trowell had become a dormitory village, with most people working in Nottingham and Ilkeston, home of textile industries that employed many women. On the other side of the valley was Stanton Ironworks, a local landmark and the centre of a distinctive community until it was finally demolished in around 1990. *The boundary between Nottingham City and Trowell will be signposted at Balloon Houses and the first approach is along the green belt known as Trowell Moor, down Pinfold Hill to Canal Bridge, where a stop should be made for the view there to be obtained. At the*

figure 1
Festival Inn sign, Trowell, about to be demolished. (Elain Harwood)

1. PRO WORK 25/241.

2. Built by H.T. Rainger, and opened by the Chairman of the Festival, Lord Ismay, Chairman of the Festival Council, on 5 May 1951. In PRO WORK 25/241.

3. Basil Taylor, *Festival of Britain, Official Souvenir Programme*, London, HMSO, 1951, p.67.

4. Trowell Official Programme, 1951, in E2/A-T, PRO WORK 25/241.

5. Alan Cook, *A History of Trowell, Ilkeston and District Local History Society*, 1995, p.78.

6. S.L.B., *New Statesman and Nation*, 23 April 1951, p.473.

7. Gerald Barry personal diary, unpublished; 15 February 1951.

bottom of the little hill and in the centre of the picture is the twelfth-century church of St Helen. Around it are the houses and in the background, dominating the scene, are the great Ironworks of Stanton with their blast furnaces and slag tips and haze of smoke – an impressive scene by day and a veritable pyrotechnic display by night. This is the England of 1951 and this is what you have come to see.[8]

On 27 July 1950 the Parish Council had held a meeting to consider what contribution Trowell could make to the Festival. A proposed levy of 2d on the rates was rejected, and instead a door-to-door collection raised £30 to promote events in the village. In addition there was an information centre and tours of the church. Leaderflush Doors, the largest firm in the village, had an exhibition of their work, with factory tours and teas after 3.30. There were bus tours of the village run daily by the Midlands Omnibus Company, with special events on Wednesday and Saturday afternoons. A series of cricket matches were organised, with the one on 23 June played in Victorian costume. Trowell's 'own concert party, The Frolics', performed on 6 June, and amateur groups from Nottingham presented *As You Like It* and an 'old English comedy', *The Dumb Wife of Cheapside*. Another amateur group, the Nottingham Starlighters, produced a revue. There were competitions for a Rose Queen, and a fancy dress parade on 7 July was judged by the Ilkeston Carnival Queen. In addition to a conventional gymkhana, opened by Herbert Morrison, the Stapleford and District Motorcycle club staged a Motor Cycle Gymkhana. The events culminated in August with the judging of the best flower and vegetable gardens, the Garden Association Show, and an 'Old Tyme Dance' and ended on 8 September with a Fancy Dress Ball.

So what came of all these events? Plans for a hotel 'designed to be in keeping with the historic corner near the church have been drawn up', to be built after the withdrawal of building licences in November 1951. The Festival Inn was duly built in a stripped roadhouse style in 1954. Until March 1995 its sign bore Abram Games's Festival logo, but even this has now gone, though the name remains. In August 1976 the Festival was commemorated by a no less ambitious series of slightly more modern events, including cricket matches, discos, and a recording by the BBC of its programme, *Any Questions?*

Assessing the Festival's successes in August 1951 the Festival Council had to admit that it had been the homegrown events organised by local town and parish councils whose success 'had far exceeded expectations'. The revival of the York Mystery Plays, the restoration of the York Assembly Rooms and buildings in King's Lynn and Norwich were singled out as special achievements.[9] Yet Trowell's modest events also took their place in the final reckoning. 'So successful was the varied and ambitious programme organised by the people of Trowell that it attracted visitors from overseas and all parts of the British Isles.'[10] The Festival Council also reported that 'in the village itself was awakened a new and lively interest in communal activity.'[11] And as Trowell sets out to celebrate its Golden Anniversary as the Festival Village, it seems that the unlikely choice was vindicated.

8. Trowell Official Programme, 1951, op. cit.

9. PRO WORK 25/43, A5/A3 FB.C (51)2, Council Minutes 15 August 1951.

10. *The Story of the Festival of Britain*, London, Festival Council, 1952, p.28.

11. ibid.

17 The Festival of Britain Special Architectural Awards

ELAIN HARWOOD

The Festival of Britain
Special Architectural Awards

ELAIN HARWOOD

O NE of the very first actions of the Festival organisers was to organise a limited competition for a 'Festival Symbol'. In June 1948 twelve designers were invited to submit ideas, among them Robin Day, Edward Bawden and Milner Gray. The winners were Abram Games and Lynton Lamb, and Games's design was eventually selected by the Festival Council in December that year. The idea of using the Symbol as the design for an award for good architecture and landscape seems first to have been proposed by Howard Lobb, Chairman of the Council of Architecture advising the Festival, at its September 1948 meeting. He 'had in mind something comparable to the R I BA Bronze Medal', or a plaque.[1] The idea was approved at the same meeting as was Games's design.

The plaque was developed from Games's motif of a Britannia-headed compass star by the sculptor H. Wilson Parker, who had worked on Norwich Town Hall and Hertfordshire County Hall and Library. He had previously designed the Wren on the farthing coin and the India General Service Medal.[2] It was manufactured by Poole Pottery, with a matt blue slip on which the Britannia symbol and the words 'Festival of Britain Award for Merit, 1951' are raised in white. The coloured slip technique was that already adopted for the commemorative plaques found across London, which Poole went on to manufacture between 1955 and 1981, but the matt finish – characteristic of Poole's post-war work – and the greater precision of the raised figure and lettering make the Festival plaques more sophisticated. Three of the Norfolk plaques were made locally, and the lower quality is immediately evident.

The Award could be made for any 'contribution to civic or landscape design, including any buildings, groups of buildings or improvements to the rural or urban scene.' Single buildings were not originally eligible for the Award, but this was modified to include individual items like schools and factories if, in the view of the Jury, they made a definitive contribution to civic design or landscape development. Individual private houses remained excluded. The change reflects the shortage of entries, and the lack of variety – for so many of the submissions were housing estates. Any scheme had to be 'visually comprehendible as a whole', so complete neighbourhoods or New Towns were also excluded. To qualify for the award, buildings had to be begun after VJ Day, 15 August 1945, to have been sufficiently completed by 1 September 1950 to be photographed, and had to be unconnected with the Festival of Britain.[3] Although the Award was aimed equally at architecture and landscaping schemes, the garden entries were particularly disappointing, and only the Memorial Gardens in Royston received a plaque.

The Council of Architecture considered setting up a special jury to make the awards, but eventually determined that as the architectural advisors to the Festival, and promoters of the competition, it was best qualified to choose the winners itself. Its membership was composed of established architects, planners and engineers: Professor H.V.A. Briscoe, F.J. Forty, William Holford, Robert Matthew, Rowland Nicholas, Sir George Pepler, and Howard Robertson, with J.M. Richards representing architectural criticism and younger ideas, and Hugh Casson as the Festival's Director of Architecture. The deadline for entries was

figure 1
Blue Plaque design by H. Wilson Parker based on Abram Games symbol.

figure 2
Blue Festival Plaque, Newbury Park Bus Station. (Elain Harwood)

1. F.B. Architecture (48) 2, 7 September 1948, in A5/E1–2, PRO WORK 25/49.
2. PRO WORK 25/19 A1/E3 'Biographies'.
3. A1/J1/2, 16 April 1951, in PRO WORK 25/20.

initially set at September 1950, but because the response was 'meagre', Casson was asked to get more publicity for the scheme. The final deadline was 31 March 1951, by which time 173 entries had been received.[4]

It was up to the architect or client to enter a building, and notable absentees include examples of Hertfordshire's prefabricated schools, now seen as among the most ambitious and distinctive buildings of the 1940s. Nevertheless, the entries offer a snapshot of building in the immediate post-war years. They reflect the early start in housing reconstruction made by the London metropolitan boroughs, who had been required by Government to make plans as early as 1943, but they also show the importance in the 1940s of rural council housing, and that small urban authorities were also producing interesting schemes. Indeed, because of subsequent cuts in Government grants, many of the best post-war housing schemes are those of the 1940s. New schools and factories featured less prominently in the submissions.

The most popular schemes, with nine votes each, were Newbury Park Bus Station by Oliver Hill, and a terrace of four houses in Asthall, Oxfordshire, by the Peter Dunham Group. It is sometimes stated that The Lawn, Harlow, has one of the Festival of Britain Awards.[5] In fact its plaque commemorates its opening in May 1951 as one of the Festival events, and it would have been insufficiently complete to have been entered into the competition in 1950. In York, too, there is a block of flats specially commissioned and built for the Festival.

Here is the list of nineteen winners.

4. F.B.A (50) 7, 21 September 1950. Special meeting of the Council for Architecture, 12 April 1951. Both in PRO WORK 25/49.

5. See, for example, Frederick Gibberd et al, *Harlow, the Story of a New Town*, Harlow Development Corporation, 1980, p.107.

Passfield, Bromley Road, Lewisham. Fry and Drew, 1949–50 This small development has stronger associations with Berthold Lubetkin's post-war flats at Spa Green and Priory Green than with Maxwell Fry's flats of the 1930s. The main block of flats and maisonettes uses Ove Arup's box-frame system of construction, and expresses it in the projecting clusters of balconies that denote the larger units. The plaque is situated on the curved wing of smaller flats to the side. Listed grade II.
Architectural Review, vol.109, no.649, January 1951, pp.7–15

figure 4
Barclay School, Walkern Road, Stevenage. Yorke, Rosenberg and Mardall, 1947–49, 1951.
(Elain Harwood)

Barclay School, Walkern Road, Stevenage. Yorke, Rosenberg and Mardall. 1947–49, 1951. This was the first significant secondary school to be built after the war. Eugene Rosenberg gave the standard light steel frame developed by Herts CC a more elaborate dress of brick, with some rough stonework at the entrance. The classrooms are arranged to allow a maximum of light and space within a quadrangular plan, and there is a mural by Kenneth Rowntree and a *Family Group* by Henry Moore. Listed grade II.
Architectural Review, vol.106, no.633, September 1949, pp.169–76

figure 3
Passfield, Bromley Road, Lewisham.
Fry and Drew, 1949–50.
(Elain Harwood)

figure 5
Flats in St Pancras Way, Camden.
Norman and Dawbarn, 1947–8.
(Elain Harwood)

Flats in St Pancras Way, Camden.
Norman and Dawbarn, 1947–8. St
Pancras was the first London borough to build large housing schemes
after the war. The layout, in rows
instead of around courtyards, but
giving on to a central garden and
play area, together with the modern
brick design, were then innovatory.
The scheme included its own electric
substation and laundry. The original
balcony fronts were of alternating
red and green sheet steel; the
present patterned balcony fronts are
a modernisation of the 1990s.
Architectural Review, vol.106, no.632,
August 1949, pp.80–5

**Old People's Housing in Crosshill
and Queen's Avenues, Glasgow.**
A.G. Jury, Director of Housing,
1949–50. This group of single-storey
dwellings set among mature trees
forms part of the massive Pollok
Estate developed by Glasgow City
Council from 1937 onwards. They
form an enclave in the development
of flats, two-storey 'cottage' apart-
ments and houses developed after
1945. Their steeply pitched tiles
roofs with little windows contrast
with the concrete block and rendered brick used elsewhere. Jury
went on to become City Architect in
1951.
Building, vol.28, no.1, January 1953,
pp.11–13

**Chaucer House, Coleridge House,
Shelley House and Pepys House,
with accumulator tower, Churchill
Gardens, Pimlico.** Powell and
Moya, 1948–50.
The first five blocks of the large
Churchill Gardens Estate built for
Westminster City Council. This was
the most prestigious competition of
the 1940s, which was won by Powell
and Moya in 1945. Its scale sets it
apart from any other scheme of the
period, though these early blocks
are largely faced in brick, save for
their glazed staircase towers, whose
repeated pattern give the long,
straight blocks their continental
character and architectural distinc-
tion. The round, glazed accumulator tower was built to store waste

figure 6
Old People's Housing in Crosshill and
Queen's Avenues, Glasgow. A.G. Jury,
Director of Housing, 1949–50.
(Corporation of Glasgow)

figure 7
Accumulator tower and flats, Churchill Gardens, Pimlico. Powell and Moya, 1948–50.

heat from Battersea Power Station, and provides a contrast. Open gardens and round bin stores complete the group. These blocks are listed, and the whole of the estate is a Conservation Area.
Architectural Review, vol.109, no.650, February 1951, pp.71–9; vol.110, no.659, October, pp.243–7.

Somerford Estate, Dalston, Hackney. Frederick Gibberd, 1947–9. An early, relatively small but intricate example of a 'mixed development', carefully designed to provide a variety of housing in interconnected urban squares, with pedestrian routes separated from traffic areas. Gibberd sought to group the five different types of housing in a series of closes, each with its own character and giving diagonal views from one to another. One of his very best schemes, the estate survives in recognisable condition, but has been spoilt by window replacement. PRO WORK 25/20 for Gibberd's own account.
Architectural Review, vol.106, no.633, September 1949, pp.144–51

Appleby Frodingham Steel Co., Scunthorpe. Frederick Gibberd, 1946–9. The award was made for an electricity sub station, which serves a steel rolling mill, offices and a

welfare centre designed by Gibberd from 1946 onwards. The building consists of a large machine room with a fan house at one end and transformers in small buildings in front. A problem was the height of the building, which Gibberd did not try to hide, but sought merely to express as simply as possible in brick and concrete. The small entrance porch was designed to give a human scale, as was the use of bright yellow door panels and blue-grey tilework.
Architectural Review, vol.106, no.635, November 1949, pp.284–9

figure 9
Appleby Frodingham Steel Co., Scunthorpe. Frederick Gibberd, 1946–9.

Rushmere Primary and Infants School, Lanark Road, Ipswich. Martin J. Slater and Birkin Haward, 1947–9. An infant and junior school for 600 pupils, built in phases. This was the first of many schools by Haward for the Ipswich Education Authority. It is a clever rationalisation of the most economic features of steel framing for schools, with classroom blocks devised on a low-cost 7ft grid, combined with traditional brick construction for 'one off' elements such as the hall. The layout is also distinctive, with folding windows giving on to quiet courtyards for outdoor teaching. Existing hedges and a small orchard

figure 8
Somerford Estate, Dalston, Hackney. Frederick Gibberd, 1947–9.

figure 10
Rushmere Junior and Infants Schools,
Lanark Road, Ipswich. Martin J. Slater
and Birkin Haward, 1947–9.

were preserved on the site.
Architects' Journal, vol.110, no.2840,
14 July 1949, pp.39–43
Birkin Haward, *Autobiographical
Notes*, unpublished memoire, Ips-
wich, 1996, pp.43–5.

**Oak Hill Court, Oak Hill, Highams
Park, Woodford Green.** F.E.
Southgate, Borough Architect for
Walthamstow, 1949–50. Three 3–
storey blocks, each of twelve flats,
were built on the site of a Georgian
house damaged in the war. The 'T'-
shaped layout was devised to preserve the mature trees on the site.
Two blocks have two-bedroomed
flats, and are linked by walkways
leading to a central pram store. The
smaller flats are to one side, with
private gardens. The blocks have
copper roofs and distinctive big

eaves and really delicately designed
porches. This is the most intimate
of a large number of flat schemes
built by Walthamstow MB immediately after the war.
The Builder, vol.184, no.5741, 27
February 1953, pp.337–40.

**Priory Memorial Gardens, Priory
Lane, Royston, Cambs.** Arthur M.
Whydale, 1947–51. Five derelict
acres in central Royston were
bought by the Parish Council in
1947, and their development was
entrusted to a local architect.
Whydale's scheme comprised ornamental gardens, a miniature golf
course, tennis courts, a 'children's
corner' and a small bird sanctuary.
This was the first attempt to give
Royston a public park, and a bowl-
ing green, lake and bandstand were
planned for the future.
A3/17 in PRO WORK 25/20

**Housing, Laleham Road,
Shepperton, Middlesex.** Basil
Spence, 1949–50. 164 houses, flats
and old people's bungalows, for
Sunbury on Thames UDC. The
dwellings have coloured walls, and
distinctive aluminium roofs and
porches, though again plastic windows have taken their toll. The flat
aluminium door hoods and big
window boxes remain the most

figure 11
Oak Hill Court, Oak Hill, Highams Park,
Woodford Green. F. E. Southgate,
Borough Architect for Walthamstow,
1949–50.

figure 12
Priory Memorial Gardens, Priory Lane,
Royston, Cambs. Arthur M. Whydale,
1947–51.

figure 13
Housing, Laleham Road, Shepperton,
Middlesex. Basil Spence, 1949–50.

distinctive features of this unusual
work by Spence, who went on to
design a similar scheme in Sunbury
itself.
Architectural Design, vol.20, no.1,
January 1950, p.24

**Newbury Park Bus Station, Eastern
Avenue, Ilford.** Oliver Hill, 1947–49
The bus station and adjoining canteen was all that was built of a bus
and rail interchange, for which Hill
was commissioned in 1937. The
simple shell vault sheathed in copper was designed so that a station
booking hall and shops could be
added later. Its simplicity and striking thinness make it such an en-
dearing landmark that it was quietly
listed (grade II) as early as 1981,
ostensibly as a 1930s' design. Hill's
curved forecourt walls have been
lost to road widening, but the shelter was restored in 1994–5.
Alan Powers, *Oliver Hill, Architect and
Lover of Life*, London, Mouton Publications, 1989, pp.51–2.

figure 14
Newbury Park Bus Station, Eastern
Avenue, Ilford. Oliver Hill, 1947–49.
(London Transport Museum)

**Paragon, Colonnade House, Para-
gon House, Blackheath.** Michael
Searles, 1794–1802, restored by
Charles Bernard Brown 1947–9.
This was an early scheme of restoration for a major Georgian set-piece,
and its conversion into flats. Nineteenth-century accretions, including blind boxes and verandahs,
were removed. 'This is a brave
attempt to rescue a corner of
Blackheath from desecration's by
the Victorians and war damage, and
to prove that flat conversions need
not ruin period houses.' The houses
are listed grade 1.
A3/17 in PRO WORK 25/20

figure 15
The Paragon, (Colonnade House and
Paragon House), Blackheath. Michael
Searles, 1794–1802, restored by Charles
Bernard Brown 1947–9. (E. Harwood)

figure 16
White City Underground Station, Wood
Lane, Shepherd's Bush. A.D. McGill and
Kenneth J.H. Seymour, under Thomas
Bilbow of London Transport, 1947–50.
(Elain Harwood)

**White City Underground Station,
Wood Lane, Shepherd's Bush.** A.D.
McGill and Kenneth J.H. Seymour,
under Thomas Bilbow of London
Transport, 1947–50. This was a
reconstruction of an earlier station
on a new site, to provide longer
platforms and to give better access
to White City Stadium through a

separate 'rush hall' that could be opened to the side on racing days. An office and canteen was also built for train crews who changed shift here. The main ticket office and platform buildings survive, still with the milky faience tiling distinctive of the period.
The Builder, vol.CLXXIV, no.5473, 9 January 1948, p.54
David Lawrence, *Underground Architecture*, London, Capital Transport Publishing, 1994, pp.156–7.

Gaer Housing Estate, Newport, Wales. Johnson Blackett, Newport Borough Architect, 1949. This is a series of 25 curved terraces, with near-flat roofs, on a big, open hillside site overlooking the Bristol Channel. At the rear of the site are a few semis, also with low roofs. Attached to the houses is a charm-

ing junior school, with porthole windows and a square clock tower. Britain's largest surviving prefab estate is alongside. J.M. Richards considered that 'this scheme wins high marks for a judicious mixture of repetition and variety, and for regarding a sequence of terraces as an architectural whole ... It is time Britain showed the world she is good at something else besides endless country cottages.' The scheme also won a Ministry of Housing medal in 1950.
Architects' Journal, vol.III, no.2867, 19 January 1950, p.73

Heath Park Estate, off Frizlands Lane, Dagenham. Norman and Dawbarn, 1949–50. 131 houses and 148 three-storey flats were built on a featureless windswept site adjoining the LCC's large estate for the

figure 17
Gaer Housing Estate, Newport, Wales. Johnson Blackett, Newport Borough Architect, 1949.

figure 18
Heath Park Estate, off Frizlands Lane, Dagenham. Norman and Dawbarn, 1949–50.

figure 19 a,b,c &d
Housing in South Norfolk. Tayler and Green, 1948–50. (Elain Harwood)

figure 20
Walker Terrace, Asthall, Oxon. Peter Dunham Group, 1947–8.

local borough council. There were also bungalows for the elderly and specially adapted ground-floor flats for the disabled. The five-storey flats, unusually high for outside London, had brightly-coloured canted balconies that are the scheme's chief feature. A laundry, social centre and the proximity of the neighbourhood shopping centre gives this estate a wider range of facilities than is usually available to such a scheme.
Architects' Journal, vol.114, no.2961, 29 November 1951, pp.645–50.

Housing in Hedenham, Geldeston, Aldeby, Wheatacre and Thurton, South Norfolk. Tayler and Green, 1948–50

Tayler and Green won awards for five groups of houses arranged in terraces. The scheme at Geldeston (1949–50) also has the pair's first bungalows for the elderly. All the dwellings are of colour-washed brick with low roofs to fit more gracefully into the long, low lines of the Norfolk landscaping. Tayler and Green's application for the award also stresses the attention given to landscaping the houses, with new trees and hedges added to the careful preservation of older specimens. The Festival of Britain could afford to send only two Poole pottery plaques; the others were made up by Loddon RDC.
Elain Harwood and Alan Powers, *Tayler and Green Architects*, London, Prince of Wales Institute 1998

figure 21
Queen Adelaide Court, Queen Anne's Road, Penge. Edward Armstrong, 1949–50. (Elain Harwood)

Walker Terrace, Asthall, Oxon. Peter Dunham Group, 1947–8.

A terrace of four cottages for Witney RDC in Cotswold stone, sited and designed to harmonise with the other buildings in this tiny hamlet. Dunham's design, like other vernacular-style housing then being built in the Cotswolds, offered an alternative to the mix of modern European and traditional elements developed by Tayler and Green. This was the first housing built in this tiny village for over a century, and was fitted into the bend of the lane behind the existing cluster of cottages. It was extensively featured in the 1949 Housing Manual.
A3/17 in PRO WORK 25/20

Queen Adelaide Court, Queen Anne's Road, Penge. Edward Armstrong, 1949–50

This was Penge's first post-war housing project, and 'one of the largest flatted schemes to have been built by an urban district council' by this date. The site had previously been occupied by 14 three-storey houses built in 1851, which had been bombed in 1940, and was replaced by seven blocks of five-storey flats arranged as a series of courtyards, with the road forming the fourth side. It is a scheme of unusual grandeur for a suburban area, but has been spoilt by window replacement and the addition of pitched roofs.
A3/17 in PRO WORK 25/20

Notes on Contributors

GAVIN STAMP is an architectural historian and writer. He is Senior Lecturer at the Mackintosh School of Architecture, Glasgow School of Art, and Chairman of the Twentieth Century Society. Amongst other writings, his books include *The Changing Metropolis: Earliest photographs of London 1839–1879*, *The English House 1869–1914*, *Alexander Greek Thomson* and *Telephone Boxes*.

SUZANNE WATERS works for English Heritage and was until recently Honorary Secretary of the Twentieth Century Society.

ALAN POWERS teaches at the University of Greenwich and is Chairman of Trustees of Pollock's Toy Museum. His recent books include *Serge Chermayeff: designer, architect, teacher* (2001).

H. T. CADBURY-BROWN worked for Ernö Goldfinger before winning a competition for railway advertising kiosks. He first worked with Hugh Casson, Misha Black and Ralph Tubbs on the MARS Group exhibition in 1938. He went on to design the Royal College of Art and buildings at Birmingham and Essex Universities.

ELAIN HARWOOD is the Inspector at English Heritage responsible for its post-1945 research and listing programme. She has written *Tayler and Green* with Alan Powers (1998), *England: A guide to post-war Listed Buildings* (2000), and she is now working on a longer study of the period for Yale University Press.

SIR PHILIP POWELL won a competition for housing in Pimlico (Churchill Gardens) with Hidalgo Moya in 1945, when upon they formed the practice Powell and Moya with Philip's brother Michael. Skylon was their second competition win. The firm went on to build extensively for Oxbridge Colleges and the National Health Service.

DAVID ROBINSON is a film critic and historian, and director of the Pordenone (Italy) Silent Film Festival. His many books include *World Cinema*, *From Peepshow to Palace* and the now classic *Chaplin, His Life and Art* on which Richard Attenborough's film, 'Chaplin' was principally based. He is old enough to remember, with affection, the Festival of Britain and the Telecinema.

ROBERT BURSTOW is Senior Lecturer in History and Theory of Art at the University of Derby. His writings have appeared in exhibition catalogues and in academic and professional journals, including *Art History*, *Artscribe International*, *Frieze*, *Perspectief* and the *Oxford Art Journal*.

PAUL RENNIE is a graphic design historian, collector and dealer based in London. He has recently contributed to the *Decorative Arts Society Journal* and has helped to curate an exhibition of German film posters from the 1920s at Central St Martin's College of Art and Design in London.

MARY SCHOSER is a freelance historian, critic and curator in the decorative arts, specialising in textiles and wallpapers. Recent work includes contributions to *Making their Mark: the workshop as Central to art, craft and design* (2000, and touring exhibition 2000–1), and preparing a study of the motivations behind current decorating trends, *More is More* (Conran-Octopus, pending).

BECKY CONEKIN is a lecturer and Research Fellow in Cultural and Historical Studies at the London College of Fashion. She was co-editor of and contributed a chapter on the Festival to *Monuments of Modernity: Reconstructing Britain 1945–1964* (1999). She is writing *The Englishness of English Dress* (Berg, forthcoming 2001), as well as *'The Autobiography of a Nation': The Festival of Britain, Representing Britain in the post-war Era* (Manchester University Press, forthcoming 2002).

ROB GILL discovered Coventry when he was a student at Warwick University. A second-hand bookseller, he has had a bookshop in the city since 1977. He is a member of the Twentieth Century Society and is a tireless campaigner for the preservation of post-war Coventry.

ANNIE HOLLOBONE has been on the Committee of the Twentieth Century Society for the past two years where she has been responsible for operating its website. She has also been involved with the National Trust property, 2 Willow Road, since it opened in 1996.

EMMANUELLE MORGAN is a casework officer for the Twentieth Century Society. She teaches architecture and design at Ravensbourne College of Design and Commerce and has organised and toured an exhibition on the work of Berthold Lubetkin.

SIMON WARTNABY works for English Heritage and is a member of the Twentieth Century Society.

Cartoon by Professor A. E. Richardson,
from 'The Gentle Art of Making Enemies', Building, August 1951, p.305.
Courtesy of Simon Houfe.